ITALIAN & ITALIAN AMERICAN STUDIES

Edited by
Stanislao G. Pugliese
Hofstra University

This publishing initiative seeks to bring the latest scholarship in Italian and Italian American history, literature, cinema, and cultural studies to a large audience of specialists, general readers, and students. I&IAS will feature works on modern Italy (Renaissance to the present) and Italian American culture and society by established scholars as well as new voices in the academy. This endeavor will help to shape the evolving fields of Italian and Italian American Studies by re-emphasizing the connection between the two. The following editorial board of esteemed senior scholars advises the series editor:

FORTHCOMING BOOKS:

Queer Italia: Same-Sex Desire in Italian Literature and Film
    Edited by Gary P. Cestaro   July 2004

Frank Sinatra: History, Identity, and Italian American Culture
    Edited by Stanislao G. Pugliese   October 2004

The Legacy of Primo Levi
    Edited by Stanislao G. Pugliese   December 2004

Representing Sacco & Vanzetti
    Edited by Jerome A. Delamater & Mary Ann Trasciatti   April 2005

Mussolini's Rome: The Fascist Transformation of the Eternal City
    by Borden Painter   July 2005

Carlo Tresca: Portrait of a Rebel
    by Nunzio Pernicone   July 2005

Frank
Sinatra

History, Identity, and
Italian American Culture

Edited by

Stanislao G. Pugliese

palgrave
macmillan

First published 2004 by
PALGRAVE MACMILLAN™
175 Fifth Avenue, New York, N.Y. 10010 and
Houndmills, Basingstoke, Hampshire, England RG21 6XS.
Companies and representatives throughout the world.

PALGRAVE MACMILLAN is the global academic imprint of the Palgrave Macmillan division of St. Martin's Press, LLC and of Palgrave Macmillan Ltd. Macmillan® is a registered trademark in the United States, United Kingdom and other countries. Palgrave is a registered trademark in the European Union and other countries.

ISBN 1–4039–6655–9

Library of Congress Cataloging-in-Publication Data

Frank Sinatra : history, identity, and Italian American culture / edited by Stanislao G. Pugliese.
    p. cm.—(Italian and Italian American studies, ISSN 1530–7263)
    Includes bibliographical references and index.
    ISBN 1–4039–6655–9
    1. Sinatra, Frank, 1915- 2. Sinatra, Frank, 1915—Political and social views. 3. Singers—United States—Biography. 4. Italian Americans—Social life and customs—20th century. I. Pugliese, Stanislao G., 1965- II. Series.

ML420.S565F735 2004
782.42164'092—dc22

                                                                2004041585

A catalogue record for this book is available from the British Library.

Design by Letra Libre, Inc.

First edition: October 2004
10 9 8 7 6 5 4 3 2 1

Printed in the United States of America.

The most despairing songs are the loveliest of all,
I know immortal ones composed only of tears.

—Alfred de Musset, *Poésies Nouvelles.*
La Nuit de Mai (1835)

Contents

Acknowledgments

*I*t has now been several years since Hofstra University organized an extraordinary three-day conference on the life, music, and legacy of Frank Sinatra. I was privileged to have been asked to assist in the planning of that conference and participated as a moderator on one of the panels. The conference could not have been successful without the dedication and professionalism of the Hofstra University Cultural Center under the guidance of Eric J. Shmertz, Distinguished Professor Emeritus of Law at Hofstra, and Ms. Natalie Datlof, director of the Cultural Center. I would like to thank my colleagues Dr. Ruth Prigozy, Dr. Jeanne Fuchs, and Dr. David Lalama for their collaboration in preparing this volume.

At Palgrave Macmillan I was fortunate to work with a fine editorial staff. My thanks go to Michael Flamini, Brendan O'Malley, Donna Cherry, and Melissa Nosal.

For their gracious assistance in the use of the photos included here, I would like to thank Charles Granata, Lenny Triola, George Kalinsky (official photographer at Madison Square Garden and "Frank Sinatra's favorite photographer"), Franz Douskey, and Tony Consiglio.

Permission to reprint John Gennari's essay "Passing For Italian" has been granted by *Transition Magazine* no. 72 (Fall 1997): 36–48; I would also like to thank Professor Philip V. Cannistraro for permission to reprint excerpts from my essay "The Culture of Nostalgia: Fascism in the Memory of Italian Americans," which first appeared in the *Italian American Review* 5, no. 2 (Autumn/Winter 1996–97): 15–26.

A generous grant from the National Italian American Foundation (NIAF) assisted in the publication of this volume. I would like to thank John Marino of NIAF for his support of this project.

In the course of preparing this volume, my children, Alessandro (now 7) and Giulia (now 4), have come to be Sinatra afficionados. Alessandro likes the music but will occasionally roll his eyes when his father starts into another rendition of "Three Coins in the Fountain." To Giulia—who still asks that I dance with her to Sinatra's music—I dedicate this volume.

—*Stanislao G. Pugliese*
July 2004

List of Illustrations

Frank Sinatra

Introduction

"I'm for anything that gets you through the night."

1

Longing, Loss, and Nostalgia

Stanislao G. Pugliese

There are almost as many Sinatras as our imaginations may will into existence: the wise-ass *scugnizzo** from the streets of Hoboken; the vulnerable crooner who made the bobby soxers swoon at the Paramount; the self-destructive moth to the flame of Ava Gardner; the eternal Maggio and the Comeback Kid; the head Rat with rock glass in hand; the original "gangsta" epitomizing cool and a certain way with women; the ferociously proud Italian American; the Chairman of the Board; Ol' Blue Eyes; civil rights spokesperson. . . . In short, Sinatra was the palimpsest upon which much of American culture was written in the second half of the twentieth century.

Author, composer, and musicologist Arnold Shaw is only partially correct in his comparison between the original leader of the Rat Pack and Sinatra:

---

* The *scugnizzi* are the infamously cunning and adaptable street children of Naples.

"If Humphrey Bogart stands forth as the existential man, viewing life with a sense of detached irony but living with courage within the human condition, Sinatra is the archetype of the romantic man, raging against the human condition," for Sinatra could and did have an ironic streak. Shaw is closer to the mark in focusing on the complex, even paradoxical nature of the Sinatra charisma: "Sinatra's appeal as a twentieth-century romantic derives from a set of clashing chords. In the hierarchy of our sex symbols and love gods, he has been the tormented lover, vulnerable as well as triumphant, hurt as well as hurting. . . . It is this constant counterpoint of toughness and tenderness that has made Sinatra a magnetic and enigmatic personality. And it was the projection of these polarities in his singing that helped make him the master singer of our time." (Shaw 1968: 3).

Sinatra's appeal rested not just on his masterful singing but on these carefully constructed images and myths. Sinatra was fully conscious of their construction although he was not always sure how much the myths depended on his consciousness of their construction. In classic postmodernist language, he remarked late in life: "Sometimes I think I know what it was all about, and how everything happened. But then I shake my head and wonder. Am I remembering what really happened or what *other* people think happened? Who the hell knows, after a certain point?" And contrary to the cocksure assertiveness of "My Way," Sinatra at the end of his life was less sure of "his way" than at any time in his life. "Maybe that's what it's all about. Maybe all that happens is, you get older and you know less" (Hamill 1998: 98, 180).

In the arena of images available to us in framing "our" Frank Sinatra, I would here suggest another possible—although admittedly flawed—construction. Sinatra conflated within himself several of the stock characters of the Italian tragicomic art form of *commedia dell'arte*. In some ways Sinatra resembles Arlecchino (Harlequin), the immigrant, with a primitive and simple personality who evolves into a smart, sophisticated character. To survive, Arlecchino must make use of his wits to best the arrogant and greedy characters he encounters. Flanking Arlecchino are the Zanni, poor immigrants, ever hungry, yet shrewd, insolent, masters at the art of *arrangiarsi* ("arranging" or "systematizing" oneself). In his own dexterous manner, Sinatra, too, exemplified the peasant and immigrant's art of *arrangiarsi*. Brighello (the name comes from *briga*, "to fight") is the first among the Zanni: Cunning and avaricious, he is the trickster who prefers young lovers. And personifying the tragicomic nature of the human condition, the Neapolitan Pulcinella. Agile, nimble, skillful, dexterous, adroit, clever, stoic yet a dreamer, Pulcinella is a victim of melancholy, the enduring disease of the *Mezzogiorno,* the Italian south. Melancholy—not to be confused with depression—can best be described as a pensive sadness or a sober musing that occasionally gives way to despair. And just as Pulcinella's *coppolone* (sugar loaf hat) came to symbolize his character, Sinatra's snap-brimmed hats, worn at various angles to indicate his mood, came to symbolize an American icon.

There is a certain character trait that is common in these personalities of the *commedia dell'arte:* they are always attempting to create and control anarchy at the same time.

Much has been written of Sinatra's paternal Sicilian origins (his mother, Dolly, was from Genoa, with an entirely different set of cultural codes and mores). On the surface, any outside observer would have thought that it was his father, Marty, who must have been from the "reserved" north of Italy and the volcanic Dolly possessing the Sicilian blood. Yet that was not the case. Southern Italians are by nature reticent and not prone to public displays of wrath or fury. Although notorious in trying to protect his privacy, Sinatra often betrayed the cult of *omertá,* the ancient Sicilian code that demands silence before strangers. No information—no matter how seemingly obvious or trivial—is to be divulged. (For example: The polished practitioner of *omertá* can and will deny knowledge of the town's fountain when it can be seen and heard gurgling behind his back.) Sinatra's betrayal of *omertá* is there on every record and radio broadcast.

In many ways, he represented the dilemma of the emigrant, torn from an impoverished, rural society that was paradoxically both intensely Catholic and yet deeply pagan, bereft of the benefits of modernity. Author and scholar Robert Viscusi has poignantly described the trauma inflicted on those who left Italy in the late nineteenth and early twentieth centuries: "A whole nation walked out of the middle ages, slept in the ocean, and awakened in New York in the twentieth century" (Viscusi 1996: 22). Under such conditions, it is not to be wondered that nostalgia is the immigrant's disease.[1] Coined by a Swiss physician in the late seventeenth century, the word "nostalgia" is derived from the Greek *nostos,* meaning "to return home," and *algia,* "a painful condition"—hence, "a painful desire to return home." *Webster's* suggests "a wistful or excessively sentimental, sometimes abnormal yearning for return to some past period or irrevocable condition." The etymology of the word can help orient us in that bewildering topography of the mind where memory and the present intersect. Where exactly is the "home" for which we are homesick? Is it some small village in rural Italy, or is it rather a highly personal, idiosyncratic conceit held together by memory, longing, pain, and loss? In the architecture of memory, "home" is truly where the heart is and remembers. As such, it is constructed both individually (in memory) and collectively (recalling those past experiences with others and thereby reinforcing their particular characteristics). Nostalgia is based on personal history and experience: One cannot be nostalgic about the Roman Empire or the medieval Crusades. In the nostalgic imagination, certain aspects of life are privileged: the family, nature (usually its abundance), childhood and youth, first loves. Yet even painful experiences can pass into the realm of precious nostalgia, as when Italian Americans of the post-1945 immigration recount their suffering during World War II. It soon becomes obvious that nostalgia is one of many strategies available to the individual and the immigrant in constructing an identity.

Nostalgia is a yearning for the past in order to rectify past and current perceived wrongs; a desire to embrace myths that are capable of regenerating society or the self. Nostalgia questions and challenges the Enlightenment tradition of scientific-technological rationality and is a manifestation of the crisis of modern individualism (Olinick 1992: 195; Rider 1992: 73). This phenomenon of being trapped in time is undoubtedly familiar to all students of immigration. An Italian scholar has called nostalgia "an ambiguous emotion" and focused on its dual components of memory and desire (Bellelli 1991: 63). Nostalgia is a rebellion, a movement of transgression against the limitations imposed physically by time and space; it is an attempt to push the parameters of possibility and impossibility (Masciangelo 1990: 549). This dialectic of presence and absence reaches pathological dimensions when that which is absent is more real than that which is before us; when our idealized image of the past, admittedly necessary for both individuals and societies, prevents us from living in the present. The fortunate immigrant passes through a mourning period that is also a process of liberation, so that there can be a sense of belonging to the new culture without giving up one's cultural heritage. The unfortunate immigrant is trapped by memory. Nostalgia, then, is a complex dialogue of the self, but also a dialogue that must engage others in the construction of an ideal past. In an age of forced mobility, uprootedness, discontinuity, and rupture, nostalgia seeks to mend the torn fabric of the fragile psyche. It may also be a rationalization and justification for an ancient transgression—the abandonment, and therefore the betrayal, of the family and the *paese*.

The literary critic Frederic Jameson, writing in regard to the cultural theorist Walter Benjamin, perceptively observed that "if nostalgia as a political motivation is most frequently associated with fascism, there is no reason why a nostalgia *conscious of itself,* a lucid and remorseless dissatisfaction with the present on the grounds of some remembered plenitude, cannot furnish a revolutionary stimulus as any other" (Jameson 1969–70: 68).

Sinatra was caught in the double bind confronted by all immigrants to America: The necessity of assimilating into American culture while retaining a distinct ancestral identity. As the late anthropologist Thomas Belmonte has written, "The predicament of the Italian-American was a predicament of loss. How to relinquish the medieval mind, with its sensuousness, its wisdom, its religious devotions, its oaths, its belief in envy-motivated magic and the power of incantation? How to become a 'modern American' and condemn the old country's traditions of blood feud and vengeance? How to downplay its emphasis on virginal chastity and maternal sacrifice? . . . America liberates. But when it liberates the Italian-American, it creates a self that is painfully divided" (Belmonte 1999: 15–16). If history is a house built on memory, nostalgia is the complicated and often painful blueprint for its construction.

The latest census figures indicate that perhaps more than 20 million Americans identify themselves as Italian Americans. Yet the overwhelming majority are the grandchildren and great-grandchildren of immigrants, and their ties to Italian American culture are tenuous at best. If Italian American culture runs the risk of degenerating into a culture of nostalgia, it also is in danger of losing its pathos to bathos.

> pathos *n.* [Gr. *pathos,* suffering, disease, feeling . . . to suffer] 1. [Rare] suffering. 2. the quality in something experienced or observed which arouses feelings of pity, sorrow, sympathy, and compassion. Not to be confused with the common usage of pathetic which in reality denotes bathos which is a false or overwrought pathos that is absurd in its effect. Poignant: a sentiment that is keenly felt, often to the point of being sharply painful. (*Webster's New World Dictionary* 1980: 1041).

Sinatra managed, for most of his career, to sing on the right side of the fine line between pathos and bathos. The quality of pathos came from longing and loneliness. Hamill comes closest to the mark in arguing that "Sinatra had only one basic subject: loneliness" (Hamill 1998: 69). Yet that is only part of the whole, for that loneliness was always accompanied by pathos, melancholy, and nostalgia for something (not just a woman) irreparably lost. In his embrace of longing, loss, and nostalgia, Sinatra gave voice to the immigrant myth. "The core of the immigration myth," writes Hamill, "is this: it was about the way people overcame misery, how they found their consolations, and, in the end, how they redeemed America in a time when America believed it was not in need of redemption" (Hamill 1998: 51). Sinatra was one of the "agents of consolation": Although he wasn't as successful, the average Italian American could look to Sinatra as one of "us" who had climbed to the top without sacrificing the ethos and mores of the *via vecchia* (old way).

The middle third of the twentieth century was a momentous time for both Sinatra and Italian Americans. Sinatra's name was synonymous with the popular music of twentieth-century America; another Italian name (Joe DiMaggio) was synonymous with the nation's pastime, and still another Italian name (Fiorello LaGuardia) was considered to be the finest mayor in the history of New York City.

Immigrants from the Italian south, who never considered themselves Italians while in Italy, rediscovered a shared cultural history in America. If

Machiavelli's *Prince* argued that the state could be a work of art (or artifice), Baldassare Castiglione's Renaissance manual *The Book of the Courtier* held that the self is a work of art. It was Castiglione who coined the term *sprezzatura* as the art of making the difficult appear easy. DiMaggio epitomized this on the ballfield while Sinatra exemplified *sprezzatura* on stage and in the recording studio. Although both were meticulous craftsmen who would work years to perfect their craft, the appearance was one of unforced and spontaneous brilliance.

Pete Hamill's *Why Sinatra Matters* (1998)—quickly recognized as the best thing written in the immediate wake of Sinatra's death—opens on a rainy, 1970 New York midnight at P. J. Clarke's saloon. Sinatra is holding court at a table attended by Hamill, the disc jockey William B. Williams, the sportswriter Jimmy Cannon, the restaurateur Jilly Rizzo, and Danny Lavezzo, manager of the bar. The conversation eventually turns into an argument over the relative greatness of Hemingway and F. Scott Fitzgerald. Cannon champions Hemingway but Sinatra—revealingly—argues in favor of Fitzgerald. Like his hero, Jay Gatsby, Sinatra "believed in the green light, the orgastic future that year by year recedes before us" (Fitzgerald 1925: 182). It was that longing for a lost future that so permeated his music and life that gave it an essential quality of longing, loss, and nostalgia.

At the end, with Ava Gardner and Dean Martin and the others of the Rat Pack all gone, Sinatra was alone in facing the tyranny of nostalgia. "So we beat on, boats against the current, borne back ceaselessly into the past" (Fitzgerald 1925: 182). Our only consolation is that, in the end, the music remains—Sinatra's siren song of nostalgia and longing, memory and desire.

The essays collected here were first presented at an international conference at Hofstra University in November 1998. From the several hundred presentations delivered over three days, the editor has selected these essays dealing with politics, history, sociology, psychology, semiotics, philosophy, architecture, cultural studies and Italian American culture: a wide net indeed.

Part I examines Sinatra's place in American history. Douglas Brinkley offers an assessment of Sinatra's place in the "American century." More precisely, he argues that Sinatra's voice "is the soundtrack of the second half of the twentieth century."

In chapter 3 Joseph Dorinson accurately describes Sinatra's political trajectory over a half century of turbulent American history and his early support of civil rights, opening the many doors of our nation's house. Much has been made of Sinatra's pendulum swing from liberal Democrat to supporter of Richard Nixon and Ronald Reagan. Some have lain this at the door of John F. Kennedy's public snub of Sinatra (supposedly at Bobby Kennedy's insistence) because of Sinatra's familiarity with mob figures. A more sociological and historical (and less personal) explanation may lie in the general political odyssey of Italian Americans from urban, blue-collar democrats when they weren't "white," to suburban, white-collar (and white) conservatives.

Chapter 4 by Leonard Mustazza, on civil rights, ties Sinatra's support of equality with an immigrant experience rife with prejudice, hatred, and even violence, and a close reading of two of Sinatra's essays: one from 1958 and the other from 1991.

Michael Nelsen writes in chapter 5 that it was Sinatra who initiated the close relationship between celebrities and political figures, beginning with the singer's endorsement of Franklin Delano Roosevelt in 1944. Nelsen, though, argues against the sociological model in explaining that Sinatra's transformation into a conservative was due largely to his personal disappointment with Democratic party leaders, especially Jack and Bobby Kennedy.

Part II opens with an essay on the phenomenon of the bobby soxers by Janice Booker. Sinatra's sensuality combined with the loneliness of the home front in a surge of emotion that was paradoxically both innocent and dangerous. Returning to the Paramount Theater two years after his epoch-making performance on December 30, 1942, Sinatra precipitated the "Columbus Day Riot" of October 1944. In its aftermath, the commissioner of New York City's Board of Education revealingly remarked: "We don't want this sort of thing going on. We cannot tolerate young people making a public display of losing control of their emotions" (quoted in Goldstein 1982: 20). That "sort of thing" translated well even in the sophisticated nightclubs of Gotham: "What his singing does to women is immoral," a male nightclubber once remarked, "but it's pleasant" (17), leading one to recall a widely held belief that most Americans born in the second half of the twentieth century were conceived with Sinatra singing on the radio. A photograph from the collection of Neal Peters depicts a small, intimate performance with Sinatra at the microphone with his back to the photographer. The real subject of the photograph is not the singer but the audience: a hundred or so fans, mostly female, with the few men pushed to the back of the small room by their wives, fiancées, girlfriends, and sisters. All have the same dreamy look in their eyes (Lahr 1997a: 102–03). Tommy Dorsey saw the phenomenon from its inception and acidly commented, "what he did to women was something awful" (quoted in Taraborrelli 1997a: 48). Booker places this "Sinatramania" in its historical, psychological, and technological context.

In chapter 7 Gaspar González looks at what the "Big Room" meant for Sinatra and others in terms of class and a changing socioeconomic reality for the millions of immigrants and children of immigrants in the post–World War II era. Here, issues of spectacle, consumption, inclusion (and, by necessity, exclusion) come to a head. González brilliantly reveals how performance and space are intimately related.

Chapter 8, by Rob Jacklosky, looks at how the early Sinatra projected images of frailty and vulnerability. These images were carefully constructed, but Jacklosky argues that they were closer to the real Sinatra than the later images crafted in the 1960s (Rat Pack), 1970s (Chairman of the Board), and 1980s (elder statesman of jazz). For Jacklosky, the Sinatra of the 1940s is "the unalloyed expression of the male anxiety of rejection and the most fully articulated expression of feminine vulnerability."

In chapter 9 T. H. Adamowski explains the elusive character of charisma, convincingly arguing that the full effect of Sinatra's charisma did not flower until after his infamous Fall, while the unimagined success of the 1960s sparked an image of the powerful patron. "No Calvinist, Sinatra was a throwback to the kind of medieval *Aristoi* who salted the earth with coins to suggest the transcendence of money." That profligacy was a gift, a *charism*, "a tribute to the working of grace in the world."

Part III collects essays examining Sinatra's ethnic heritage and his impact on Italian-American culture. In chapter 10, "Sinatra at the Table," father and son restaurateurs Joe and Sal Scognamillo recall scenes from their landmark, Patsy's. Here, we are privileged to see Sinatra act according to the codes of *amicizia* (friendship), the *bella figura* (to cut a beautiful figure), *comparaggio* (godfatherhood), *furbizia* (cunning), *omertà* (the ancient code of silence), *onore* (honor), and *rispetto* (respect).[2]

Chapter 11, by John Gennari, probes Sinatra's problematic relationship with his mother, the indomitable Dolly. Gennari uses the particular Italian mother-son dynamic of *mammismo* as a framing device. (*Mammismo* is the noun; *mammissimo,* the adjectival form.) *Mammismo* is the "cult of the mother, particularly as reflected in the privileged relationship between mother and son" (D'Acierno 1999: 739). Of course, *mammismo* is never far from the *Madonna-puttana* complex, in which men trap women in an impossible either-or scenario: mothers, wives, daughters are immaculate *Madonne,* while all other women fall into the latter category and are hence "fair game." To compensate, the "mamma's boy" often adopts the posture of *menefreghismo,* or "I don't give a damn."

In chapter 12 Thomas Ferraro, employing the work of the late sociologist Herbert Gans, shows how Sinatra adhered to the tightly woven codes of Italian American urban behavior. As first Gans and now Ferraro demonstrate, Sinatra was the first Italian-American public figure who was not only not embarrassed by his ethnic heritage, but was willing "to countenance offending the genteel sensibilities of an Anglo American cultural elite." Paradoxically, that Anglo American cultural elite was struck by Sinatra's "class" in his singing but repulsed by his "boorish" behavior off stage. Ferraro writes that Sinatra, initiated early into the rituals of *bella figura* and Italian American performance, reproduced those rituals in altered form in his singing. In a most intrepid reading, Ferraro argues that Sinatra created a cultural *corpus christi:* "a community of wonder produced out of disparate conditions . . . in mystical relation to one another and the body social."

Gennari's second essay in this collection, chapter 13, examines the influence of Sinatra on African American "gangsta" culture, where the image is inseparable from the music.

In chapter 14, Pellegrino D'Acierno argues that Sinatra claimed a song in ways matched only by Enrico Caruso and Billie Holiday. Surely it is no co-incidence that the two people in the same category as Sinatra are a Neapoli-tan singer dead of pleurisy at age forty-nine and an African American female singer who saw the worst of both American and African American culture. Sinatra was able to attach his name to his singular triumphs as well as his very public defeats. Or, as D'Acierno acutely observes, Sinatra was able "to place his name on the extraordinary narrative of self-creation through which he achieved America." The Sinatra name and narrative have "rewritten the hegemonic American immigrant myth in a way that exposes the alienation and self-alienation intrinsic to Immigrant American and the myth-function of American exceptionalism." In a way that could not be fulfilled through the cool and classical DiMaggio or the lovable LaGuardia, Sinatra laid bare the Italian American psychic identity. For D'Acierno, Sinatra was/is the ve-hicle for an Italian American psychic identity's "conflicted passage from im-migration and exile" into the common culture. It is this "negative experience" that makes Sinatra our "crazy mirror" reflecting both an au-thentic self and one that is simultaneously distorted and displaced by the dominant culture.

Rocco Marinaccio relates, in chapter 15, how Sinatra and his music functioned as a "potent marker of my ethnicity and class background" and how the reactions to that marking from friends and colleagues have changed over two decades. Marinaccio reveals how the academy, as a mi-crocosm of the larger society, demands that one abandon overt expressions of class and ethnicity to foster a convenient myth. Marinaccio, like Sinatra, refuses these demands. Sinatra, by refusing to give up the name, and with an insistence on adhering to the old-world dictates of *rispetto, bella figura, omertà,* and all the rest, thereby becomes dangerous to the dominant cul-ture. Marinaccio also courageously points out the discrepancy between what the academics were doing at the Hofstra conference and what those in attendance wanted to hear.

Functioning as a coda, chapter 16 by Edmund Santurri concludes the volume with a semiotic study of Sinatra and the myriad ways the singer has been represented in American popular culture and mass media. Sinatra's polysemous character is neatly captured here, as is the complicated manner in which the media have constructed various images of Sinatra through the years. Santurri also lays out the Italian-American aspect of these images and insists that "American bourgeois society has something to learn morally from the Mediterranean ethos reflected in much of Sinatra's behavior." He concludes that Sinatra was "the master of the zeitgeist of the twentieth century." For Santurri, Sinatra was a "postmodern Prometheus."

Perhaps it is fitting that we end with this image, for, by stealing the songs of the gods, Sinatra has given us both light and heat.

Notes

1. Elsewhere I have written on Italian American culture as a "culture of nostalgia." See "The Culture of Nostalgia," in *Italian American Review* 5, no. 2 (Autumn/Winter, 1996–1997): 15–26. I gratefully acknowledge the permission to reprint sections here.
2. Here and below I make use of the invaluable "Cultural Lexicon" compiled by Pellegrino D'Acierno in his *The Italian American Heritage* (1999: 703–66).

Part One

History and Politics

"We've made only small, suspicious progress toward international understanding while the world festers with racial and religious discontent."
—Frank Sinatra (1947), quoted in Mustazza essay

2

Frank Sinatra and the American Century

Douglas Brinkley

Should we take Frank Sinatra seriously? The answer, for me, is a resounding yes. I feel those who are critical of studying American popular culture at Harvard or Yale or other prestigious institutions will be studying Frank Sinatra fifty years from now. So it is possible that Hofstra was ahead of the curve by conducting a conference and by reflecting on Mr. Sinatra.

For all he brought to America's understanding of "cool" over the last fifty-odd years, the bedrock legacy of Francis Sinatra will always remain his hypnotic singing style: the impeccable spacing of words and breath and the unmatchable ability to make any lyric his own that defined the no-nonsense, Jersey-bred crooner in the snap-brim fedora, swinging in the spotlight to the rhythms of the twentieth century as they poured out from his Horatio Alger soul. Put more simply, Sinatra was the best singer with impeccable taste, whose voice is the soundtrack for the second half of the twentieth century.

Now, of course, the last century produced other great pop vocalists—for example, Delta bluesman Robert Johnson, scat wizard Ella Fitzgerald, the heartbreaking Judy Garland, raw and raspy Ray Charles, the always smooth Tony Bennett, and, among so many others, Minnesota folk-rock legend Bob Dylan. Interestingly enough, only Frank Sinatra managed to embrace all these musical elements and stir them into that cocktail-culture coolness, brimming with urban sophistication, that defined much of the American century. If modern jazz is twentieth-century America's great gift to the world, then we must salute Sinatra for being the supreme vocalist of that particular art form.

The great saxophonist Lester Young, the father of cool jazz, once said, "Really, my man is Frank Sinatra."[1] Whatever his personal peccadilloes and choices of associates, it was still Sinatra who taught an entire generation of jazzmen to study a song's lyrics before improvising on it with the extravagant recklessness that could bare the music's soul. In the course of his long career, Sinatra's name became synonymous with "pop singer," while excelling as a movie actor, director, producer, and Las Vegas showman. Sinatra was never a songwriter, never a source of music in the manner of George and Ira Gershwin, Jerome Kern, Cole Porter, and Harold Arlen, but, in a way that no other interpreter was able to, Sinatra made their songs his own. He was, therefore, the master of the lyric.

It's stunning now to think how many strong personas Sinatra leaves behind: the Crooner, the Swinger, the Brawler, the Chairman of the Board. More surprising is how he made these various selves work together in such harmony. Not unlike America itself, Sinatra was a great paradox: tough and tender, the hard-luck boy from Hoboken who made it to the top of the Land of Milk and Honey. As Pete Hamill recently noted, Sinatra was believable as both Maggio in *From Here to Eternity* and as the ultimate TV ham, standing on two chairs singing, "I've Got the World on a String" (Hamill 1998: 5). Somehow Sinatra got away with being both the little guy who bucked the establishment and a charter member of that same prevailing culture; a frequent guest of any number of presidents at the White House, where, in fact, he received the Presidential Medal of Freedom from Ronald Reagan in 1985. Considered a close friend of President John F. Kennedy and President Richard Nixon as well, Sinatra was also the performer the American people felt most comfortable with for the longest period of time. He made Elvis Presley appear, by contrast, like a flash in the pan. Frank Sinatra never knew a generation gap.

I personally like to think of Sinatra as *the* voice of the American century. If one had to select a most apropos pop anthem of this century, I don't believe it would be Dylan's "Like a Rolling Stone" or Woodie Guthrie's "This Land Is Your Land," but Sinatra's bold version of Paul Anka's "My Way." When he died on May 14, 1998, I read about a dozen obituaries and none of them was satisfactory. Certain biographical facts about his life were new to me, and I marveled at the longevity of his career, but what I actually craved was his voice. Television reports of his death were terribly deficient. Sinatra in sound bites was unfulfilling. Only—and a point that Pete Hamill makes in his 1998 book—radio really captured the essence of Sinatra's art. That evening of May 14, Sinatra's voice froze America in its tracks as a thousand radio stations played Sinatra all night. I was in Atlanta at the time, the evening of his death, in a taxicab. I distinctly remember riding along Peachtree and hearing on the radio "Cycles," one of the songs I truly love, as I consider his version perfect. Two hundred years from now, generations of new Americans will try to emotionally understand the American century by listening to Frank Sinatra. Sinatra turned pop art into high art, his voice showing the human dimensions behind modernity, the soul that can be found in a skyscraper, the loneliness of the American interstate at night, the beautiful vibe of what Langston Hughes called "the sweet flypaper of life."

Now, true, I think Frank Sinatra doesn't quite make it in Hank Williams country, as it's hard to imagine Sinatra's voice on an Iowa farm. But as I thought about that, I would say it's only on an Iowa farm during the day. I think Sinatra's voice at night, in the Midwest, when it's dark in any type of home, would capture a certain American essence. I also think that, in a way, Sinatra's voice has brought generations of Americans together, because it's accessible, recognizable, and as lonely as the sound of the automobile racing down a back road at times. Sinatra himself once noted—in fact, he embraced it as a motto—"I'm for whatever gets you through the night."

One of the other remarkable things about Sinatra's image, which I repeat, is how it spans generations. It would be difficult to find an American who didn't pull for the guy, so powerful and yet somehow always the underdog at the prize fight. "Sock it to 'em, Frankie boy!" shouted five generations of fans, and Sinatra always replied, "You bet." The lasting appeal of Sinatra is that of the unpredictable individualist who was also money in the bank. Nobody, at any point in Sinatra's career, ever left a Frank Sinatra concert disappointed. America has always loved a maverick, and Sinatra gave them one in spades. Much more than a matinee idol or the king of swoon that women found so irresistible, he was—in a way—the personification of Norman Mailer's "white Negro" for every generation since World War II. Remember Sinatra's World War II V-disc recordings? Those recordings had a definite impact. I'm director of the Eisenhower Center for American Studies. My colleague Steve Ambrose and I have recorded the voices of the veterans of D-Day and the Battle of the Bulge. It is amazing that, when they tell stories of music and what it meant in their lives as eighteen-, nineteen-, or twenty-year-old soldiers—whether they were in Belgium, France, or the Pacific, or soldiers fighting the Nazis in the Ardennes Forest or the Japanese on flyspeck Pacific islands—they all came back loving Frank Sinatra. Men who had their legs blown off at Iwo Jima were said to break into their first smiles when hospital radios began to blare "The Story of a Starry Night" or "I Couldn't Sleep a Wink Last Night." The GIs may have loved Bing Crosby's singing just as much, but in Frank Sinatra they recognized themselves, and so did we all. I was told by one conference participant that, on D-Day, there was a group of soldiers whose code phrase to recognize each other, as opposed to the enemy, was "Who's the great American singer?" The answer was "Frank Sinatra." This occurred on the beaches of Normandy on D-Day sixty years ago.

With World War II ending sixty years now, what's so amazing is that Sinatra is more popular than ever with young people. In fact, there is no cultural icon who better personifies both formalism and recklessness—and I stress those paradoxical words. They're the reasons why Frank Sinatra has such staying power with the post–Generation X hipsters. With his fusion of perfect style and imperfect behavior, Sinatra is a practical and natural hero for a generation that resents regulation yet at the same time yearns for structure. Swing clubs—like the Derby in Los Angeles, the Red Room in New Orleans, the Lucky Strike Room in San Francisco—have become youth meccas now, where Sinatra is in vogue and the Billboard top-ten hits are out. Young people want Frank Sinatra style and pathos. These young embracers of swing today agree with the sentiment that Emily Dickinson once stated: "After a time of great pain, a formal feeling comes." And I think it's applicable to Mr. Sinatra.

Sinatra has remained, I believe, *the* voice of contemporary America. He is loved for having recorded music about anguish and love, and for understanding that, at the end of the road, all that's left is what Jack Kerouac called "the forlorn rags of growing old." What makes Sinatra such a transcendent artist is that, from his barstool of anguish, he also embraced dynamism. He celebrated success. He reminded us that right now matters because right now is all we have that is certain.

What may be most remarkable about Frank Sinatra is that, in our throwaway culture, where neon always dies, Sinatra never became a has-been. To the end, he remained the Man, swaggering according to the inscription on Balzac's walking stick, which said, "Whatever gets in my way, I crush." After all, the entire history of America has been the story of crushing whatever blocked its path, be it mountain ranges, Native Americans, or foreign nations with ideas of their own. There's always been something haunting and, at times, even beautiful about America's relentless march to progress. In the postwar years, that spirit found its voice in Frank Sinatra, via the radios and phonographs that had just become commonplace when he happened upon the scene.

He is gone, but his voice will long remain both timely and timeless, thanks to the more than two hundred albums he recorded in his remarkable career and also because, as poet Archibald MacLeish once wrote of Ernest Hemingway, "His is the one intrinsic style that our century has produced."

Notes

1. "One Of Jazzdom's Greats Reminisces, Evaluates And Chats," interview with Lester Young, <http://www.downbeat.com/default.asp?sect=stories&subsect=story_detail&sid=422>

3

🎤

Frank Sinatra's House

Pride, Passion, and Politics

Joseph Dorinson

*O*ur house, the Bible teaches, is one of many mansions. Frank Sinatra began his great ascent to the room at the top in 1935 when he broke into show business on *Major Bowes' Amateur Hour*. His rise, over Judy Garland's rainbow, personifies the American dream. His achievements have earned this self-styled saloon singer a permanent perch among the icons in our pantheon. Most studies of Sinatra, however, pay little attention to his politics; hence this effort to shed some light on a neglected but important subject.

Sinatra's political education started at home in Hoboken, New Jersey, where his mother, Dolly Graventi Sinatra, functioned as a ward heeler. In return for favors extended to recent immigrants who flocked to Hudson County, she garnered votes for the Democratic machine. Realizing that politics is the art of accommodation, Dolly filled a vacuum that our founding fathers and their progressive children had created in rigid deference to their waspish values. Thus, when semiliterate indigent newcomers needed coal to heat their cold-water flats, turkeys to feed their hungry children at Thanksgiving, or jobs for family survival, they turned to the urban bosses. High-minded sentiment and lofty sermons on rugged individualism, moral responsibility, and civic duty did not suffice. Following in the wake of Irish politicians, Dolly Sinatra was always there: to help as well as to reap rewards. She got her husband, Marty, a job in the local fire department and opened a saloon during the era of Prohibition. And in 1932, at the height of the Great Depression, she bought a four-story house (Clarke 1997: 7–11).

Daughter Nancy describes her father's political odyssey in a colorful way (N. Sinatra 1995: passim). Identifying with marginal Americans, Sinatra supported Franklin Delano Roosevelt's New Deal, actively campaigning for the president in 1944 at considerable risk to his high-flying career. The president took Sinatra to tea on September 28, 1944, at the White House. Invited along with saloonkeeper Toots Shor and comedian Rags Ragland at the suggestion of Democratic National Committee chair Bob Hannegan, the crooner sang Roosevelt's praise: "The greatest guy alive." Bantering with reporters upon leaving, he endorsed Roosevelt for reelection and joined the campaign. He spoke at rallies and on radio. When he put his money, $5,000, near his mouth, the kid from Hoboken elicited condemnation from right-wing journalists like Lee Mortimer and Westbrook Pegler.

This acrimonious exchange marked the end of Sinatra's honeymoon with the press and the beginning of a long feud with the fourth estate. The singer resented the double standard imposed on him. When Ginger Rogers and George Murphy (later elected to the U.S. Senate from California) campaigned for Republican candidate Tom Dewey, no adverse commentary surfaced. To his critics, Sinatra shot back: "My first real criticism came from the press when I campaigned for President Roosevelt in 1944. A few columnists took me to task insisting that entertainers should stick to entertaining. They also realize it is bad public relations to indulge in politics because you may lose fans who don't agree with you. However,

I feel it is the duty of every American citizen to help elect the candidate of his choice" (Howlett 1980: 44).

Sinatra made his political debut on October 31, 1944, at Madison Square Garden flanking Harry Truman and Fiorello LaGuardia. The rally, sponsored by the Liberal party (not a dirty word in the halcyon 1940s), attracted many famous people. Senator Robert Wagner, Vice President Henry Wallace, entertainers Ethel Merman, Benay Venuta, and Victor Borge drew cheers from twenty thousand in attendance (Adams 1944: 16). Bill "Bojangles" Robinson, the fabulous black dancer, swapped roles with the young singer from Hoboken. Sinatra danced; Robinson sang. Warned that his political activities would hurt his career, Sinatra countered: "Well, the hell with that. I'm more interested in good government than in my own future" (quoted in ibid.). At a loss for words without music, Sinatra appeared emotionally drained. All that the crooner managed to say about FDR was: "He is good for me and my kids and my country" (Howlett 1980: 44). At subsequent rallies he teamed up with Orson Welles, a dynamic duo that excelled on radio. A largely Republican press aimed their barbs at Sinatra. Happily, the nation's youngsters, "bobby soxers," mostly poor, adored "the Voice." Despite his fragile physique and because of his enormous success, he embodied their quest for power and articulated their need for heroes. Author Bruce Bliven, from whom this last observation is borrowed, had it right: "Perhaps Frankie is more important as a symbol than most of us are aware" (Petkov and Mustazza 1995: 30–33).

After the election, Sinatra embarked on a crusade against intolerance. Mentored by the politically liberal jazz vocalist George Evans, Sinatra talked to Bronx high school students about juvenile delinquency, a prime concern on the home front during World War II. He received coverage on the front page of the *New York Daily News*. This led to a nationwide tour of ten cities. Not all newspapers responded favorably. For example, bilious and bibulous Westbrook Pegler of the Hearst Press took potshots at the popular singer.

In 1945 Frank Sinatra garnered laurels for his work against prejudice from the National Conference of Christians and Jews. To promote this worthy cause, producer Frank Ross suggested a film with a song. "Putting his convictions on the line," writes daughter Nancy Sinatra, "Dad played himself, preaching tolerance to a group of boys in *The House I Live In,* a 10-minute short for RKO . . . on the theme of racial tolerance" (N. Sinatra 1995: 66). This mini-masterpiece was the product of Lewis Allen, composer Earl Robinson, and screenwriter Albert Maltz. Allen had written the blistering attack on lynching, "Strange Fruit," so hauntingly sung by Billie Holiday. Earl Robinson had teamed up with John Latouche to write a one-act oratorio, "Ballad for Americans," first recorded by Paul Robeson and, later, Bing Crosby (Friedwald 1995: 323).

Directed by Mervyn LeRoy, the film was shot in two days in May 1945, soon after the death of President Roosevelt. Sinatra introduced the song in August, the month of Hiroshima and Nagasaki. Sinatra recorded it with Columbia and featured it on the "Old Gold" radio program between 1945 and 1947. Both Sinatra and LeRoy received Oscars in 1946 for this film, a powerful and friendly persuader against racism. Years later Sinatra informed Edward R. Murrow in a televised interview that he prized this Oscar more than the one *From Here to Eternity* (Friedwald 1995: 324–25).

Note the moral of the film: "Look, fellas," Sinatra reasons, "religion makes no difference except to a Nazi or somebody as stupid. . . . Don't let them make suckers out of you." In this remarkable venture, great music resonated with good politics in this apotheosis of postwar America when "Our House" began to open its doors to "strangers in the night."

Sinatra recorded another commentary on racial politics in 1946. Kurt Weill and Maxwell Anderson wrote "Lost in the Stars" three years before the musical drama of the same name reached Broadway. The song exemplifies a progressive social and musical ideology. Drawing on African folklore, it delivers a powerful message in three minutes and thirteen seconds (Friedwald 1995: 325). Sinatra practiced what he sang. When he learned that the Lakeside Country Club had a membership policy that excluded Jews, he followed another gentile member, Darryl Zanuck, in joining the Hillcrest Country Club (N. Sinatra 1995: 63). In another instance, Orson Welles, Frank Sinatra, and a black driver entered a restaurant. A giant waiter refused to serve the chauffeur. Welles remembered that Sinatra reared up, grabbed the server, and insisted: "You're serving coffee for three." By "sheer force of character," Frank triumphed (ibid.: 68). Each incident, however, drew fire from the conservative press.

Picture, if you will, "Autumn in New York," 1947. Frank Sinatra encouraged Sammy Davis Jr. to perform with him at New York's Capitol Theater. The Hearst Press replaced a favorable review with a hostile one coauthored by Lee Mortimer and Jack Lait, who blasted Sinatra's performance (Howlett 1980: 44) and gloated when attendance sagged (N. Sinatra 1995: 49). Eventually Mortimer would earn a well-aimed sock on the jaw from the explosive singer.

The Hoboken heartthrob was also a writer. In a series of essays, Sinatra crafted eloquent pleas for ethnic understanding and racial tolerance. As a victim of prejudice during the 1920s and 1930s, he identified with the outsiders: Dostoyevsky's "insulted and injured." He urged his young readers to be smarter than their contemporaries (Mustazza 1998b: 5–9; Wiener 1986: 21–23). Of particular significance is Sinatra's open letter to Henry Wallace published in the *New Republic* on January 6, 1947, but written one month prior. Calling for world peace and the right (inclined to the left) leadership to achieve this goal, Sinatra sang the praises of the former vice president and exhorted him to seek the presidency in 1948. Using a star's "bully pulpit" to frame political solutions to political problems, the celebrated crooner created a precedent. And this act of courage coupled with conviction brought "heat" from the house of F.B.I. Director J. Edgar Hoover. The notorious "Red Hunter" and homophobic closet queen joined forces with the House Un-American Activities Committee to pillory Sinatra as a "pinko" (Mustazza 1998b: 8; Clarke 1997: 94).

No stranger—night or day—to controversy or confrontation during the "Organization Man" 1950s, Sinatra subverted the cultural code. Although he extolled "Love and Marriage," he thundered against the "Tender Trap." He deviated from the sing-along thrust of Mitch Miller. As living standards rose, musical standards declined. Sinatra, Friedwald persuasively argues, maintained high benchmarks in popular song. Recruited by friend Peter Lawford, Sinatra joined the Kennedy bandwagon in 1960. In the struggle for the presidential nomination, daughter Nancy reports that her father secured the support of mob boss Sam Giancana in the crucial West Virginia primary. His mother, Dolly, helped to swing the Hudson County delegation issuing from Jersey City (N. Sinatra 1995: 146). His hit song "High Hopes" was altered for and tailored to the Kennedy campaign. Sinatra also commissioned a pro-JFK libretto from another buddy, the "Irresponsible" Sammy Cahn. In 1961 this led to the "Old Jack Magic." Distanced by allegations of Mafia guilt by association, Sinatra remained a Kennedy devotee. He sang melancholy songs following the assassination of both Kennedy brothers evoking that "brief shining moment" (Friedwald 1995: 301).

According to Alan King—comic, actor, producer, friend—the break with the Kennedys was strictly personal. For years Sinatra had been an ardent Democrat and zealous fund-raiser. He orchestrated the entire pre-inaugural gala, which featured a true galaxy of stars, among them: Ethel Merman, Nat King Cole, Louis Prima, Helen Traubel, Leonard Bernstein, Frederick March, Anthony Quinn, Bette Davis, Sidney Poitier, and Laurence Olivier, flanked by the Mormon Tabernacle Choir and Nelson Riddle's orchestra. But trouble, like Herbert Hoover's vaunted prosperity, was just around the corner. When Sinatra invited President Kennedy to stay at his Palm Springs estate, the chief executive gladly accepted. But, pressure from the Justice Department, headed by brother Bobby, compelled the captain from Camelot to alter course. At the behest of Hoover and his brother, both concerned with the Sam Giancana–Frank Sinatra mob connection, Kennedy stayed at the estate of Bing Crosby, a registered Republican. A fuming Sinatra neither forgot nor forgave the Kennedys. Nevertheless, King asserts that in his heart, Sinatra remained a Democrat (King 1996: 117–20; Reeves 1993: 289, 292–93).

He also retained his core values. Even when he reinvented his artistry and refashioned his politics, Sinatra remained "a fighter against his times." As Mustazza reminds us, he opened doors for black performers as guests at the Copacabana and as entertainers in Las Vegas. Black artists, such as Nat King Cole and Sammy Davis Jr., and black athletes, such as Joe Louis and Sugar Ray Robinson, all benefited from the saloon singer's largesse. Sinatra put his money to work in behalf of causes that he publicly supported. In addition, he performed at benefits for organizations as diverse as the NAACP, the Simon Wiesenthal Center, and the Southern Christian Leadership Conference (Mustazza 1998b: 9–11).

The Rat Pack phenomenon deserves attention in this context. This stage in Sinatra's life has attracted increasing interest stimulated by several made-for-TV films. On the surface, it appears as a case of arrested juvenile development. Certainly an element of residual adolescence lays at the heart of Sinatra's capers. But the antics have deeper significance.

The idea started with Humphrey Bogart. At his home in Holmby Hills, California, Bogie and his wife, Lauren Bacall, hosted a bunch of hard-drinking nonconformists. In 1955 they headed for Las Vegas to watch Noel Coward at the Desert Inn. With Sinatra, Judy Garland, David Niven, Irving "Swifty" Lazar, Jimmy Van Heusen, and Angie Dickinson in tow, they cavorted in Glitztown. When Bacall saw them inebriated in the casino, she remarked, "You look like a goddamn rat pack" (Bogart 1995: 53–56; Rudin 1998: 43).

After Bogie's death of lung cancer in 1957, Sinatra, who had served as "Pack Master," assumed leadership. A new court formed around Frank. It included Joey Bishop, Sammy Davis Jr., Dean Martin, and Peter Lawford as the core group, or two Jews, two Italians, one African American, and one WASP.

"The Rat Pack show," said Max Rudin, "featured—even flaunted—race and ethnicity. Bishop, dressed as a Jewish waiter, warns the two Italians to watch out" for the Matzia, his own group (Bogart 1995: 57). When John Kennedy took a breather from the presidential race in 1960, Martin picked up Davis and offered him to the candidate as an award from the NAACP. The Pack, unlike the silent generations that preceded, paraded their ethnicity. Davis quipped, "I'm colored, Jewish and Puerto Rican. When I move into a neighborhood, I wipe it out" (Bogart 1995: 57). No longer victims of prejudice, they used humor to lash out at prejudice. And Peter Lawford, the only WASP (though a convert to Catholicism, a product of a marriage to Kennedy's sister, Pat), became the comic foil. His pompous British persona sparked mirth in others.

In the political arena, throughout the 1960s, Sinatra hated Richard Nixon. He could barely shake his hand at Toots Shor's in 1962; he campaigned for Pat Brown against Ronald Reagan for governor of California in 1966. He brought fellow rat-packer Dean Martin along for the political ride. After the Watts riot in Los Angeles in 1965, Vice President Hubert Humphrey praised Sinatra for teaching tolerance and preaching against prejudice among young people. Both promoted a series of concerts to raise money for voter registration drives to implement the Voter Rights Act of 1965 (N. Sinatra 1995: 200, 206).

In the early 1970s he buddied up to Spiro Agnew first and Nixon, too, appearing at a White House reception on April 17, 1973. How does one explain this defection? Daughter Tina, a staunch McGovern supporter, was appalled, reports her sister, Nancy, "with the laughing face" (N. Sinatra 1995: 226).

Sinatra's switch to conservative Republican politics is both baffling yet understandable. A self-made man, his great ascent in American popular culture carried him inexorably to the right. Although he supported Pat Brown for reelection as governor of California against the successful challenger, Ronald Reagan, in 1966, Sinatra was already "turned off" by the radical politics in the 1960s. A man of deep personal loyalties and visceral dislikes, "Old Blue Eyes" followed his impulses. Never a consistent thinker (the "hobgoblin of little minds") or a political sophisticate, Sinatra enjoyed golfing with Spiro Agnew in Palm Springs. This led to the recruitment of disaffected Democrats to the Republican banner in 1972. Ironically, as the Watergate felons were thrust out of office in disgrace, Sinatra remained faithful to his fallen comrades. He also decided to return to public performance. Admirable moves, to be sure; but an incident in 1960 reveals a less noble side to the Sinatra persona.

Albert Maltz, a victim of the "Red Scare" of the 1950s, wrote a script, "The Execution of Private Slovik," at the behest of Sinatra. The Catholic hierarchy in New York balked at the rehabilitation of this communist writer. Cardinal Spellman communicated his opposition to Joseph Kennedy, who feared ugly repercussions on his son's bid for the presidency. Bowing to pressure, Sinatra sacrificed Maltz on the altar of political expediency (Howlett 1980: 148; N. Sinatra 1995: 148). It was not his finest hour.

Abruptly, Sinatra moved to the right of the political spectrum. Clearly, he had switched houses. Less obvious are the causes of this departure. A number of Frankophiles have fixed on the Joe Kennedy–orchestrated break because of Sinatra's alleged Mafia links. In various television documentaries that aired following Sinatra's death, Peter Lawford was cited as both the matchmaker and the messenger (of bad tidings) that initially attracted and later repelled—indeed expelled—Sinatra from the inner sanctum. Perhaps. But other, more cogent reasons animated the move.

In a 1997 book about blacklisted artists, *Tender Comrades,* authors McGillan and Buhle single out Sinatra for his humane treatment of those who were victimized by the "Red Scare." Independent filmmaker and art critic Faith Hubley recalls his kindness and quotes Lionel Stander, that gravel-voiced, one-eyed character actor, to the effect that Sinatra not only read Karl Marx, but "Old Blue Eyes" was the only actor who could "comprehend it" (292, 542). Whatever the underlying reasons, Sinatra's Democratic residence was part of a distant past. Wooed by Agnew, courted by Nixon, seduced by Reagan, the kid from Brooklyn by way of Hoboken climbed luxury's ladder to embrace fat-cat politicos and conservative leaders as his boon companions. Vintage Sinatra, say around midnight of 1945, had a better voice in this writer's judgment and, bereft of sour grapes, sounder politics.

Brooklyn's best writer, Pete Hamill, has the last word: Sinatra mattered because he was the first artist/entertainer to get involved, politically, proudly, and passionately (Hamill 1998: 136–37). Hurt as a little boy by the hate-filled epithets hurled at him, he never forgot. Sinatra signed petitions. Throwing caution to the summer wind, he threw his hat into the arena. He supported candidates. He spoke out. A new breed of entertainer, he refused to play the "invisible man" or sit on the political fence. Surrounded by hostile children, that vulnerable boy on the ledge represents everyone who was marginalized in America: blacks, Jews, Catholics, immigrants, Hispanics, and gays. Happily, we all found a champion in a self-styled saloon singer from New Jersey. Because of his powerful voice, the doors in our nation's house opened and the walls of bigotry started to crumble. And America, in the eloquent words of poet Langston Hughes, "became America again."

4

🎤

Frank Sinatra and Civil Rights

Leonard Mustazza

*I*f bandleader Harry James had had his way back in 1939, the legendary performer the world knows as Frank Sinatra might have been known to us as Frankie Satin, or Frankie Trent, or some other such catchy and easily pronounced name. On the other hand, perhaps his name would not be so well known if he had acquiesced in the pressure to submerge his ethnic identity in the insipid melting-pot stew—a pressure to which popular performers would continue to succumb through the decades following and to this very day. That decision was deliberate and emotional, as Sinatra once admitted to writer Pete Hamill:

> "Of course, it meant something to me to be the son of immigrants. How could it not? How the hell could it not? I grew up for a few years thinking I was just another American kid. Then I discovered at—what? five? six?—I discovered that some people thought I was a dago. A wop. A guinea." An angry pause. "You know, like I didn't have a fucking *name*." An angrier pause.

"That's why years later, when Harry [James] wanted me to change my name, I said no way, baby. The name is Sinatra. Frank fucking Sinatra." (Hamill 1998: 37–38)

To be sure, Frank Sinatra's fame rests on his greatness as an entertainer. However, talent alone is not enough to account for his professional longevity, much less his transition from pop performer to cultural icon. That status was achieved as much by the media persona he projected and the values he endorsed over the course of some sixty years in the public eye. Among the most culturally significant of those values was his outspoken belief in the basic dignity of all human beings, regardless of race or ethnic origin or religion. The early decision to maintain his Italian surname was merely the first symbolic assertion of this now-fashionable principle.

During the period of his phenomenal rise in the 1940s, again following his comeback in the 1950s, and for the long stretch of time until his death in 1998, Italian Americans, American Jews, Irish Americans, Polish Americans, and other clearly identifiable ethnic groups have regarded him as *their* star, someone who, unashamed, retained his ethnic identity, who, despite his great fame, spoke *like* them and *for* them, who held out the hope that they, too, could aspire to better positions in our often parochial society. As Pete Hamill notes in his excellent little book *Why Sinatra Matters,* "the life and career of Frank Sinatra are inseparable from the most powerful of all modern American myths: the saga of immigration. Because he was the son of immigrants, his success thrilled millions who were products of the same rough history" (1998: 37).

Sinatra's defense of the social "underdog," moreover, was not limited to ethnic whites. Early on he also took up the banner of racial equality, a decidedly unfashionable stance that came not without cost to him personally and professionally but one that he steadfastly maintained for his entire career. His efforts did not go unnoticed. For years now, the black community has applauded his pioneering efforts on their behalf. In 1987, for instance, the magazine *Jet* did a story on Sinatra's relationships with blacks in response to Kitty Kelley's character assassination of the singer in her unauthorized biography published in 1986. It has not been widely reported, the magazine noted, that Sinatra had written a piece for *Ebony* magazine in 1958 entitled "The Way I Look at Race." The editors of *Jet* called it "the most significant stand taken by a famous white person since Mrs. Eleanor Roosevelt . . . gave support to the cause of racial justice and equality" (*Jet* 1987: 56). In the days following his death, a good many African Americans echoed this sentiment. New York columnist Stanley Crouch wrote that Sinatra "was a man who seemed absolutely free of ethnic or religious bias. It wasn't that he didn't love being an Italian-American; it was just that he didn't love it so much that he couldn't like or love anybody from a different background" (Crouch 1998: 49). *Baltimore Sun* writer Gregory Kane called Sinatra "a veritable one-man Hollywood civil-rights squad, hiring blacks for his films long before it became considered the fair and moral thing to do" (Kane 1998: 1). And Maria Cole, the widow of the great Nat King Cole, was among the many American blacks who spoke of his courage in battling racial prejudice in the 1940s and 1950s. "There was no question he despised bigotry," she told the *Boston Herald*. "And he had no bigotry in him. None at all" (Mueller: 1998: 50). It is clear, therefore, that through his words, his art, and his deeds, Frank Sinatra advanced multiculturalism long before it became the right thing to do. Given this vigorous defense of Americans' basic rights, is it any wonder that he was chosen to receive some of the nation's highest honors, including the Freedom Medal (Philadelphia, 1977), the Medal of Freedom (Washington, 1985), and, posthumously, the Congressional Gold Medal?

Although this essay generally considers Frank Sinatra's advancement of racial, ethnic, and religious freedom throughout his long and distinguished career, it is specifically concerned with the least known of Sinatra's activities on behalf of his values—his own published writings on the subject. I would like to focus on four articles in particular—two of them published in 1945, when the singer was a young idol to millions; one of them in 1958, when, having made his spectacular comeback, he sat atop the entertainment world; and the final one in 1991, when he was generally regarded as the elder statesman of show business. The message heard in these writings is totally consistent, but, as we shall see, the writer's tone, diction, and approach to his subject change considerably during that fifty-six-year period.

The earliest stories about Sinatra's direct championing of civil rights date back to his days as the boy singer with Tommy Dorsey's band in 1940 to 1942. One such incident, dramatically portrayed in the 1992 television miniseries *Sinatra,* involved Dorsey's talented African American arranger, Sy Oliver, with whom Sinatra offered to share a hotel room on their road trips. When a hotel clerk refused to allow Oliver to stay in the whites-only hotel, Sinatra was outraged, and he responded the way he always did when he was outraged—swiftly and viscerally. He pulled the morally benighted clerk across the counter and threatened to tear up the hotel if the man did not give Oliver a room key immediately. As critic Andrew Sarris pointed out in his liner notes to the 1986 Columbia package *The Voice,* "An early victim of anti-Italian bigotry, there has never been in him the slightest trace of anti-black bigotry." It's true, and there were many such stories of his courageous action at the time. As was once noted, "At a time when segregation was virtually a way of life in the U.S. and Black entertainers couldn't stay in hotels where they performed, Sinatra put his career on the line to try to make things better for many Black performers of the '40s and '50s" (*Jet* 1987: 56).

To be sure, those actions earned the young performer the respect of those who themselves felt ethnically and racially oppressed and, on the other extreme, the ire of right-wing elements in our society, not the least of these elements being the conservative and potent Hearst press. In fact, it is no mere coincidence that the lurid press accounts of Sinatra's unsavory associations with shady characters began to appear in the 1940s, a time when the singer had the audacity not only to take a stand on the question of race but also to support the liberal policies of the Roosevelt administration, going so far as to name his only son after the president he so admired (Wiener 1998: 38; Wiener 1986: 21–23; Vare 1995: 64–69).

Interesting in this regard is the fact that the greatest concentration of his public work on behalf of racial and religious "tolerance" (the term in vogue at the time) came in 1945, the year of FDR's death and the end of World War II. Using his famous name and his vast influence among young people, he engaged in a variety of activities designed to promote this important social value. That year he starred as himself in a short RKO film titled *The House I Live In.* Directed by Mervyn LeRoy and written by Albert Maltz (who would soon make it onto Senator Joe McCarthy's infamous Hollywood blacklist), the film has Sinatra lecturing a group of prejudiced boys about the injustices of moral and religious bias. It concludes with his singing the title song, a number he would do in concert right up through the end of his long career— further evidence of his deeply held, lifelong commitment to this principle.

Also in 1945, he toured the country giving lectures to high school students about tolerance, acceptance of individual differences, and celebration of the diversity that makes America great. The most famous of these lectures occurred during a racially charged incident at Froebel High School in Gary, Indiana, in November of that year. The white students of the school staged a strike to protest the new principal's "pro-Negro policies" of allowing the school's 270 African American students to participate in the student government association, to use the school pool, and to play in Froebel's orchestra. Although black students made up 50 percent of the school's enrollment, white students and their parents wanted them barred from extracurricular activities, fearing that such accomplishments might give blacks some competitive advantage in the job market, notably jobs in Gary's steel mills. While the popular Sinatra was able to attract a large crowd of white students and to deliver his message, *Life* magazine (whose reporting on the young idol was never favorable in those days) claimed that "Frankie" only "made some vague references to the American way of life and the Hot Dog" and ultimately failed to prevent the strike (*Life* 1945: 45). Of course, the *Life* reporter didn't interview any of the students to determine whether the young Sinatra's message got through to some of them; the story merely reports on the strike, which, by all indications, was primarily arranged and promoted by the white students' parents.

Apart from personal appearances and film work, Sinatra also became a writer on this subject in 1945. He published two short articles, one in a now-defunct periodical titled *Magazine Digest* and the other in the student publication *Scholastic*. Although these writings are perhaps the least known of his pro-tolerance activities, they provide interesting insights into his view of America and the modes in which he communicated that view to two distinct audiences: adults and teenagers, whom he influenced most and who, he hoped, would influence their parents in turn.

The first of these articles, titled "Let's Not Forget We're *All* Foreigners," appeared in the July 1945 issue of *Magazine Digest*. The three-page piece features a drawing of the young Sinatra's head next to which there appears a quote from the article: "Wops, dagoes, kikes, and niggers are America." The magazine's identification of the author reads, accurately though somewhat ironically: "Although Frank Sinatra is known as the world's No. 1 'swooner,' he is working equally hard at another job which he considers just as important—that of bringing to the attention of America the vital question of racial tolerance." The dependent clause of this statement is, by today's standards, amusing, but it is also revealing when we consider the time during which it was composed. No one today would say that a famous person had taken a political or moral stand *although* that person is really a singer or actor or athlete. We've come to expect our celebrities to endorse values and thereby influence people, just as surely as their paid product endorsements are used for this purpose. But such was not the case in 1945, and this curious caveat subtly indicates just how unique Sinatra's moral stand was for its time. When performers wanted to be known merely as pleasant entertainers and steer clear of controversy, it took a good deal of conviction on Sinatra's part to come down squarely on one side of a controversial issue. But, then again, this was Sinatra, albeit a young one, and the world would later have ample opportunity to learn that this performer would never shy away from controversy, particularly those involving his own deeply held beliefs.

Written in a colloquial style and aimed at an adult audience, the article is divisible into three parts. The first is concerned with name-calling, and Sinatra asserts that, contrary to the old saying about "sticks and stones," names *can* hurt when those names are aimed at an individual's race, ethnicity, or religion. He knows, he says, because he was himself the victim of such treatment growing up in Hoboken in the 1920s and 1930s. Extrapolating from that experience, he asks the reader to imagine what it feels like to be categorized in this way and, adding insult to injury, to have stereotypical modifiers added to the epithet—*dirty* nigger or *greasy* wop or *stingy* kike. The second movement of the piece is concerned with the Nazis and their claim of being a "master race," a concept that Sinatra scoffs at. "Every race produces men with big brains and men with small brains; men with big strong muscles, and men like me," he writes self-effacingly but boldly (9). Finally, quoting Lincoln's Gettysburg Address and the Pledge of Allegiance, Sinatra defines America as a pluralistic society in which no manner of prejudice has any place.

Two months later, on September 17, 1945, he published virtually the same article in *Scholastic,* a magazine aimed at young people. To tailor the message for this audience, he changed the title to the more colloquial "What's This About Races?" and added a different introduction. Ironically, he begins by telling readers that what he has to say ought really to be aimed at their parents. That he has already done so in the *Magazine Digest* piece is deliberately not mentioned. In fact, of the two audiences that Sinatra addresses in these articles, this youthful one is far more promising in terms of beneficial social change than the adult group, whose prejudices are likely to be more set. Again using a self-deprecating persona, he asserts that kids at the time were a lot smarter than those of his own generation and were accordingly fit for the kinds of future changes he wanted to see effected. "After all," he writes, "you are the parents of tomorrow. You'll be around here longest. So it's most important to you that some things which aren't quite the way they should be now get going right—and stay right" (Mustazza 1998: 23–25).

Whether these missives to his admirers made for any widespread social change is hard to determine. Nevertheless, Sinatra pushed on, reaching well beyond parents and their offspring. On January 6, 1947, he published a letter in the *New Republic* to former vice president and liberal presidential hopeful Henry Wallace. Written on December 7, 1946—the fifth anniversary of the Japanese attack on Pearl Harbor—he invokes, paradoxically, brutal memories of the war[1] and warm associations with that Christmas season to make his point about tolerance:

> Mutual respect, whether it's on the slum level of one little kid for another or at the top of the ladder where it's one government for another, one race for another or one belief for another, is nothing but tolerance. . . . It is now 15 months after the defeat of powers that laughed at tolerance and planned to enslave the world by setting one faith against another and one nation against another. And what have we? We've made only small, suspicious

progress toward international understanding while the world festers with racial and religious discontent. . . . May we find [the right leadership] before another December 7 catches up with a world almost oblivious to the fact that only 18 days separate the anniversaries of peace on earth and war on earth. (Sinatra 1947: 3, 46)

It is fascinating to watch the young and idealistic Sinatra use the "pulpit" of his fame for a good cause—something that performers would learn to do with greater frequency in the future. Even more interesting is the evolution of Sinatra's influence as his career and power grew. Before long he would use a good deal more than words to get his message across.

In 1953 Frank Sinatra did an extraordinary thing—he reinvented himself as an artist. Out of the ashes of a ruined career, he rose to the top of several entertainment realms. The dreamy crooner gave way to the singer of jazzy swing and heartbreaking ballads; the screen song-and-dance man came back an Academy Award–winning actor; the radio personality was now *seen* and heard coast to coast on a new invention called television; the bobby-sox idol became an adult audience's swingin' hero. And yet for all of these changes, it is clear that his core values remained unaltered, notably his commitment to civil rights in America. From his perch atop the entertainment world, he used his considerable drawing and earning power to open doors for black performers, who, as outrageous as it seems from our own perspective, were not allowed to dine or live at the venues at which they played as entertainers. Sammy Davis Jr., for instance, was allowed to dine at New York's Copacabana as Sinatra's guest only after Sinatra threatened not to sing for the hundreds who'd lined up to see him perform. Likewise, he threatened not to perform at the Sands in Las Vegas because Nat King Cole and other black performers were not allowed to stay at the hotel or eat in the dining room. "I'll burn it down before they do that to him again," he once raged. "I own this bar joint. If he does not eat in the dining room, I don't work here anymore" (Mueller 1998: 50). Stories of this sort are legion in the entertainment business.

It was from this influential position in 1958 that Sinatra again committed his thoughts on the matter of race to paper. The piece, as told to Allan Morrison, appeared in *Ebony* magazine that July under the title "The Way I Look at Race." Unlike his 1945 writings on the subject, this later piece is lengthy (eight pages) and noticeably more mature, serious, even aggressive in tone, diction, and outlook. It begins not with idea that we are one big American family; rather, it sounds a more elemental note—that of friendship:

> A man's friends are probably the most precious things he has for they give his life warmth and meaning and excitement. Without real friendship life would be a pretty empty experience. . . . In one of Shakespeare's most famous plays, *Hamlet,* he wrote the following wonderful words of advice to a son from his father:

> > The Friends thou hast, and their adoption tried,
> > Grapple them to thy soul with hoops of steel.

> Now I'm no scholar—singing is my business—but these lines beautifully answer for me the ageless question of how a man should choose his friends, and keep them. . . . A friend to me has no race, no class and belongs to no minority. My friendships were formed out of affection, mutual respect and a feeling of having something strong in common. These are eternal values that cannot be racially classified. . . . The fact is that I don't "like" Negroes any more than I "like" Jews or Moslems or Italians or any other group. . . . My personal relationships are not determined by the boundaries of a country or what society thinks of certain kinds of human beings. (Sinatra 1958: 35)

Unlike the earlier essays, in which Sinatra's point is the general theme of American democracy and the benefits to it of inclusivity, this one is decidedly personal. Accordingly, the personal "voice" articulated in these opening paragraphs is sustained throughout the essay, moving through a variety of issues:

- His then most recent film, *Kings Go Forth,* which dealt with the problems associated with interracial romance.
- His own experiences with racial prejudice growing up in Hoboken, New Jersey.
- His professional experiences with racial and religious intolerance, involving both himself and close friends, including Louis Armstrong and Nat Cole.

- His personal friendships with black entertainers and sports figures, including Sammy Davis Jr. and Joe Louis.[2]
- The influence of black entertainers in his own development as a musician. The list of such entertainers is long, including the likes of Louis Armstrong, Duke Ellington, Billie Holiday, Ella Fitzgerald, Count Basie, and Miles Davis.
- The slow but steady erosion of segregation in America.
- The fact that Hollywood and, to a lesser extent, television, were working to eradicate racial and religious stereotyping.

The final page of the article sounds much more like the earlier essays, involving as it does an indirect plea to American youths to eradicate the hatreds and biases passed along by "prejudiced parents and politically inspired agitators" (Sinatra 1958: 44). When people are brought together, he concludes, only then will all Americans be regarded not as members of minorities but as human beings.

Over the course of his next four decades in public life, Sinatra's formal politics would make the long journey from Kennedy Democrat to Reagan Republican. And yet this conservative affiliation did not affect in the least his lifelong liberal belief in the basic rights of all human beings. The 1960s began with a curiously little-known honor paid to the singer by the black community. He was awarded an honorary Doctor of Humanities degree by Wilberforce University for, in the words of *Jet* magazine "practicing what he preached 26 years ago." In presenting this honor, President Rembert Stokes declared that the degree recognized Frank Sinatra's "practice of true democracy" (*Jet*, 1987, p. 56). And practice such democracy he would continue to do, placing his fame, his example, and his talent at the service of his beliefs. Among his charitable activities in the decades to come were performances to benefit national organizations like the NAACP, Martin Luther King's Southern Christian Leadership Conference, and the Latino organization Nosotros. He also did work on behalf of causes and issues that moved him personally. In March 1981, for instance, he joined Sammy Davis Jr. in a benefit performance at Atlanta's Civic Center to help finance the investigation into the serial murders of children in that city.

And yet, like everything else in the life and career of this feisty, principled man, even his stance on civil rights was not without controversy. When the Los Angeles chapter of the NAACP presented Sinatra with its Lifetime Achievement Award on May 14, 1987 (ironically, Frank Sinatra's death would come on that same date eleven years later), several civil rights activists nationally and a small group of protesters outside the venue of the award, the Century Plaza Hotel, objected, citing his appearance in 1981 at Sun City, a resort in apartheid-torn South Africa. While not excusing his decision to perform there except to say that South African prime minister Pieter Botha "is a bum," the seventy-one-year-old Sinatra did say something about his publicly held convictions of the past half-century: "Those of you who know me feel pretty secure about the way I think, the way I am. As far as anyone else is concerned, if my lifetime—more than half a century lived in the spotlight of public life—if those 50-plus years are not enough to show my covenant on the issue of civil rights, I am not going to waste my time defending the obvious or itemizing a laundry list of my deeds to benefit the brotherhood of man. Even saying this much embarrasses me" (Greenwood and Stein 1987: 22).

Several of those in attendance spoke up in his defense,[3] although the one he offered—his lifelong "covenant," as he aptly put it—was better than any of theirs.

On July 4, 1991, a few months before his seventy-sixth year of life and more than fifty years since he first began his advocacy of civil rights, Frank Sinatra sounded off again in print on the question of race in America. This one-page piece, his final public utterance on the subject, came in a *Los Angeles Times* editorial titled "The Haters and Bigots Will Be Judged." Of the four essays discussed here, this one is clearly the most aggressive, as if he were asking, "Are we *still* talking about this subject after all these years?" Using the Independence Day holiday as a fitting occasion to question what ought to be fundamental American values, he begins with what amounts to a frontal assault—a verbal barrage whose strident language and tone are a far cry from the youthful "hip" pleas found in his 1945 essays: "We are created equal! No one of us is better than any of us! That's the headline proclaimed in 1776 and inscribed across centuries in the truth of the ages. . . . Then why do I still hear race- and color-haters spewing their poisons? Why do I still flinch at innuendoes of venom and inequality? Why do innocent children still grow up to be despised? Why do haters' jokes still get big laughs when passed in whispers from scum to scum? . . . As for the others, those cross-burning bigots to whom mental slavery is alive and well, I don't envy their trials in the next world, where their thoughts and words and actions will be judged by a jury of One" (5).

What is unique to this piece is its metaphysical emphasis. In keeping with its allusive title, there are numerous references to religion generally and to God specifically. It might be argued perhaps that, at nearly seventy-six, his own advanced age prompted his turn toward the consolations of religion and hence his use of the deity now in his condemnation of bigots. In fact, on a purely personal note, he even claims at one point in the essay that he is "no angel," that he'd done things in his life of which he was not too proud. On the other hand, there is also a genuineness and appropriateness in his use of this religious motif. After all, despite its separation of church and state, America *is* a religious country, a fact that is evidenced in its most cherished recitations, anthems, and songs, on its monetary currency, in its everyday life. And so, since American freedom, justice, individuality, and constitutional equality are the common themes in all of Sinatra's writings and pronouncements on the subject, it is hardly surprising that he should turn to a decidedly religious theme as support for his position.

As noted earlier, it is impossible to gauge just what social benefits and attitudinal changes, if any, have occurred as a result of Frank Sinatra's occasional writings on the subject of racial, ethnic, and religious bigotry. Indeed, the writer himself qualifies just about every article with the assertion that he's "just a singer," but we've also found increasingly in our celebrity-admiring society that people are often much more willing to listen to the moral "lessons" of entertainers (for better or worse) than they are to the teachings of those who profess to be moralists by trade.

There is a fascinating short poem published by Gerald Early in *The Prairie Schooner* in 1989. Titled "Listening to Frank Sinatra," it concerns a man who encounters some grotesque people working in a carnival sideshow. When one of these people is asked how he spends his day, he asserts that he listens to Frank Sinatra. The speaker ponders this paradox: The notion that these unusual individuals get through their existence by listening to the eternal wisdom they find in the music of this singular man. And, the speaker concludes, if listening to Frank Sinatra could speak so inspiringly to the man who was the "horror of horrors," just imagine what such listening could do for the rest of us (Early 1989: 11; Mustazza 1998: 109–10). If even a fraction of Frank Sinatra's many admirers over the course of some sixty years also *listened* to and took to heart his more didactic lessons on fairness and equity, then, in more than one respect, he left the nation a better place than the one he was born into more than eighty years ago.

Notes

1. Ironically, while Sinatra obliquely invokes memories of the Nazi atrocities during the war, many historians have also pointed out that, for many African Americans, World War II also provided an eye-opening expression of American prejudice. For instance, in his book *Promises to Keep* (1995), Paul Boyer notes that "for the nation's African-American population, the war brought about changes heavy with implications for the future. Although the military services remained segregated, for some of the 1 million blacks in uniform the experience provided glimpses of European societies less rigidly racist than the United States" (20). Curiously, France, Italy, and other European countries proved to be far more accommodating than the very nation these service personnel were fighting to defend.

2. For an interesting personal reminiscence about the relationship between Sinatra and Louis, see Betty DeRamus's article, "Sinatra Helped Sick Joe Louis Keep on Fighting in Las Vegas" (1998).

3. Among those who defended Sinatra were Stevie Wonder and Sammy Davis Jr., who said, "I've never asked him for anything for my people in 40 years that he did not do. There'd be little film on me if it hadn't been for him" ("L.A. Branch of NAACP Give Sinatra Achievement Award," 1987).

5

Frank Sinatra
and Presidential Politics

Michael Nelson

The close relationship between celebrities and politicians has become so familiar a part of the American political landscape as to seem unremarkable. The motives of each party to this relationship are clear. On the Hollywood side, as Ronald Brownstein has written, "Celebrities look to politicians to validate them as part of the company of serious men and women" (1990: 10). One thinks, for example, of Charlton Heston's earnest defense of gun owners as head of the National Rifle Association, or the relentless grilling on the issues to which the Hollywood Women's Political Caucus regularly subjects endorsement-seeking Democratic presidential candidates.

On the political side of the relationship, Brownstein notes, "politicians look to celebrities to validate them as part of the company of the famous"

(10). As political parties have declined in influence among voters, politicians have been encouraged to link themselves in the public's mind with stars and with the courage, intelligence, compassion, and other qualities that people associate with them because of the roles they play. Thus in 1976 Jimmy Carter involved the Allman Brothers in his presidential campaign as a way of softening his otherwise straitlaced public image. Twelve years later George H. W. Bush enlisted country music stars and Arnold Schwarzenegger in his run for the presidency in the hope that they would mute the public's impression of him as effete and elitist. Politicians also look to celebrities to help them raise money for their campaigns.

As in music, so in politics: Frank Sinatra paved the way, in this case for the intertwining of celebrities and politicians that has become so prominent a feature of modern politics. Prior to Sinatra, mainstream entertainers shied away from partisan political activity for fear of complicating their public images and alienating a large portion of their audience. (Studio executives were heavily involved, but quietly and mostly as a way of promoting and protecting their business interests [Brownstein 1990: ch. 1–4].) Sinatra broke the mold in 1944 with his active support of Franklin D. Roosevelt's bid for a fourth term as president and his public campaign for civil rights. For the next quarter century, he continued to work for Democratic candidates, especially John F. Kennedy in 1960 and Hubert H. Humphrey in 1968, as well as for select liberal political causes. During the 1970s Sinatra became a Republican for a complex set of reasons that had less to do with his turning conservative than with his personal disappointment with the Democrats.

Sinatra's Early Years

Pathbreaking as Sinatra's political involvement was, abstention from politics would have been unnatural to him. Sinatra grew up in a highly political home in a politics-dominated community. His father, Marty Sinatra, worked for the city of Hoboken, New Jersey, as a fireman, eventually rising to the rank of captain. More important, his mother, Dolly Sinatra, was a leading cog in the Hudson County political machine of Mayor Frank ("I Am the Mayor") Hague. Extraordinarily for her time—women could not yet vote—Dolly was named leader of the Third Ward in Hoboken's Ninth District because of her familiarity with the many dialects of Italian that were spoken in the immigrant-dominated neighborhood. Her job was to help her poor neighbors in their dealings with city hall, then round them up to vote on election day (Hamill 1998: ch. 2–3).

Sinatra was that rarest of things in an Italian neighborhood: an only child. Because Dolly's political activities kept her so busy, often his only alternatives as a young boy were to stay at home by himself or to tag along with his mother. "I've been campaigning for Democrats ever since I marched in a parade for Al Smith when I was a twelve-year-old kid [in 1928]," he liked to say as an adult (Taraborrelli 1997a: 224). Even earlier, says daughter Tina Sinatra, "Dad says he was carrying placards for candidates when he couldn't read what was on the signs" (Hersh 1997: 139). During an April 1973 concert at the White House for Italian prime minister Giulio Andreotti, Sinatra told the audience, "When I was a kid back in New Jersey, I thought it would be a great boot if I could get a glimpse of the mayor of Hoboken in a parade" (Taraborrelli 1997a: 397). John F. Kennedy introduced Sinatra at the 1961 inaugural gala as one who, "long before he could sing, used to poll a Democratic precinct back in New Jersey" (Kelley 1986: 285). In truth, once Dolly became reconciled to Sinatra's passion to sing professionally, she booked him at local Democratic party events. By some accounts, she used political influence both to get Sinatra into the singing group the Three Flashes, which (as the now-renamed Hoboken Four) was about to make some movie shorts with entertainment impresario Major Bowes, and to arrange the landmark 1938 booking at the Rustic Cabin nightclub in nearby Englewood Cliffs that earned Sinatra his first notice as a singer (Levy 1998: 17).

Dolly Sinatra gave her son more than an exposure to politics and a boost in his career. As the journalist Pete Hamill has written, "she also gave him some of her values. . . . From adolescence on, Sinatra understood patronage." Specifically, "She knew how to get a lawyer or a bailbondsman," according to Hamill. "She showed up at weddings and wakes. She was generous with her personal time, repeatedly helping those neighbors who were less fortunate than the Sinatras" (Hamill 1998: 78). "Just as her son would become years later," Sinatra biographer Randy Taraborrelli has added, "she was practically a *padrone*" (Taraborrelli 1997a: 27).

Sinatra and Franklin D. Roosevelt

Sinatra's meteoric rise in show business (by the mid-1940s, he was "a bigger star in more media than anyone else in the world" [Levy 1998: 20]) did not affect his sense of himself as a little guy who was represented politically by the Democratic party and, in particular, by Franklin D. Roosevelt. FDR had first been elected president in 1932, when Sinatra was sixteen years old. On January 10, 1944, Sinatra named his newborn son after the president: Franklin (not Francis) Sinatra.

Sinatra's first personal encounter with Roosevelt left him star-struck. On September 28, 1944, in the company of New York restaurateur Toots Shor, Sinatra met the president at a White House tea. Referring to the singer's recent appearances at the Paramount Theater, Roosevelt jokingly commended him: "Fainting, which once was so prevalent, has become a lost art among the ladies. I'm glad you have revived it." Sinatra was awed: "I thought here is the greatest guy alive today and here's a little guy from Hoboken, shaking his hand. He knows about everything, even my racket" (Shaw 1968: 77).

Sinatra's visit with the president was controversial. Politicians and columnists denounced it. Senator Kenneth Wherry, a Nebraska Republican, scoffed, "That crooner! Mr. Roosevelt could spend his time better conferring with members of the Senate." Westbrook Pegler scornfully labeled Sinatra "the New Dealing crooner," and others questioned the propriety of the president honoring someone who had neither served in the armed forces (Sinatra was 4-F) nor gone overseas to entertain the troops. (He made a USO tour the following year.) Nearly all of Sinatra's advisers urged him to withdraw from partisan politics lest, as Sinatra himself summarized their views, "you may lose fans who don't agree with you" (Shaw 1968: 77–78).

Instead, Sinatra campaigned widely for Roosevelt in 1944, singing and speaking to audiences all over the country. The first politically active star with an appeal to young people, he told audiences, "This peace will depend on your parents' votes on November seventh." He donated at least $5,000 to the Roosevelt campaign and, in a nationally broadcast election-eve rally at Madison Square Garden (from which many pro-FDR entertainers had begged off, fearing that they would alienate half of their fans), he told an audience of millions: "Since he is good for me and my kids and my country, he must be good for all the other ordinary guys and their kids" (Kelley 1986: 94; N. Sinatra 1985: 63–64; Wilson 1976: 64).

Sinatra, Civil Rights, and the Left

Sinatra's early political involvement was not confined to presidential politics. Beginning in the 1940s, a decade when civil rights was not a popular or prominent political cause, he campaigned ardently for racial and religious toleration. "What other star at the top of the charts had thrown himself into the civil rights struggle so directly?" asked the historian Jon Wiener in a 1991 book (265). His answer: none.

Wiener recalled the annual screening of the movie short, *The House I Live In,* in his St. Paul, Minnesota, Sunday school class. Sinatra, screenwriter Albert Maltz, composers Lewis Allan and Earl Robinson, and director Mervyn Leroy, supported by RKO, had donated their time and talent to make the ten-minute film in 1945. In it Sinatra steps outside from a recording session for a cigarette, sees some kids taunting a Jewish boy, and intervenes to preach tolerance in word ("Look, fellas, religion makes no difference except to a Nazi or somebody as stupid) and song ("All races and religions,/That's America to me"). Prejudice was unpatriotic and alien to traditional American values, Sinatra argued. The eighth-grade-educated singer, on the advice of his publicist George Evans, had been reading books such as sociologist Gunnar Myrdal's *An American Dilemma*. Evans, an ardent liberal, was the only Sinatra adviser who supported his political activism (Wiener 1991: 105–106; Levy 1998: 68; Kelley 1986: 105–106).

Sinatra's opposition to discrimination was long-standing. Even as a six-year-old, he intensely disliked the ethnic name-calling that was so widespread among the boys in his neighborhood and argued with his mother when she questioned his bringing home a Jewish friend. On stage and in the recording studio, he changed the opening line of "Old Man River" from

"Niggers all work on the Mississippi" (or even "Darkies all work," which lyricist Oscar Hammerstein had substituted) to "Here we all work." He slugged a southern counterman who refused to serve a black musician in his orchestra. Sinatra's civil rights work and, subsequently, his highly visible friendship with entertainer Sammy Davis Jr., always reduced his popularity in the South (N. Sinatra 1985: 7–8, 62, 214; Shaw 1968: 84; Kelley 1986: 107–109). He appeared in person to urge tolerance at numerous high schools where racial or religious tensions were running high. "Your dad was a hero to these kids and he took this powerful message right to them," Vice President Hubert H. Humphrey later wrote to Sinatra's daughter, Nancy. "I am convinced that this early dedication and activity personified by your father helped create the political climate that made possible the passage of the civil rights legislation in the 1960s." Humphrey, who was the mayor of Minneapolis at the time, believed that "[t]housands and thousands of boys and girls in the 1940s who have become parents in the 1960s had their eyes opened for the first time to the evils of prejudice by your dad" (N. Sinatra 1985: 214).

Sinatra's crusade for civil rights came at considerable professional cost. To be sure, Ed Sullivan, then a New York columnist, defended Sinatra ardently. Rebuking stars such as Al Jolson and Rudy Vallee for not yoking their celebrity to a social conscience, Sullivan wrote: "Some performers will suggest that Sinatra is stupid to step out of character, suggest that singing and social significance shouldn't be coupled. But it seems to this observer that Sinatra instead has added something new and important to popular singing, a species of disinterested public service we should all render to the things we believe" (Shaw 1968: 97).

But Sullivan's praise for Sinatra was drowned out by a barrage of angry criticism. In 1946 the notoriously racist leader of the America First party, Gerald L. K. Smith, told the House Un-American Activities Committee (HUAC) that Sinatra "has been doing some pretty clever stuff for the Reds." Indeed, during the eight years that followed the release of *The House I Live In,* Sinatra was labeled a communist before HUAC twelve times. In 1949 the California State Senate Committee on Un-American Activities charged Sinatra with having "followed or appeased some of the Communist party line program over a long period of time." Columnists for conservative newspaper chains joined the chorus. Sinatra was "one of Hollywood's leading travelers on the road to Red fascism," charged Hearst writer Lee Mortimer. Later, on the basis of a tip from a source in the federal government's Bureau of Narcotics, Mortimer and Scripps-Howard columnist Robert Ruark tried to discredit Sinatra in their readers' minds by reporting on his 1947 trip to Havana, where he was seen in the company of mobster Lucky Luciano (Shaw 1968: 84; Wiener 1991: 263–64; Rockwell 1984: 101; Hamill 1998: 144). The story was the first of many that linked Sinatra with organized crime.

Nonetheless, Sinatra remained active and outspoken for civil rights. "When I was young," he later recalled, "people used to ask me why I sent money to the NACCP and, you know, tried to help in my own small way. I used to say, Because we've been there too, man. It wasn't just black people hanging from the ends of those fucking ropes" (Hamill 1998: 45). The ending of Sinatra's 1958 movie, *Kings Go Forth,* left little doubt that the character he portrayed would marry a black woman. In 1961, within a few days of the inauguration eve gala he had organized for President Kennedy, Sinatra did a benefit concert at Carnegie Hall for Martin Luther King Jr. and the Southern Christian Leadership Council. By the time other mainstream stars became publicly involved in the civil rights movement during the early 1960s, Sinatra had been active for nearly twenty years (Brownstein 1990: 169).

Sinatra also worked on behalf of other liberal causes. In 1944 he had moved from New Jersey to California in furtherance of his burgeoning movie career. After FDR died in 1945 and the country's wartime alliance with the Soviet Union was ended, much of Hollywood, led by a growing cohort of New York writers and actors who had moved west with the advent of the "talkies," shifted their political allegiance to the radical left. Sinatra shifted with them. In July 1946, at the same meeting of the newly formed Hollywood Independent Citizens Committee of the Arts, Sciences, and Professions (HICCASP) that refused to adopt a resolution rejecting communism "as a desirable form of government for the U.S.A.," Sinatra was elected vice president of the organization. Like most HICCASP members, he supported Henry A. Wallace when President Harry S. Truman fired the left-leaning secretary of commerce in September. In a letter to the *New Republic,*

Sinatra even urged Wallace to "take up the fight we like to think of as ours—the fight for tolerance, which is the basis of any fight for peace." He publicly blasted the right-wing Spanish dictator Francisco Franco. In 1947 Sinatra slammed the ongoing HUAC investigation of communist influence in Hollywood. "Once they get the movies throttled," he asked, "how long will it be before the committee gets to work on freedom of the air? . . . If you can make a pitch on a nationwide radio network for a square deal for the underdog, will they call you a commie?" (Patterson 1996: 189).

For all the seriousness of his reading, Sinatra was, in his own words, "Not a heavy thinker." "I'm not the kind of a guy who does a lot of brain work about why or how I happened to get into something," he said. "I get an idea—maybe I get sore about something. And when I get sore enough, I do something about it." By 1948 Hollywood was feeling beleaguered by the assault from Washington. So was Sinatra, but in his case beleaguerment over politics was compounded by growing criticism of his alleged mob ties, his marital infidelity, and his weakening (at least by the standards of the newest fad: Frankie Laine–style belters) singing voice. "I don't like communists," Sinatra now said, "and I have nothing to do with any organization except the Knights of Columbus." Although he did not actively campaign for Truman in 1948, neither did he support Wallace, who was running as a left-wing third-party candidate (Kelley 1986: 110).

The 1950s

The left may have been in retreat in Hollywood after the HUAC hearings, but liberalism was not. In the early 1950s, as Sinatra was struggling to restore his singing and acting career, he fell in with the Holmby Hills Rat Pack, a group of show business and literary friends who gathered around the actors Humphrey Bogart and Lauren Bacall. According to Bacall, to be a member, "[o]ne had to be addicted to nonconformity, staying up late, drinking, laughing, and not caring what anyone thought or said about us." Sinatra fit in so well that he was made "pack master" of the group. One also had to be politically liberal. As the actor William Holden observed bitterly, "The Rat Packers are only interested in being with people who think exactly as they do. You have to believe in the same things, support the same political candidates, have the exact same politics." Adlai E. Stevenson, the Democratic governor of Illinois and a rising favorite among liberals, often visited the group when he was in Los Angeles (Quirk and Schoell: 1998: 56, 61–62).

Sinatra joined Bogart's Rat Pack in strongly supporting Stevenson in his losing bids for president against Dwight D. Eisenhower in 1952 and 1956. On October 27, 1952, at the height of public notoriety over his stormy second marriage to the actress Ava Gardner, Sinatra sang and spoke for Stevenson at a large election-eve rally at the Hollywood Palladium. (Gardner introduced him to the audience, prompting headlines of "Frankie, Ava Kiss and Make Up" that eclipsed Stevenson's speech and the rest of the rally.) In 1956, having regained his popularity as an actor and singer, Sinatra not only campaigned for Stevenson but was invited to sing the National Anthem at the opening session of the Democratic National Convention. According to *Look* magazine writer Bill Davidson, Speaker of the House Sam Rayburn, a Texan, slung his arm around Sinatra's shoulder as he stepped down from the microphone and burbled, "Aren't you going to sing 'The Yellow Rose of Texas,' Frank?" Sinatra's alleged reply (both he and Rayburn denied the story, but Davidson had an eyewitness) was, "Take the hand off the suit, creep" (Shaw 1968: 230).

After Stevenson lost the election, it became apparent that the real story at the 1956 convention had been the young senator from Massachusetts, John F. Kennedy, who, when Stevenson threw the vice presidential nomination open to the floor, ran a surprisingly strong second and was pleasingly graceful in publicly conceding defeat. As the convention wore on, Sinatra, who had met the senator in 1955, spent more and more time with Kennedy and his political lieutenants. He was impressed with the degree of organization the family applied to the campaign. He also took note when he heard Robert F. Kennedy, the senator's younger brother and campaign manager, tell people, "O.K. That's it. Now we go to work for the next one" (Brownstein 1990: 147; Levy 1998: 69).

Sinatra and John F. Kennedy (Candidate)

"In the long history of Hollywood's relationship with politics," Ronald Brownstein has written, the coming together of Sinatra and Kennedy "was probably the pivotal moment" (1990: 155). Sinatra's relationship with

Kennedy, both in public and in private, was the closest in history between a major party presidential nominee and an entertainer, then or since.

By the late 1950s Sinatra had reached the peak of his popularity in show business. Close association with Kennedy's 1960 presidential campaign promised to open additional doorways for him, to power and, above all, to respectability. "What could be better than being Frank Sinatra?" the writer Leonard Gershe wondered at the time. "Being Frank Sinatra walking along with the president" (Brownstein 1990: 155). Sinatra's long political experience and loyalty to the Democratic party provided an additional motive to support Kennedy. "Jack knew how to use power and Stevenson didn't," he told actress Shirley Maclaine, who, like most of liberal Hollywood, was still "Madly for Adlai" (Brownstein 1990: 156).

The basis of Kennedy's attraction to Sinatra was more complex. Kennedy hagiographers tend to stress the innocence of it all. Sinatra was "fun," according to one (Brownstein 1990: 155). "Sinatra told him a lot of inside gossip about celebrities and their romances in Hollywood," a second has written (O'Donnell and Powers 1970: 183). Still another, in the course of describing the troubled marriage between actor and Sinatra friend Peter Lawford and Kennedy's sister Pat, quotes Kennedy as saying that "Sinatra is the only guy who gives Peter jobs. And the only way I can keep this marriage going is to see that Peter gets jobs. So I'm nice to Frank Sinatra" (Klein 1996: 307).

Less partisan observers have emphasized the lures of Sinatra's freewheeling lifestyle, which he gladly shared with Kennedy when the candidate visited Las Vegas and Palm Springs. With Bogart dead, the ethos of Sinatra's reconstituted Rat Pack was unbridled hedonism. To Sinatra, Davis, Lawford, and singer Dean Martin, fame entitled one to freedom from rules or restrictions on personal behavior. Kennedy liked to join the ongoing party now and then, and when he did, according to Lawford, "Frank was Jack's pimp" (Kelley 1986: 269). On February 7, 1960, for example, Sinatra introduced Kennedy to Judith Campbell when the senator stopped in Las Vegas between campaign appearances in Oregon and New Mexico. An affair between Kennedy and Campbell began on March 7 in New York and continued into the White House (Brownstein 1990: 154; Parmet 1983: 117–118; T. C. Reeves 1992: 165). A few days after the Kennedy introduction, Sinatra introduced Campbell to the Chicago gangster Sam Giancana, and another affair was begun.

But just as Sinatra's attraction to Kennedy was based in part on explicitly political motives, so was Kennedy's attraction to Sinatra. In the summer of 1959 the candidate's father, Joseph P. Kennedy, met with Sinatra to ask him to help raise campaign funds, recruit other celebrities to the Kennedy campaign, and record a theme song. Sinatra agreed and was invited to sit in on several West Coast political strategy meetings with the candidate. Joseph Kennedy also asked Sinatra to speak with a number of labor and crime figures, all of whom were wary of the senator because of Robert Kennedy's recent attacks on mob influence in the unions as a Senate committee staffer. For example, according to Tina Sinatra, Joseph Kennedy told her father to ask Giancana to arrange Teamsters union support for Senator Kennedy in the politically crucial West Virginia primary and, during the general election, in Chicago. Federal Bureau of Investigation (FBI) wiretaps subsequently revealed large Mafia donations to the Kennedy campaign. According to former federal prosecutor G. Robert Blakey, the money went from Giancana to Sinatra to Joseph Kennedy. In return, Blakey says, Giancana and his colleagues were convinced that "the Kennedys would do something for them," namely, reduce FBI pressure on their activities (Taraborrelli 1997a: 216; Brownstein 1990: 147; Hersh 1997: 137, 140; Levy 1998: 166).

Sinatra's public role in the campaign (apart from his recorded voice on "High Hopes," which blared constantly from Kennedy sound trucks) was focused on fund-raising. From 1920 to 1950 the cost of presidential campaigns, measured on a per capita basis, had essentially remained constant. But during the 1950s American politics entered the television age. (In 1950 nine of ten American homes did not have a television set; in 1960 nine of ten American homes did.) By the time Kennedy ran for president, the cost of campaigning had skyrocketed to pay for political advertising on the new medium, generating unprecedented demands for political funds that, in Kennedy's case, Sinatra helped to meet (Heard 1960: 403). He marshaled a small army of Hollywood stars to entertain at a convention-eve fund-raising gala for the Democratic party. Nearly three thousand people paid $100 per plate to attend the July 10 event in Los Angeles, and Sinatra reveled in his presence at the head table with Kennedy and other party luminaries. During the fall campaign Sinatra performed at several fund-raisers and at a huge election-eve rally in Newark, New Jersey.

Kennedy's aides fretted about their candidate's relationship with Sinatra. They feared that the Mafia-Sinatra linkage that existed in many voters' minds would sully Kennedy's reputation for honesty, and worried that the Rat Pack image would undermine their efforts to make the forty-three-year-old senator seem mature and experienced. (Sinatra did not help matters when he temporarily redubbed the Rat Pack the Jack Pack.) On one occasion campaign staffers Harris Wofford and John Siegenthaler advised Kennedy not to meet "in public" with Sinatra at a conference that both men were scheduled to attend in New York. Siegenthaler added in a memo: "It is hoped that Sinatra would realize his own worth and keep his distance from the senator." He went on to recommend that Sinatra be deployed to help a voter registration drive in Harlem, "where he is recognized as a hero of the cause of the Negro" (E. Wilson 1976: 169).

Sinatra was willing to do almost anything to accommodate the Kennedy campaign. In March 1960, for example, after signing blacklisted Hollywood Ten screenwriter Albert Maltz, his collaborator on *The House I Live In,* to write the screenplay for a movie version of William Bradford Huie's novel, *The Education of Private Slovik,* Sinatra was publicly chastised by conservatives. "I wonder how Sinatra's crony Senator John Kennedy feels about him hiring such a man," actor John Wayne snarled to an interviewer. Sinatra fought back with a *New York Times* ad that said: "I do not ask the advice of Senator Kennedy on whom I should hire. Senator Kennedy does not ask me how he should vote in the Senate" (Wiener 1991: 266–67). But when the Roman Catholic cardinals of Boston and New York expressed their displeasure with the Maltz hiring to Joseph Kennedy and, through him, to Sinatra, he paid the screenwriter in full and abandoned the project. Sinatra also endorsed, albeit unenthusiastically, Sammy Davis Jr.'s decision to postpone his wedding to the white actress May Britt from October 16, 1960, until after the election in deference to a request from the Kennedy campaign. Sinatra had agreed to be Davis's best man, and Kennedy's aides feared that the public would draw a Davis-Sinatra-Kennedy interracial marriage connection. Later Sinatra did not stand in the way when

Davis was dropped from the program of the inauguration eve gala (Levy 1998: 168; N. Sinatra 1985: 144–45).

Unfortunately for Sinatra, the relationship between him and Kennedy was inherently asymmetrical. Sinatra regarded Kennedy as a friend as well as a political leader. Kennedy enjoyed Sinatra's company and appreciated the glamour that the singer brought to the campaign, along with his behind-the-scenes work with organized labor and organized crime—but that was it. Affection, fellow feeling, even gratitude were nothing compared with political expediency. In September, two months after Sinatra had enthused to Peter Lawford on the night of Kennedy's nomination, "We're on our way to the White House, buddy boy!" the candidate told a columnist, "He's no friend of mine. He's just a friend of Pat's and Peter Lawford's" (Brownstein 1991: 151).

Sinatra and John F. Kennedy (President)

Kennedy's election did not alter his fundamental attitude toward Sinatra (enjoy him, use him, then deny him if the political price gets too high), but it did raise the stakes. As president-elect, Kennedy prevailed on Sinatra to organize a preinaugural gala, which the singer did to wonderful effect. Yet during the Kennedy years, as Lawford recalled, Sinatra "never flew on Air Force One and was never invited to any of the Kennedy state dinners or taken to Camp David" (Kelley 1986: 291). Eventually he was snubbed by the president in a more public and thus a more humiliating way.

January 20, 1961, the day of Kennedy's inauguration, marked a fundamental divide in his relationship with Sinatra. The inauguration-eve gala that Sinatra organized at Kennedy's behest was a remarkable entertainment event for which he pulled out all the stops, flying in Ella Fitzgerald from Australia, Sidney Poitier from France, and Gene Kelly from Switzerland, and buying out the Broadway show *Gypsy* for one night so that Ethel Merman could appear. The *New York Times* said that the gala "may have been the most stunning assembly of theatrical talent ever brought together for a single show" (Alter 1998: 64b). Not incidentally, it raised $1.4 million for the Democratic party. The next night Kennedy briefly excused himself from the official round of inaugural balls so that he could spend some time at a private party that Sinatra was giving at the Statler Hilton Hotel.

But Kennedy did not see Sinatra again until September, at his family's compound in Hyannis Port, Massachusetts. Accounts differ about whether Sinatra, who had been under pressure from Giancana to ask the Kennedys (especially Robert Kennedy, the new attorney general) to repay what Giancana regarded as their election debt to him by muzzling the Justice Department's investigation of organized crime, actually spoke to the president, his brother, or his father about the matter. But an FBI wiretap in December recorded a Giancana lieutenant quoting Sinatra as saying that he had given Robert Kennedy a piece of paper with Giancana's name on it and said, "This is my buddy, this is what I want you to know, Bob" (Brownstein 1990: 162). Wiretaps also revealed the Sinatra-Giancana connection with Judith Campbell, whom both Kennedy and Giancana were continuing to see. FBI director J. Edgar Hoover, no friend to either Kennedy brother, visited the president on March 22, 1962, to tell him that he knew about Campbell and Giancana, as well as about Sinatra's role as intermediary between each of them and the president (Reeves 1993: 289).

Hoover's meeting with Kennedy had its intended effect. Robert Kennedy urged his brother to break not just with Campbell (whom the president called for the last time a few hours after Hoover left) but also with Sinatra: "Johnny, you just can't associate with this guy" (Reeves 1993: 289–91). The Sinatra-Kennedy relationship had already been drawing public criticism from conservative politicians and newspapers for other reasons, ranging from the military limousine that Sinatra had used while organizing the inaugural gala to the propriety of hosting the exemplar of Rat Pack hedonism at the Kennedy's private home. Now the stakes became considerably higher.

Kennedy resolved to cut Sinatra loose. "It meant nothing [to him]," according to White House aide Richard Goodwin. "If Kennedy . . . thought it would even in the slightest wound his presidency, of course he would cut it off; he would cut off people a lot closer than Sinatra if he had to" (Brownstein 1990: 166). The coup de grâce came soon after Kennedy's meeting with Hoover: Sinatra was informed that, contrary to previous assurances, the president would not be staying at his much-refurbished (in anticipation of the visit) Palm Springs home when he visited California. Instead, for "security reasons," Kennedy would stay with the singer Bing Crosby (a Republican!).

Although Sinatra blamed Robert Kennedy and other Kennedy advisers more than the president himself for the change in plans, he felt personally betrayed and publicly humiliated. His embarrassment was compounded when White House press secretary Pierre Salinger, asked at a November briefing whether the president had seen a chrysanthemum-covered rocking chair that Sinatra had sent him for his birthday, said, "No, it was sent straight to Children's Hospital with other birthday flowers and the president never saw it." The final humiliation came when Sinatra was not invited to Kennedy's funeral after the president was assassinated on November 22, 1963. "He's already been too much of an embarrassment to the family," said Peter Lawford (Levy 1998: 260).

The Post-Kennedy 1960s

Sinatra's relationship with John F. Kennedy was sadly ironic. Sinatra had hoped that his association with the leader of the free world would replace public perceptions of him as an underworld figure and a libertine with a more respectable image. Instead, the old perceptions were reinforced. If Kennedy dropped Sinatra, the public seemed to think, all the sordid stories about him must be true. As Brownstein has written, "By standing next to Kennedy, Sinatra may have hoped to surmount his past; but he was only stamped with it more indelibly than ever" (1990: 167).

But Sinatra's disillusioning experience did not prompt him to retreat from Democratic party affairs. He was heartened when California Democrats chastised the White House for the decision to send Kennedy to Crosby's house (Brownstein 1990: 165–66). More important, he remained a strong liberal. In a February 1963 *Playboy* interview, for example, Sinatra denounced "practiced bigots," especially "that leering, cursing lynch mob in Little Rock reviling a meek, innocent little twelve-year-old girl as she tried to enroll in a public school" in 1957; said that "[o]ur concern over a Sovietized Cuba ninety miles from Key West must be equated with Russian concern over our missile bases surrounding them"; and called on Americans to cure "the cancers of starvation, substandard housing, educational voids and second-class citizenship that still exist in many backsliding areas of our own country." In a revealing comment, Sinatra added that "the only chance the world has for survival" may be to lock up "all the leaders in every country in the world" and "then—boom! Somebody blows up the mother building." Among those he mentioned as belonging in the building was Kennedy ("*Playboy* Interview," 1963).

Sinatra did withdraw from national politics for a time. He did not campaign for Lyndon B. Johnson in 1964, and the one personal encounter he had with Kennedy's successor was unpleasant. Toward the end of his presidency, when Sinatra came to Washington at Vice President Humphrey's request to do a charity concert, Johnson reluctantly agreed to see him. Sinatra, who was hoping for a picture of himself with the president, found Johnson naked on the massage table, awkwardly traded complaints with him about the unfairness of the media, and was escorted out after fifteen minutes. Reportedly, Johnson still resented Sinatra's brusque treatment of his fellow Texan Rayburn at the 1956 Democratic convention (Berman 1979: 96, 135; Kelley 1986: 384–85, 405).

Even during his hiatus from national politics, however, Sinatra was a mainstay of the California Democratic party. In 1964 he publicly opposed Proposition 14, which would have nullified the state's new fair housing law, and supported Pierre Salinger's unsuccessful candidacy for the U.S. Senate. In 1966 he campaigned hard on behalf of Governor Pat Brown's reelection bid against movie actor–turned-conservative activist Ronald Reagan. Sinatra disliked Reagan intensely—"almost as much as Richard Nixon," said Lawford (Taraborrelli 1997a: 357). For a time, he even added, "Hates California/It's Reagan and damp," to concert versions of the Rodgers and Hart song, "The Lady Is a Tramp." Along with 147 other actors, Sinatra signed a newspaper ad that declared: "[W]e believe very strongly that the skills an actor brings to his profession are NOT the skills of governing" (Kelley 1986: 361). Nonetheless, Reagan was easily elected.

Distaste for Robert Kennedy's candidacy for the Democratic presidential nomination in 1968 ("Bobby's not qualified to be president" [Kelley 1986: 383]) helped motivate Sinatra to return to the national political arena. He had gotten to know Kennedy's major rival for the nomination, Vice President Humphrey, in 1966, and the two had liked each other. Sinatra, one of the few major stars to support the vice president, did ten fund-raising concerts for the Humphrey campaign and, in frequent conversations, advised him on matters such as makeup and lighting for his television appearances. Sinatra even opened his home to groups of Black Panthers, urging them to support Humphrey for president. Yet at a time when many movie stars, including Warren Beatty, Paul Newman, and Marlon Brando, were not only getting involved in politics but also speaking out on the issues, Sinatra confined his public political role to singing and raising money (Brownstein 1990: ch. 7).

Humphrey's nomination at the 1968 Democratic convention (Robert Kennedy had been assassinated in June) marked the high point of Sinatra's relationship with him. Sinatra certainly did not lack for enthusiasm: "I'll do anything to defeat that bum Nixon," he pledged (Kelley 1986: 388). But, as had President Kennedy's advisers eight years earlier, Humphrey's aides now warned their candidate to stay away from Sinatra, citing the singer's alleged Mafia connections, which were being rehearsed again in newspapers like the *Wall Street Journal* ("Sinatra's Pals—Gangster Friendships Cause Singer Trouble but He Isn't Fazed," read the *Journal* headline). "It was an old story," Lawrence Quirk and William Schoell have written. "Politicians always wanted Frank to use his showbiz connections to get entertainers from all across the world to campaign and entertain for them, but once they were in office their advisers would remind them of Frank's mob ties. In other words, Sinatra had served his purpose and it was time to give him his walking papers" (Quirk and Schoell 1998: 330–31).

In this case, Sinatra kept walking, right into the arms of the Republican party.

Becoming a Republican

Sinatra's conversion to Republicanism was not sudden. In 1970 he endorsed Reagan's candidacy for reelection as governor of California and raised $500,000 in benefit concerts for the Republican incumbent's campaign fund. But he did so as the co-chair of Democrats for Reagan. "I'm an Italian Democrat all the way," Sinatra affirmed. "On that score I could never change" (Kelley 1991: 189). Indeed, he accompanied his endorsement of Reagan with public support for several California Democratic candidates, such as Jerry Brown, the son of former governor Pat Brown and the party's nominee for secretary of state, and Senator John Tunney, for whom Sinatra raised $160,000. In addition, Sinatra tempered his endorsement of Reagan by declaring that "if Reagan ran for president against Humphrey, I'd come out for Humphrey" (Kelley 1991: 186). In that context, the July 9, 1970, *Los Angeles Times* headline that accompanied Sinatra's Reagan endorsement—"Sinatra Explodes Political Bomb"—may have overstated the extent of his transformation.

Similarly, although Sinatra formed a close friendship with the controversial Republican vice president, Spiro T. Agnew, when they met soon after the 1970 elections, he did not embrace the ticket of which Agnew was a part. "Now Nixon scares me," Sinatra said of the president. "He's running the country into the ground" (Kelley 1991: 181). The Sinatra-Agnew connection prompted Nixon's chief political adviser, Charles Colson, to urge the president to try to woo Sinatra into the administration's political camp in early 1971. "Sinatra is the most important person in the Hollywood entertainment community," Colson wrote in a White House memo, adding (perhaps less realistically): "[H]e has the muscle to bring along a lot of the younger lights" (Oudes 1989: 211). The memos stopped after Sinatra retired from show business in June 1971. But as late as September 1971, Nixon fretted in a taped conversation with his chief of staff, H. R. Haldeman, that "[Edmund] Muskie used Frank Sinatra's plane in California" (Kutler 1997: 32). At the time, Muskie was the front-runner for the Democratic nomination to run against Nixon the following year.

Nonetheless, by 1972 Sinatra was firmly in the Republican camp. His final reservation about the president was removed when Nixon decided to keep Agnew on the ticket. (Sinatra actually financed a pro-Agnew write-in campaign to rouse support for the vice president.) He contributed $53,000 to Nixon's reelection campaign, campaigned with Agnew, and briefly abandoned his retirement to sing at a Young Voters for Nixon rally at the 1972 Republican Convention in Chicago.

What explains Sinatra's political conversion? His own answer was that his views on the issues had changed. "The older you get, the more conservative you get," he frequently told his daughter Nancy Sinatra (N. Sinatra 1985: 226). He liked the way Reagan had stood up to student demonstrators at the University of California during his first term as governor. In addition, according to Agnew, "we hated the way the left-wingers were constantly running down the competitive, free-enterprise system that was the real strength of America" (Agnew 1980: 205). Yet Sinatra was not consistently conservative. When he learned about Governor Reagan's anti-abortion, antiwelfare policies in 1970, he urged him to moderate them. Part of his attraction to Nixon in 1972 was the president's bold opening to Communist China, something that Sinatra had urged President Kennedy to undertake in 1963 (N. Sinatra 1985: 225).

A second explanation for Sinatra's move to the Republican party is less ideological than populist. In speaking out for Roosevelt in 1944, Sinatra had said of the president, "He's for the little guys like me" (Shaw 1968: 77, 79–80). Big business seemed to pose the biggest threat to the common people in the 1930s and 1940s; active government seemed to be their defender. At some level, despite his success, Sinatra continued to think of himself as a little guy for the rest of his life. But by the 1970s Sinatra and many other erstwhile New Deal Democrats, most of them white ethnic Catholics like himself, had come to regard big government as their nemesis. In particular, the journalist John Rockwell has written: "From Sinatra's point of view, his constant battles with state and federal officials over his alleged Mafia ties were proof of government malevolence" (1984: 211).

A third, and perhaps deeper, explanation of Sinatra's political conversion may lie in an aspect of his character that almost all close observers of him have noted. Loyalty was the supreme virtue in Sinatra's code of morality. He was "*Il Padrone,*" in the writer Gay Talese's marvelous phrase, a man of "fierce fidelity . . . This is the Sicilian in Sinatra: he permits his friends, if they wish to remain that, no easy Anglo-Saxon outs. But if they remain loyal, then there is nothing Sinatra will not do in turn—fabulous gifts, personal kindnesses, encouragement when they're down, adulation when they're up" (Talese 1966/1995: 99, 102). To Sinatra, loyalty had to be unconditional and would always be rewarded; disloyalty was unacceptable and must be punished.

Thus, when comedian and songwriter Steve Allen published an open letter in 1970 calling on Sinatra to put aside "Sicilian vengeance" and return to the Democratic fold, he was on to something. Jesse Unruh, Reagan's Democratic opponent in that year's California gubernatorial election, had violated the code of loyalty, in Sinatra's view. Unruh, an ardent supporter of Robert Kennedy in 1968, had done nothing to help Humphrey when he won the Democratic presidential nomination. "Unruh hurt my man badly in Chicago [at the Democratic convention]," Sinatra said. "In fact, he hurt the whole Democratic party. Humphrey didn't lose. His people lost for him" (Kelley 1991: 192). In contrast, Reagan defended Sinatra when he had a public run-in with the staff at Caesar's Palace in Las Vegas: "Why don't you ask about the good things he's done?" the governor asked reporters. (Democrats Brown and Tunney, whom Sinatra also supported in 1970, were the sons of old friends and thus fit objects of his loyal support.) As for Agnew, even though "political allies of mine did everything possible to persuade me that Sinatra was a political liability because of the controversy that always surrounded him," the vice president stood up publicly for his friend when Sinatra was called before the Select Committee on Crime of the U.S. House of Representatives in 1972 to answer questions about a race track investment (Agnew 1980: 205). Nixon telephoned Sinatra to congratulate him on his testimony, which was a public relations triumph (Kelley 1986: 410, 405). Republicans, it seemed to Sinatra, understood loyalty in the same way that he did, and the Democrats did not.

The Republican Years

If Sinatra had set out to test Nixon's loyalty, he could not have chosen a better way to do so than his behavior on the eve of the president's second inauguration in 1973. When Secret Service officials, citing insufficient time to run a security check, refused to let Sinatra add comedian Pat Henry to the bill of the American Music Concert at the Kennedy Center, which Sinatra was scheduled to emcee for an audience that included the Nixons, he stormed out of the theater. Later that night, at a party, Sinatra exploded at *Washington Post* society columnist Maxine Cheshire. "Get away from me, you scum," he shouted. "Go home and take a bath." Then (to cite the PG-rated version of the story) he added, "You're nothing but a two-dollar broad. You know what that means, don't you? You've been laying down for two dollars all your life." Before stalking off, Sinatra stuffed two one-dollar bills into Cheshire's drink glass (E. Wilson 1976: 270–73).

Washington was shocked by Sinatra's behavior, and Nixon was enraged to have his inauguration sullied by such crude antics. Yet the president refused aides' advice to cancel Sinatra's upcoming April 17, 1973, appearance at the White House to sing for the Italian prime minister. (It was to be his first White House concert ever.) Nixon had even less use for the *Post* than Sinatra; later that year he sardonically (and privately) remarked to confidant Bebe Rebozo that Cheshire's true price was "two bits, not two dollars" (Kutler 1997: 621). On the night of Sinatra's White House performance, Nixon compared him to the Washington Monument—"The Top." Indeed, Sinatra turned out to be, if anything, the less loyal member of the relationship with Nixon. He never publicly abandoned the president during the Watergate affair ("Nobody's perfect," he would remind Nancy Sinatra), but after it was over he told Pete Hamill, "You think some people are smart, and they turn out dumb. You think they're straight, they turn out crooked" (Taraborrelli 1997a: 396–97; N. Sinatra 1985: 226; Hamill 1998: 180).

Sinatra's fidelity to Agnew never flagged, however. Agnew stayed with him at Palm Springs many times; as an indication of where Sinatra's political loyalties now lay, he even renamed the guest house he had built in 1962 in anticipation of Kennedy's visit Agnew House. When press reports broke in 1973 about a federal criminal investigation into bribe-taking by Agnew, Sinatra flew to Washington, made his lawyer Mickey Rudin available to the vice president, and phoned him every day to buck up his flagging spirits. After Agnew resigned on October 10, 1973, as part of a plea bargain and became the object of Internal Revenue Service scrutiny, Sinatra made him an unsolicited, pay-when-you-can loan of $200,000. Agnew dedicated his memoirs to Sinatra, describing him as being "in a special bracket, a bracket of one" (Agnew 1980: 177–80, 203–204).

After Nixon and Agnew's exit from politics, Sinatra renewed his ties with Ronald and Nancy Reagan. He sang at a 1974 fund-raiser for Reagan's bid for the 1976 Republican presidential nomination, substituting "Nancy Reagan" for his own daughter in "Nancy With the Laughing Face" (Kelley 1991: 212). Reagan narrowly lost the 1976 nomination to President Gerald Ford (whom Sinatra then supported in the general election), but when he ran again in 1980, Sinatra campaigned hard. At one Boston concert he raised $250,000 for the Reagan campaign. As usual, however, the same audiences that thrilled to Sinatra's singing at political events winced at his spoken comments. "He wants to be reelected," Sinatra said of Reagan's opponent, President Jimmy Carter. "We should string him up" (Kelley 1991: 455–56).

Sinatra's close relationship with the Reagans prompted criticism and concern in some quarters. One critic compared the 1981 inaugural gala, which Sinatra organized at the president-elect's request and which raised half of the inauguration's $10 million cost, to "a cross between Dial-a-Joke and 'Hee Haw.'" During Senate confirmation hearings, Reagan's attorney general designate, William French Smith, was taken to task by *New York Times* columnist William Safire and Wisconsin senator William Proxmire for attending Sinatra's sixty-fifth birthday party a few weeks after the 1980 election (Kelley 1986: 457–58). Incredibly, a rumor spread that Reagan was going to appoint Sinatra as ambassador to Italy. The Italian newspaper *La Stampa* was worried enough to huff: "If the American government thinks of Italy as the land of mandolins and La Cosa Nostra, then Sinatra would be the appropriate choice" (Alter 1998: 64b).

Ignoring the criticism, the Reagans remained loyal to Sinatra. When he applied for a Nevada gaming license in 1980, Reagan listened to his wife instead of to his close political adviser, Ed Meese, and wrote a strong character reference for Sinatra (Kelley 1991: 265–66). The president awarded Sinatra the Medal of Freedom in 1985. Sinatra was a frequent guest, especially of the first lady, at the White House, for both official events and personal visits. After Reagan was reelected in 1984, Sinatra was invited to organize the 1985 inaugural gala.

As always with Sinatra, loyalty to him was reciprocated with loyalty from him. In 1981, responding to Screen Actors Guild (SAG) president Ed Asner's oft-expressed hostility to the president, Sinatra and others formed a group called Actors Working for an Actors Guild and ran candidates for the SAG board. He ardently defended Nancy Reagan against press criticisms of her extravagance in clothes and china. He helped the White House staff to improve its lighting and sound system for evening entertainments and arranged concerts by artists ranging from Zubin Mehta to Mel Tillis. ("I've already checked your schedule," Sinatra told Tillis, "and you are free" [Kelley 1986: 493]). In 1984 Sinatra raised money for the Reagan campaign at a series of cocktail parties and accompanied the president on a frenzied campaign visit to the Festival of St. Ann in Hoboken. With keen understanding of the purpose of the appearance, Governor Mario Cuomo of New York, a leading Democrat, complained that Reagan was using Sinatra to pander to Italian American voters. In 1988, when former Reagan chief of staff Donald Regan's tell-all memoir, *For the Record,* was published, Sinatra decried the disloyalty of insiders who reveal the secrets of their erstwhile bosses. "I'm saying they're pimps and whores," he charged. "They're the ones who write the books about people with whom they had a kind of privy association and suddenly they're out making a buck because they got a pigeon" (Kelley 1991: 91).

Conclusion

The story of Sinatra and the American presidency is interesting because of what it tells about Sinatra, especially the code of loyalty that seems to have animated every aspect of his life. The story is important because of what it tells about the American presidency. Sinatra's participation in the Roosevelt and Kennedy campaigns opened the floodgates for celebrity involvement in presidential politics. As journalist Jonathan Alter has written, "Sinatra forever changed the relationship between Hollywood and Washington" (1998: 64b).

Broadly speaking, the motivation for celebrities such as Sinatra to seek out politicians has been less economic self-interest than a personal and ideological attraction to particular candidates and a desire to seem like serious public figures. The motivation for candidates to seek out celebrities has been to bask in their glamour and to obtain help in fund-raising. Yet Sinatra's experiences with Kennedy and Humphrey reveal the fault line that underlies the association: Whenever a celebrity's public image becomes controversial, candidates may cut him or her loose.

Beyond that marriage of self-interest, however, may lie a deeper source of what Brownstein has called the "Hollywood-Washington connection." Entertainers and politicians face similar challenges. Whether on screen or on the hustings, they must woo the public, balance private life with life in the media spotlight, and adjust to changes in style and taste. Thus, they can not only help but also empathize with each other in a way that few outsiders can.

Part Two

Identity and Representation

"I knew Maggio. I went to school with him in Hoboken. . . . I might have been Maggio."

6

Why the Bobby Soxers?

Janice L. Booker

he time was the beginning of World War II, with the country emerging from the Great Depression. Young teenagers had not experienced either of these events directly, but were aware that their families had suffered, and the world crisis was their daily fare. The frenzy that was part of the Sinatra experience provided an opportunity to concentrate on something else, someone else, apart from family separations and potential danger. It was also the time between childhood and adulthood, when young girls—and boys—needed to find something that belonged only to them, a road to separation and independence. This adoration of Sinatra touched emotions in themselves that many did not yet understand.

Psychologists explained the Sinatra phenomenon as a result of the war: working mothers, absent fathers, and boyfriends. Perhaps the scarcity of eligible young men made it safe to sublimate sexual fantasies on an unobtainable object.

Frank Sinatra commented on his appeal to teenage girls: "Psychologists have tried to go into the reasons why. With all sorts of theories. I could have told them why. Perfectly simple: It was the war years, and there was a great loneliness. I was the boy in every corner drugstore, the boy who'd gone off to war" (N. Sinatra 1995: 55).

Yet many of the bobby soxers were too young to date within the mores of the time, too young to feel the absence of eligible boys. They were at the end of latency, at the threshold of their sexual quest. Sinatra could represent to them what they were feeling but not yet understanding.

Since young women begin their trek into adulthood a few years before their male contemporaries, those "little boys" who sat next to them in class were not ready to cope with the burgeoning sexuality or the romantic fantasies of their classmates and neighbors. Frank Sinatra was someone on whom those fantasies could be focused; yet he was safe because he was unattainable; unattainable because he was a celebrity, and unavailable because he was married with children. Troubling situations with boyfriends were absent in this crush. No decisions had to be made about where to go or what to do. No problems could arise about dating, meeting parents, or any of the ordinary issues that become heart-wrenching to teenage girls. They could explore romance from a distance, daydream to his romantic songs, attach the lyrics to the love of the moment, but dismiss the realities that the boy next door might present.

Sinatra's choice of songs, with the lyrics delivered in his precise, haunting, and lyrical way, were compelling. Sensuality was his byword as each song was personalized. Intimacy was possible even with an icon. The expression of emotion through the tantalizing lyrics and delivery could express feelings just coming to the surface. Pete Hamill, New York journalist and friend of Sinatra, has this view of "the Voice": "[T]here was a tension in Sinatra, an anxiety that we were too young to name but old enough to feel." Hamill talks about the sounds of anguish, loss, and loneliness evident in Sinatra's voice, and about the women whose husbands and boyfriends were off to war, and adds, "[I]t was Frank Sinatra who was giving words and voice to the emotions of their own roiled hearts. . . . He inhabited a song the way a great actor inhabits a role, often bringing his own life to the music" (Hamill 1998: 27, 28, 116).

Sinatra said, about his own voice: "I think my appeal was due to the fact that there hadn't been a troubadour around for ten or twenty years, from the time that Bing had broken in and went on to radio and movies. And he, strangely enough, had appealed primarily to older people, middle-aged people. When I came on the scene and people began noticing me at the Paramount, I think the kids were looking for somebody to cheer for. Also the war had just started. They were looking for somebody who represented those gone in their life" (N . Sinatra, 1985 41).

He made eye contact with his audience. His outstretched arms called to each and every teenager in that audience: "I mean *you*." He personified love and desire. Perhaps without verbalization, the bobby soxers understood that his projection of masculine sensuality was what they were seeking, in another man, some day. Sinatra was always considered a master of lyric construction, his poetic interpretation. His phrasing, pitch of certain notes, and "teasing" the rhythm was exemplified by his always considering the microphone as an instrument. His hanging on to the microphone was not a visual ploy; he virtually seduced the microphone to extract from it the nuances that he wanted his lyrics to have. He mirrored the complexities of love, longing, and lust that were at the threshold of teenage initiation. The sense of melancholy that permeated so many of the ballads reflected the polarity of feelings that typify teenagers. You don't sigh; you cry. You don't talk; you yell. Emotions are on the surface of the skin, erupting as virulently as acne. The quality of loneliness in his voice evoked the feelings of teenage isolation—the ambivalence of wanting to be independent yet still in need of family support.

That special voice with its special purity. The stance, the lean body, echoing the microphone, and the broad-shouldered jacket, making him a triangle. The quivering lower lip. The expressive hands. The sweet speaking voice. The shyness. The vulnerability. Every girl wanted to take care of him. The needy, hungry quality. Every girl wanted to feed him (N. Sinatra 1985: 49).

The screaming and moaning was a legitimate, socially acceptable catharsis for budding sexual longings, at a time when emotion was more internalized, when expressions of feeling were more constrained, when sexuality for young teenagers was not expressed as blatantly as it is now. The obvious but unexpressed passion that was heard in the moaning and screaming and fainting could sublimate the desires that in most cases were below consciousness. His voice was like a caress, the lyrics touched those places in the fans that would later respond to the ecstasy of a personal romance. For now Frank Sinatra embodied those emotions. The saloon singer was also a bedroom voice.

For teenage girls, his emotional articulation of lyrics that spoke of love, longing, betrayal, and love lost was an eye opener. They were of a generation that inculcated the idea that males did not display emotion, that only women loved with all their heart, that only women suffered when love was lost. Sinatra's poignant portrayals of desire and longing perhaps helped, in some way, to pave the way for these women, when they were mature, to have expectations of intimacy and emotion on the part of their men that heretofore had remained dormant. That males, even young boys, could show pain at the dissolution of a love affair or the fruitless quest for one, coming from a very masculine, sexual man, gave males permission to be emotional about love.

Although there were boys who liked the way Sinatra sang, it wasn't the same. That young men, too, were admirers, is evidenced by their aping of his fashion style. His wide-shouldered jackets and bow ties were copied all over America.

Participation in the bobby soxers phenomenon was a bonding experience for young women. Forty years later it might have been called "sisterhood." The "Sinatra thing" that girls shared was special; it didn't involve their mothers, brothers, or neighbors. This was an emotion shared only with their peers. They understood each other because they could express their feelings about Sinatra to each other. They wanted to assert their individuality while at the same time they longed to be part of a group.

What is more important to a fourteen- or fifteen-year-old than her circle of girlfriends? Sinatra was like a glue for these friendships. Wanting to be part of a larger membership is central to the development of young teenagers. Sinatra provided this vehicle: an opportunity for conversation and being together to listen to his records. Listening to his radio program or the Saturday night Hit Parade was a perfect prelude to a sleepover. A trip to a neighborhood dance where only his music was featured could be planned.

This joint experience of a shared identity provided a clublike atmosphere for teenage girls for which the only entrance requirement was adoration of Sinatra. You could not be blackballed from this club.

The combination of his blue-collar undercoating and his sophisticated manner appealed across class lines. Being a Sinatra fan as a bobby soxer offered the chance to affiliate with girls unlike themselves, crossing social lines, economic classes, ethnic differences, and school cliques. Whoever was a Sinatra fan was a friend, at least for the length of a concert or the time it took to share a new song. Differences faded in the avid pursuit of his photo in the latest movie magazine, his newest album, and whatever gossip followed wherever he went. Even hurried exchanges about Frank created a sense of special, joined identity.

Psychiatrist Clifford Anderson, in his book *The Stages of Life*, says: "The main impetus is toward forming relationships with others 'like me.' At this point in life it is easier for the mind to borrow from others who are similar in appearance and who are continuously available. Thus, by mid-adolescence one's primary relations are with one's peers" (Anderson 1995: 115).

Picture the early 1940s and how a young teenager spent her leisure time. The parents are out of the house; the younger brother is asleep upstairs. She turns on the console that houses an elaborate radio and record changer. The 78s are stacked on the spindle, dropping automatically until the pile is exhausted. The Sinatra records are arranged in no specific order, just ballad after ballad—"Dancing in the Dark," "All or Nothing at All," "Embraceable You." Later he would call them "saloon songs." She wouldn't have understood the term at that innocent time in her life. As the first song begins, she arranges herself on the sofa, prone, eyes closed, thinking whatever romantic fantasies she permitted herself.

The term "bobby soxers" came from the uniform of the day for teenage girls: white ankle socks worn with brown and white saddle shoes or penny loafers, pleated skirt, pastel sweater. The advent of the swooning bobby soxers surfaced at the Paramount Theater in New York on December 30, 1942 (some sources list the date as December 31), when Sinatra was at the bottom billing of the marquee, noted as an "extra added attraction." Benny Goodman was the big band leader on stage—Goodman had never heard of

Sinatra—and Bing Crosby starred in the movie on the screen. When Sinatra walked out on stage, the audience, filled with thirteen- to fifteen-year-old girls, broke into shouts, screams, and whatever vocal expressions of excitement could fill the theater. Benny Goodman was startled.

Most Sinatra biographers agree that somewhere along the line George Evans, Sinatra's able and skilled press agent, created a public relations spin with whirlpools that still eddy about the pop music culture. The story goes that Evans saw this inexplicable group passion and decided that screaming adulation was the key to his client's success. So, for another performance, he hired twelve young girls to feign fainting when Sinatra started to sing. His twelve did their job, but thirty swooned. Some suggest that Evans created the first burst of screams and then it got out of control, but most biographers agree that he merely capitalized on what happened spontaneously. Jack Keller, Evans's partner, said, "The dozen girls we hired to scream and swoon did exactly as we told them. But hundreds more we didn't hire screamed even louder. It was wild, crazy, completely out of control" (Lahr 1997b: 82).

Fans could be part of the audience all day; the theater never went dark. In the Earle Theater in Philadelphia, with the same kind of shows the Paramount had in New York, teenagers lined up early in the morning, brown-bag lunches in hand, standing in line for the first show. This was no polite entrance; fleet feet catapulted down those narrow aisles, shoulders blocking other shoulders, hurling bodies into seats, to get as close as possible. But it didn't matter; if you were prepared to stay all day, and many were, you sat through the movie, the shorts, the news, and then the show. When seats in front emptied out (not everyone could spend the day), the mob surged forward to get even closer, sitting through, once again, the movie, the shorts, the news, and, happily, the performance. So what happened on school days? The obvious. Classes were forgotten. Irrelevant. Tomorrow there would be more classes, but who knew when Frank Sinatra would be back at the Paramount or the Earle?

In his next appearance at the Paramount, almost two years after the first, the line began forming before dawn and soon swelled to approximately thirty thousand fans, packed six abreast. Many members of the audience for the first show wouldn't leave the theater, and the frustrated crowd outside went berserk. The situation became known as the Columbus Day Riot.

This Columbus Day riot preceded the political and racial riots of the 1960s; nonetheless, it created the same headache for police and participants. Inside the Paramount, three thousand women squealed and swooned. Outside, on the streets, thirty thousand women who couldn't get in rioted.

Richie Lisella, Sinatra's assistant road manager, remembers that day: "Outside the Paramount the lines started at eleven o'clock at night for a show eleven o'clock in the morning. They'd be there all night. When they saw him they'd get wild. I saw fans run under the horses of mounted policemen. I saw them turn over a car" (Sinatra 1986: 47).

The manager of the Paramount tried to empty the place after each show and, to discourage long-term seating, asked the bobby soxers to store their box lunches in the back of the theater. It didn't work. Even though he put the worst films on the screen, the audience managed to smuggle sandwiches and other food in their clothing so they could stay all day.

The 3,600 seats did not empty out easily. The custom was that a seat holder could stay put as long as she (he) didn't leave the seat. On October 12, the day of the riot, only 250 patrons left after the first show. Thirty thousand waited outside and couldn't enter. They clogged the streets surrounding the Paramount, and when they realized they weren't getting in to the theater, they rioted, breaking windows, and creating gridlock on the streets. Hundreds of policemen were called in to deal with the hysteria.

The bobby soxer craze spread throughout the nation. Fan clubs proliferated, numbering in the thousands. Fans were frantic for a glimpse of him and for some souvenir. We know how young girls treasure photos, revere scrapbooks, collect mementos of their idols. Some of them followed Sinatra in the snow, collecting his footprints in a block of ice and preserving them. Ashes from his cigarettes became a treasure. Fans sent him handmade sweaters and wrote hate letters to critical reviewers. In a 1968 biography Arnold Shaw wrote: "Girls hid in his dressing rooms, in his hotel rooms, in the trunk of his car" (N. Sinatra 1995: 53).

The phenomenon was called "Sinatramania." These teenage girls wrote his initials on their clothing, bribed hotel chambermaids for the chance to lie on his bed, inscribed his song titles on their jackets. When they could actually accost him, they tore pieces of his clothing, focusing especially on his floppy bow ties.

He averaged five thousand letters a week from fans, with an estimated 40 million admirers in the country. Letters included phrases such as, "I shiver all the way up and down my spine when you sing, just like I did when I had scarlet fever" (N. Sinatra 1995: 53).

"Sinatra's fans . . . were so flamboyant in their affection, so boisterous in their enthusiasm, so extreme in their numbers, that they called unprecedented attention to themselves as well as Sinatra" (Rockwell 1984: 82). The bobby soxers may have been the first to bring attention to young teenagers as a group to be recognized, a group that had purchasing power—witness the avalanche of fan magazines, Sinatra sheet music, and records that they paid for themselves. They may also have awakened a consciousness on the part of the adult population that teenagers not only had money to spend, they could also create a popular icon. Later teenagers found new idols, and more attention was paid to the fans of Elvis Presley, the Beatles, and rock and roll in general, because a real audience made its presence known.

In 1946 an essay contest entitled "Why I Like Frank Sinatra," sponsored by a Detroit radio station, named a winner who wrote: "He is one of the greatest things that ever happened to Teen Age America. We were kids that never got much attention, but he made us feel like we were worth something" (N. Sinatra 1995: 53).

The Sinatra craze coincided with a burst of new technology. Perhaps television and more sophisticated communication vehicles helped bring this experience to the public with more immediacy than would have been possible at a previous time. This information explosion may have been a factor in the group identity process and in bringing to the attention of the general population that this group of young teenagers had clout, presence, buying power, and the ability to create a commodity.

Some personal reminiscences are in order. I was a serious bobby soxer. My first piece of published writing was in a fan magazine with Sinatra as the subject. I was fifteen years old, and this recognition solidified my view of myself as a potential writer. It was my first work that appeared in a publication other than a school newspaper.

A year earlier, Frank Sinatra had performed in a concert at the Philadelphia Academy of Music—I believe it was a USO benefit. I wrote him a fan letter at the hotel where I knew he stayed when in town, expressing my disappointment at not being able to attend. The day of the concert, when I was home from junior high school for lunch, his agent, that same George Evans, called me and offered two seats, free of charge, for the event. He cautioned me to bring one friend and not tell anyone else. That caveat was disregarded the moment I returned to school; how could I resist? He told me: "Mr. Sinatra received a lot of letters today, but he liked yours the best and wants you to hear the concert." An irresistible invitation! Following Mr. Evans's instructions, my best friend and I arrived at the side entrance of the Academy of Music promptly at eight-fifteen. I announced my name and the guard nodded. "You're the one, follow me." A minute later we were seated in the second row.

This incident, I believe, speaks to Sinatra's lifelong appreciation of the bobby soxers. He never patronized them, never found them a nuisance, and always appreciated that their adulation was the key that opened the eyes of the rest of the world to his unique talent. As the bobby soxers aged, involved in their own careers and families, and perhaps incorporating the dark side of Sinatra that seemed always in the news, the infatuation didn't fade. That kernel of time, encapsulated in their youth, special and unique to their generation, remained in their hearts as a reminder of their introduction to romance. And that's why today, many a grandmother, perhaps more sedately than fifty years ago, still does a silent swoon at the sound of Sinatra's romantic voice.

7

🎤

Playing the "Big Room"

Frank Sinatra, the Fontainebleau Hotel, and the Architecture of Inclusion

Gaspar González

*T*he opening credits of director Frank Capra's 1959 film *A Hole in the Head* roll against the backdrop of the postwar Miami Beach skyline while Frank Sinatra's "All My Tomorrows" plays on the soundtrack. In the film Sinatra plays Tony Manetta, a small-time hotel owner, forever on the brink of bankruptcy, who dreams of one day opening a Disneyland on South Miami Beach. He dreams of the good life, of making it big like his old friend Jerry Marks, "one of the biggest promoters in the country." Throughout the film the recurring symbol of Tony's aspirations is the Fontainebleau Hotel, then in its infancy but already one of the most famous resorts in the world. The 500-room Fontainebleau represents, for Tony, affluence on a grand scale, the (then) new Miami Beach. It's where Tony insists on meeting a prospective investor (who complains about the $1.25 cup of coffee), where Jerry Marks stays when he is in town. The Fontainebleau Hotel forever hovers at the edge of Tony's world: a promise of riches, social acceptance, and fulfillment.

Sinatra's association with the Fontainebleau Hotel, of course, extends well beyond *A Hole in the Head*. Sinatra was a featured performer in the Fontainebleau's ballroom throughout the 1950s and 1960s. Indeed, this essay will argue that the Fontainebleau is as significant a venue in Sinatra's career as any Las Vegas or Atlantic City casino or hotel for a number of reasons: for the similarities—both structural and symbolic—between the career of Sinatra and that of the Fontainebleau's architect, Morris Lapidus; for the ways in which the building itself constituted a kind of architectural analog to Sinatra's performance philosophy; and for the degree to which the confluence of performer and venue constituted a powerful expression of the postwar American dream of prosperity and inclusion (the dream that sustains Tony in Capra's film).

The similarities between Sinatra and the Fontainebleau's architect are numerous and instructive. Like Sinatra, Morris Lapidus was the son of immigrants. Born in Odessa, Lapidus was brought to the United States as an infant by his parents in 1903. His family settled in Brooklyn, not very far from the Hoboken into which Sinatra was born to Italian immigrants a little more than a decade later. Lapidus graduated with a degree in architecture from Columbia University in 1927, and his early work—from 1927 until 1945—was, as he himself has pointed out, "All stores and shops." Indeed, during this period, Lapidus was more commercial artist than architect. "I was their captive architect," he recalled years later (speaking of a building firm for whom he worked for roughly fifteen years). "All they did was build stores and showrooms. . . . I felt that I had sold my birthright for a mess of pottage. I didn't meet architects; I didn't talk to architects. . . . I felt that what I was doing was not architecture because I wasn't building buildings. I was designing stores" (Cook and Klotz 1973: 150). Lapidus's lament—the lament of an aspiring artist and innovator who found himself trapped in an almost mercenary occupation—is reminiscent of Sinatra's own oft-quoted comments on his early days as a saloon singer, his repeated recollections of singing all night for "sandwiches and cigarettes."

If Lapidus's tenure as a store designer was analogous to Sinatra's early career as a saloon singer (to the degree that both were, in the strictest sense, "commercial" artists), it is also true that Lapidus, like Sinatra, used his time as an apprentice to develop an artistic repertoire and vocabulary. "I could experiment with a shop and it might be torn down five years later," explained Lapidus, "but no architect would experiment with a building." In time, Lapidus's experiments led to stylistic signatures that were the architectural equivalent of Sinatra's phrasing and diction: slight but ingenious variations on established forms. The editors of *Interiors* magazine referred to Lapidus's aesthetic flourishes as bean poles, cheese holes, and woggles. Lapidus deciphers the terminology: "The 'bean pole' because I used a lot of stemmed things in interiors, the 'cheese hole' because I designed decks with holes in them, and the 'woggle' because I refused to stick to the rectangle" (Cook and Klotz: 1973: 150).

Sinatra and Lapidus continued their respective apprenticeships throughout the 1930s and 1940s. Lapidus's apprenticeship, of course, lasted longer than Sinatra's. By 1952, when Lapidus received his first exclusive commission, Sinatra had already become "The Voice," had lost the voice, and was on the verge of a comeback of staggering proportions. There appeared to be little chance that the culture would ever associate the two men or their work. Little chance, that is, until Morris Lapidus's first independent commission turned out to be the Fontainebleau Hotel in Miami Beach.

In 1952 Miami Beach was benefitting from the postwar economic boom. The epicenter of the resort capital had shifted from South Beach farther north, to an area that had once been the domain of the Beach's moneyed elite. The Fontainebleau was to go up on the site of the Firestone Estate, in the vicinity of Collins Avenue and 44th Street. The Firestone Estate had been, as historian Ann Armbruster explains, "a symbol of the best [automobile tycoon and city pioneer] Carl Fisher had hoped for Miami Beach—that it become the winter residence of wealthy American industrialists, à la Palm Beach" (1995: 135). That vision, of course, eventually gave way to that of businessmen and advertisers who sought to turn the beach into the preferred destination of middle-class vacation seekers. The Fontainebleau, as the centerpiece of this project, would have to contain just the right combination of the popular and the refined, a conception of luxury at once exclusive and accessible. To construct such a vision, Morris Lapidus was hired. He recalled his first creative run-in with his employer, Ben Novack:

> When I started the Fontainebleau, it was going to be contemporary.... I drew the first sketches and [Novack] said, "You must be crazy. I don't want this. I want French Provincial . . . not that old-fashioned French Provincial. I want that nice modern French Provincial." Now try and solve that. I figured I had to produce what he thought was modern French Provincial or French something. My client was just as illiterate and uncultured as many of his guests (Cook and Klotz 1973: 156).

Novack may or may not have known French Provincial, but he knew what he liked and what his guests would want. Lapidus caught on quickly:

> [The hotel] had to be *fabulous*. It had to live up to this dream picture, the dream drawn by the advertising people. Where do these people get their culture? I finally came to the conclusion that most of them get their culture not from school, not from their travels, but from the movies.... Suppose a director came to me with a script that called for a fabulous, luxurious tropical hotel setting.... All right, I'll design a fabulous movie set. And that's what I did . . . this was wonderful nonsense. I gave [Novack] his French, which is not French. I gave him fluted columns which are not contemporary. They are not French.... All through the interior I created a potpourri of anything I could put my hands on (Cook and Klotz 1973: 156).

Lapidus encased this potpourri in a thoroughly modern skin, in a curved fourteen-story building that dominated the beachscape (and overlooked not only the ocean, but a four-acre French parterre and a 60-by–120-foot pool).

The sheer magnitude of the project suggested a virtual democratization of leisure. There were 49,000 square yards of carpeting, 2,000 mirrors, 22 carloads of furniture and antiques, 200 phones, 847 employees (1.4 per guest). There was an underground shopping arcade. Even the room closets, again in the words of Ann Armbruster, "were twice the size of a normal hotel closet; no one needed that much space, but it gave guests a feeling that they were the kind of people who *could* fill it" (1995: 139).

By appropriating the iconography of high culture and translating it into a popular idiom—that of the movies—Lapidus created an ideal leisure space for the postwar white middle class and an ideal performance space for the poet of that ever-expanding middle class, Frank Sinatra. Sinatra, in his art, after all, had done much the same thing as Lapidus. He had taken the sophisticated lyrics and melodies of the great American songwriters he so admired and made them the building blocks of a personal style accessible to a wide audience. As Sinatra biographer John Lahr has written, "[Sinatra] brought a special urgency to his [musical] proprietorship. The songwriters he embraced, especially after he went solo—[songwriters like Ira Gershwin, the Yale-educated Cole Porter, and Sammy Cahn]—were the voices of the educated middle-class mainstream, whose sophisticated wordplay, diction, and syntax had an equipoise that contrasted with the social self-consciousness that so bedeviled Sinatra" (Lahr 1997b: 83). Sinatra, like Lapidus, was an architect, building not literal but figurative and emotional spaces for the postwar middle class—for the young lovers, the swingin' lovers, and the lonely of his 1950s album titles. His approach to these long-playing records was nothing if not architectural. Sinatra exploited the new technology, leading the listener from song to song as if from room to room, in the process creating a coherent structure of feeling.

Like Lapidus, Sinatra relied on the movies, or at least on the idea of the movies, for his architecture. Fellow entertainer Steve Lawrence, echoing the sentiment of countless music critics, once described a typical Sinatra performance as a series of "three-and-one-half minute screenplays." This is a reference, of course, to the manner in which Sinatra not only presented but inhabited a song, literally acting it out. This cinematic approach was most explicit in his presentation of saloon songs such as "One for My Baby." The following introduction to the song, from a 1962 Paris show, is typical. Sinatra segues into the number by (literally) setting the scene: "The lyric of this song concerns a young man who's fractured, stoned . . . fairly mulled . . . drunk! . . . All night long, he's been going from one bar to another bar to another bar . . . it's obvious what his trouble is . . . girls . . . (then) . . . 'It's quarter to three . . . '" (*Sinatra Live in Paris,* 1994). If Sinatra approached his musical material much like an actor approaching a role, what more appropriate place for this than a luxury hotel in which every guest was invited to become an actor of sorts? Lapidus explains the theatrical (if not cinematic) rationale behind his most famous design features, the steps and staircases "to nowhere":

> At the Fontainebleau . . . the entrance to the restaurant, a very lavish, elaborate restaurant, is on the same level as the lobby. You really should walk right in. But what I did was walk people up three steps, bring them out on a platform, and then walk them down three steps. . . . Why walk up, walk across, and walk down? And yet no one has ever realized that there was absolutely no reason for it at all, except as a dramatic entrance to the restaurant. . . . It's straight showmanship. I put those people on stage and they love it. (Cook and Klotz 1973: 157)

The function of these spaces—and of the Fontainebleau as a whole—was almost purely performative, a stage upon which, and through which, guests could write themselves into a dominant cultural narrative of prosperity and belonging. Indeed, the hotel may have first functioned in this capacity for its creator. Thinking back on the hotel's opening night in 1954, Lapidus, once again employing the acting metaphor, remembers: "It was time for him to go in [to the ball]. [He] wiped away a few tears. Why in the world should [he] be crying at a moment like this? [He] had dreamed of an acting career [as an undergraduate at NYU], of making his appearance on stage, entering stage right. Well, it was time for [him] to make [his] entrance, not on stage as an actor but into a glamorous luxury hotel as its architect" (Lapidus 1979: 160).

   That first grand entrance into the Fontainebleau Hotel confirmed Lapidus's professional and cultural status. With it the Russian-born son of Jewish immigrants became the very (commercially) successful designer of resort hotels for an increasingly mainstream audience: an audience that, on numerous occasions throughout the first two decades of the Fontainebleau's existence, packed its supper club in anticipation of a Frank Sinatra show. Sitting side-by-side in their best clothes, these men and women (many, like Sinatra and Lapidus, the children of immigrants) could enact a dream of belonging. The resort setting rendered hometowns equally irrelevant. Distinctions between old and new money, if they did not melt away in the Florida sun, nevertheless proved less pernicious. Even ethnicity was less important than it had once been. The featured performer had himself once been—a long time ago, it seemed—an Italian boy singer. Now forty- or fifty-something, he was a man of distinction, troubadour to the middle-class jet set.

The "big room" was really the "old neighborhood"—reconstituted and brought into the symbolic center of the culture.[1] Symbolizing the myth of inclusion that marked the immediate postwar period, the big room projected an illusion of almost perfect democracy (albeit one largely predicated on whiteness and the ability to consume). Like the closets in the hotel's rooms upstairs, the big room simultaneously conveyed a sense of great space and great possibility, and gave guests (and, for that matter, Sinatra himself) "a feeling that they were the kind of people who could fill it." If the architecture of the Fontainebleau was all-inclusive, encouraging every guest to take center stage, so, too, was Sinatra's singing style, a delivery that rarely failed to convey the illusion of direct address. To "play" the big room, then, for both singer and audience, meant participating—performing—in a spectacle of mutual affirmation.

In retrospect, perhaps the most poetic (and prescient) moment at any of these Sinatra shows in the Fontainebleau's La Ronde supper club would have come with the first orchestral strains of Cole Porter's "I've Got You Under My Skin" (a perennial Sinatra concert favorite and a song he undoubtedly performed at the Fontainebleau many times). The song's title recalled both Morris Lapidus's professional ambition ("skin" is architectural jargon for a building's nonstructural facade) and the promise of inclusion and consensus at the heart of the American century. The illusion of consensus, of course, would be shattered as the decade of the 1960s wore on—shattered on the streets of southern towns like Selma and Birmingham and northern cities like Newark, Detroit, and Chicago. But Porter's song would appear to have anticipated even *that* possibility, its "warning voice" entreating unsuspecting listeners to "Wake up . . . [to] step up . . . to reality."

Today the Fontainebleau is a Hilton and much of what made it unique is gone—not just Lapidus's decorative excesses but, seemingly, the very culture of the inclusive spectacle. And what of the "big room"? Pete Hamill, grasping for a sufficiently evocative metaphor to mark the passing of his old acquaintance, appears to offer us an unintended but definitive answer to the question. "Now Sinatra is dead," writes Hamill, "and it's like a thousand people have just left the room" (Hamill 1998: 32).

Note

1. The metaphor of the "old neighborhood" was suggested to me by Howard Klein, senior vice president of marketing at the Claridge Casino Hotel in Atlantic City and a member of my panel at the Frank Sinatra Conference.

8

🎤

Someone to Watch over Him

Images of Class and Gender Vulnerability in Early Sinatra

Rob Jacklosky

By the 1950s the iconic Sinatra image is established: raincoat slung carelessly over the shoulder, a fedora tipped back, and a tumbler of scotch near at hand. It is at once romantic and sexual, worldly and ultra-American, and it has dominated recent representations of Sinatra. Films like *Swingers* (1996), books like Bill Zehme's *The Way You Wear Your Hat* (1998) and Shawn Levy's *Rat Pack Confidential* (1998), and biographical movies that glorify the Rat Pack years all go back to this as well: Sinatra at his peak, the grown man, singing grown-up songs. The likeliest theory explaining why this has become the primary Sinatra image is the wistful psychoanalytic one: Uncertain men of the 1990s, it goes, use Sinatra as the lens for looking back fondly on days when men could behave badly and be applauded for it.

But a decade before, there was another, younger Sinatra—the 1940s Sinatra built on vulnerability rather than bravado. This image—the skinny, boyish innocent yearning for love—was arguably fabricated by publicists and every bit as constructed. But then again it may also be more organic, may hew more closely to the core reality of the young Sinatra, the one built on vulnerability rather than bravado: an intersection of dependence on a domineering mother and his own feelings about himself that grew up from his working-class background.

Sinatra was always aware of how his own image was constructed. Indeed, he acutely analyzed his own experience in the 1940s: "It was the war years," John Lahr quotes him as saying in *Sinatra: The Artist and the Man,* "and there was a great loneliness. I was the boy in every corner drugstore who'd gone off, drafted to the war. That was all" (1997a: 34). Certainly that was much of the reason for the frenzied reaction to the young Sinatra, and his choice of the word "boy" is exactly right: In women he produced a protective, mothering reaction that was due to his boyish "undersized [and] underfed" appearance, as one contemporary observer put it (Shaw 1995: 26). And it was something that did not go unnoticed by psychologists of the era. As Arnold Shaw points out in his essay "Sinatrauma," one psychologist "argued that Frankie's appeal was a product of the maternal urge 'to feed the hungry.' In the yearning, beseeching quality of his voice, 'almost like the plaintive cry of a hungry child' the doctor found an amazing auditory equivalent of Sinatra's famished appearance. This particular analyst felt that any noticeable increase in weight could destroy Sinatra's magical appeal" (27). Writers of the period also routinely mentioned his "fragility" or his being "bashful," "clumsy," or "frightened" on stage (Bliven 1995: 32–33; Shaw 1995: 21) as the reason for the hysteria he produced in women. Of course, tracing the vulnerability to a single physical quality—weight, voice—or sociohistorical fact such as the war is too simple an answer.

In the gradual construction of the "early Sinatra" image there was much more intentionality than Sinatra or the psychologists mention. The manufacture of this image of innocence and yearning certainly had something to do with the subject positions available to Sinatra and to all young "crooners" in the 1930s: a position that was more or less invented and occupied by Bing Crosby. Crosby, of course, was Sinatra's first inspiration and a role model in those early years. The vocal intimacy he invented, Sinatra continued. Sinatra was aware that he would have to distinguish himself from Crosby, and made constant reference to the fact. Take, for instance, the joke lyric that he sings in "Dick Haymes, Dick Todd and Como": "I'll never sing like Bing, I know I don't compare."

One way Sinatra transformed the role of the crooner was through his choice of songs. In the Columbia years, from 1942 to 1950, he sings an overwhelming number of songs about the uncertain love of a powerful or potentially indifferent woman (notably predating his relationship with the powerful, often indifferent Ava Gardner). From "I Guess I'll Have to Dream the Rest," to "I Should Care," to "You Go to My Head," we are given an image of an overmatched man who "hasn't a ghost of a chance" and goes "around weeping." Visually, this image was underlined by roles in films like *Reveille with Beverly* (1943), which featured the physically fragile Sinatra outnumbered by a troop of piano-playing women or, later, *The Kissing Bandit* (1948), which almost emasculates the hero via wardrobe: Throughout the film, Sinatra is seen in a series of spangled, skin-tight costumes (the worst offender being a flouncy powder blue suit with floppy tie, white gloves, and pointy hat). Sinatra can't be blamed for the clothing in the latter film (the wardrobe department victimized the whole cast), but his own early personal self-presentation also relied on a "dapper, plentiful wardrobe," prompting the neighborhood boys to call him "Slacksey," as John Lahr points out (1997b: 78). Even as a very young man, Sinatra's famously floppy bow ties, silky shirts, and draping pants self-consciously proclaimed "I am in the Hoboken working class but not of it."

Cornell University English professor Roger Gilbert has argued that the 1950s Sinatra "fully articulated [the male image's] contradictions, anxieties and ambivalences" (Scott 1998: B9). The 1940s Sinatra is, however, the unalloyed expression of the male anxiety of rejection and the most fully articulated expression of feminine vulnerability. In films like *Anchors Aweigh* (1945) and *The Kissing Bandit,* Sinatra plays radically insecure men who need the constant reassurance of more masculine role models like Gene Kelly to literally force him to pursue women. He's the kissing bandit who won't kiss or the sailor who can't score. The plots of both films revolve around Sinatra's character being intimidated by women, perhaps ironically, given his ladies' man image. Examples range from the thoroughly unthreatening Katherine Grayson as a self-confident soprano who overshadows the bashful singer, to a more physically threatening woman who, in a stage show, does a "whip dance" in front of a hilariously cowed Kissing Bandit. The Bandit sits quivering in a chair as the whip cracks around him.

The studio system certainly limited Sinatra's control of the image he projected on film, but when taken together with his choice of songs (an arena where his control would be greater although not absolute, as he collaborated with Harry James, Tommy Dorsey, and Axel Stordahl), it seems certain that this was an image which Sinatra at least tacitly endorsed.

This image grew "naturally" out of the lush, quivering, melancholic vocal timbre, but it also grew out of a very real childhood vulnerability. In anecdotes described by John Lahr, and in Sinatra's own recollections, we see that Sinatra's headstrong mother Dolly was a "force," not only providing a shy young Frank with his wardrobe, car, and cash for orchestrations and equipment, but also with his earliest performance opportunities. Dolly produced his first "break" when she pressured the vocal group the Three Flashes into changing its name to the Hoboken Four and taking Sinatra with them on the *Major Bowes' Amateur Hour*. Dolly's preemptive strikes at making a way in the world for her little boy could serve only to exacerbate her son's sense of class vulnerability.

In Will Friedwald's book *Sinatra! The Song Is You,* the trombonist Milt Bernhart remarks, "[Sinatra] sings with the grace of a poet, but when he's talking to you, it's New Jersey. It's remarkable" (Friedwald 1995: 35). The construction of the articulate, sensitive, even posh Sinatra was very much a disguise of his class background, much like his boyhood wardrobe. And in his early spoken introductions to songs on the radio and on V-discs, we can hear him straining after some version of educated eloquence to hide the "New Jersey" in his voice. In the interstices—between the film images, his dandified style of dress, the insecurity of his vocal persona, and his efforts to project polish—we have the story of an evolving image construction that is still conditional enough to fail and rupture.

I will rest my argument on several very pointed examples from early in Sinatra's radio career that will draw out the strain in the competing "vocal images" he is manipulating, sometimes simultaneously. Occasionally, in films like *The Kissing Bandit,* you might catch Sinatra violating the movie's stilted nineteenth-century diction with a Hobokenism like "No, Chico, it's all over WID," but it is audio recordings I'm interested in because of their scripted pretense of naturalness.

In listening to V-discs from 1944, we see this early tension expressed in his very brief spoken introduction to "Long Ago and Far Away," first broadcast on CBS's *The Vimms Vitamins Show.*[1] Sinatra says in an eager, ingenuous tone, "Gentlemen of the Armed Forces, this is the hoodlum from Hoboken. I'd like to sing a tune for you and I hope *youse* like it, hey." Sinatra constructs himself as the "hoodlum from Hoboken"—establishing his humble origins and a connection with the "gentlemen" of the armed forces and, in one phrase, elevates them while minimizing his own position. The final mock, ungrammatical "hope *youse,*" linked with a now-forgotten, all-purpose youth slang suffix "hey," is an audio wink to the radio audience that Sinatra knows what he is doing: playing with his class background. When he launches into the song, he abandons the ingenuousness of his spoken intro-duction and assumes the commanding, completely articulate "Voice." Apologies for Sinatra's class origin, questionable to begin with (and likely pushed by his scriptwriters), drop away in the context of a song. It is telling that in the early 1940s, years before the media would attempt to connect Sinatra with crime bosses, and while he was still comfortably ensconced in his image of boyhood innocence, Sinatra would embrace the term "hood-lum." But then one thinks of what this term does for a slight boy, perhaps mindful of his class position and still-recent dependence on his mother. It casts him in a dangerous light: lower in social stature, perhaps, but tough, street-smart, dangerous, and rising. Furthermore, to a working-class city boy who knows that he has had the "meanness" of the streets softened for him

by a confident, politically connected, and overweening mother, the term
"hoodlum" is preferable to "mama's boy," and "up from the streets" is infi-
nitely preferable to "out from behind her skirts." In these early recordings,
the claim to being a "Hoboken hoodlum" is contradicted by everything from
the solicitousness of the spoken introductions to the delicacy of the songs.
From "I'll Never Smile Again" to "Homesick, that's All" and "I Couldn't
Sleep a Wink Last Night," Sinatra establishes himself, over and over, as lost,
neglected, and disconnected from home and the one he loves. To the
wartime audience of soldiers toward whom these V-discs are directed, however, there is power in the position of a son longing for his mother, a boy
longing for a girl. Much has been made of Sinatra's emotional expressiveness,
his ability to generate feelings of "intense intimacy" with an audience (Kahn
1995: 36; Shaw 1995: 28–29), but even those, like Shaw and Friedwald,
who describe this talent so intelligently, treat it as something that is a "talent" or one of Sinatra's particular gifts, as if it is one of many masks he wore.
To me, the vulnerability seems a heroic and even dangerous admission by
Sinatra. And one cannot overestimate how courageous it is for Sinatra to
admit even a portion of his early vulnerability.

Because Sinatra is—and was even at the start of his career—completely
at home in a song, he turns this vulnerability to a strength as a way of con-
necting with the audience. His performances are commanding, perfectly as-
sured—for all intents and purposes, classless. It is in between the songs, in
introductions written for him, in the comments made by interviewers, that
his class origins become an issue. His Academy Award–winning defense of
racial tolerance, *The House I Live In* (1945), is rightly pointed to as a moment when Sinatra makes his most public statement on progressive politics.
But for Sinatra, every verbal exchange was a comment on class. Ritualistic
mentions of Hoboken (the town becomes a kind of code for Sinatra's
working-class roots) pepper every verbal set piece. In addition to the "Hoboken hoodlum" reference already mentioned, band leader Tommy Dorsey, in
their farewell appearance together, refers to Sinatra as "the Hoboken bronco-
buster." After surprising someone with his intelligence, Sinatra would say in
mock defensiveness, "You're talking to a graduate of Hoboken High" (the
bittersweet irony is, of course, that he attended Hoboken High for little over

a month). Indeed, the habitual mentions of Hoboken are a constant and literal reminder of where he has come from. The hyperpolite speaking voice
and diction Sinatra adopts in radio scripts end up being both a camouflage
for and a reminder of the distance Sinatra is covering in these years. In the
habitual references to Hoboken and Sinatra's dangerous past, there is also an
implicit warning that, despite the lip service paid to equal opportunity for
all in wartime and postwar America, there was discomfort in the fact that
Sinatra had leapt in a matter of years the distance you were supposed to take
a generation to cover. After fighting his way from Hoboken to Hollywood,
Sinatra knew that slipping all the way back down the scale was always a possibility. John Lahr writes that, "as an adult, Sinatra often referred to his
hometown as a 'sewer'" and that "to forget the deadliness of the place took
Frank Sinatra most of his lifetime" (1997a: 3). Little wonder, because the
radio scriptwriters and other on-air personalities seemed intent on remind-
ing him.

In the context of all these reminders of his roots, even playful exchanges
summon a quick-to-fight reputation before the reputation was earned. Take
this exchange on his own radio program, the Old Gold–sponsored *Songs by
Sinatra,* on January 30, 1946.[2] After Sinatra references his "fighting weight,"
his guest Benny Goodman initiates this dialogue:

> BG: Say, how about that Frank, they tell me you are right handy with your
> dukes.
> FS: Oh, I toss a little leather, now and then, yes.
> BG: Well, then, if you were ever caught in a dark alley, you wouldn't have any
> trouble defending yourself, would you, huh?
> FS: It all depends, Benny. With Margaret O'Brien, no. With Lana Turner,
> possibly.

This moment of quickly deflated mock "toughness" is just one of many
"voices" that Sinatra tries on during this thirty-minute radio program. In the
introduction, he adopts a jazzy-cool hep-cat voice and pretends to fumble
his introductory remarks: "Well, thank you all Marvin Miller, and while you
all're goin' to see if that big clarinet tycoon Benny Goodman and the Goodman sextet are ready, I'll *axe askel.* [GIRLS' LAUGHTER] I'll *askel axel.*

[MORE LAUGHTER] Silly, I mean I'll *askel askel.* Hey, Stordhal, get me off. Play something, will ya?" In another exchange with Goodman, Sinatra complains that Goodman is playing too slowly: "Ain't that a little pokey for me, Benny? After all, man, I'm a cat. Stuff's gotta move or I goes right by. I sings by jet propulsion, man. . . . Play something for me that really romps, kid." His perfect reading of these tongue-twisting lines give the lie to his un-ease with proper English. But so does nearly every verbal exchange, which plays with some kind of vernacular. The uncertain young man is clearly his default mode, designed to appeal to bobby soxers, and is best exemplified in exchanges with a character called Teenage Tina, in which he mimics her in an Elmer Fudd–like voice. When he demurs from singing another song, Tina begs him, saying that he's "got to," and Sinatra responds: "Tina says 'I got to,' Benny. Put me in a purty mood, Benny." He also traffics in a nearly impenetrable teenage slang,[3] as in the following exchange where Sinatra uses the abbreviation "O.G." in a way that seems like a plug for his sponsor, Old Gold, but then replaces the plug with a winsome good night, and interrupts it all with that ubiquitous teenage suffix, "hey": "We're saying thanks and *O.G.* That 'O.G.,' *hey,* isn't [a] commercial. It stands for 'Oh, Goodnight.'" Rounding out his repertoire is tough-guy slang ("I've thrown some leather"), the aforementioned hep-cat slang, even country-rube slang. Throughout the script, written by Glenn Wheaton, there is an insistent emphasis on differ-ent vocal positions. The script keeps foregrounding Sinatra's comfort with them, even as you can sense that he is completely comfortable with none.

Finally, in a salute for Franklin Delano Roosevelt's birthday, he adopts this poetic and boyish tone:

> Underneath the frozen earth at Hyde Park today a great man had a birthday. And the little path that leads down to his grave was narrow and cold. On earth, this man walked a path that was warm and wide. Whole nations were lined up on either side, and they felt the warmth. And so did lots of us little people. I for one thought the world of this man. I think he was a magnificent human being. I suppose he had his share of human weakness, but he sure had more than his share of human strength. What I admired most about him [pause] was the way he had of [stumbles, pause] of making [pause] every American feel welcome here (Wheaton 1946).

Sinatra is at his most sincere in this tribute to a man he greatly admired, and yet he must adopt an inflated style with which he is not completely comfortable. It is the vernacular of exalted seriousness. Only in the plain-spoken last line, which breaks free of the turgid poeticism of the introduction, does he seem to speak, haltingly, in his own voice. It is significant that the moment in which Sinatra transitions from the "epic" style to the simple and personal is at the words "little people." When he follows "little people" quickly with "I for one," we see that here is the point at which he feels most closely connected with FDR and the New Deal's frontal assault on privilege based on class and wealth. It is as if remembering the dignity that Roosevelt recognized in all classes, "making every American feel welcome here," allows Sinatra to speak in an undisguised way out of his own class.

Throughout these very scripted early exchanges, one gets the feeling of a man playing against perceptions of himself as a working-class boy. Whether owning up to a "tough-guy" past or submerging it under politeness, he is always wrestling with it. Sinatra's mania for reading and intellectual self-improvement that would later produce impressively thoughtful commentary on his own work would always carry with it the slight self-consciousness that one hears very strongly in the early Dorsey broadcasts and even in his own radio programs. It is the carefulness that autodidacts from Thomas Hardy onward shared: a vocabulary too formal, a deliberate speaking cadence that was a half-step slower in unscripted public situations.

It is little wonder that Sinatra said of his singing, "When I sing, I believe, I'm honest. If you want to get an audience with you, there's only one way. You have to reach out to them with honesty and humility" (Mustazza 1995: 6). In his singing, with a Porter or Gershwin lyric in hand, he is most able to relax, to be himself, to put aside the different vocal personae and to be honest with his audience. He is not, in those moments of elegantly perfect phrasing, being reminded of "where he has come from."

Notes

1. Didier Deutsch and Gary Pacheco, *Frank Sinatra: The Columbia Years: The V-Discs* (New York: Sony Music, 1994), disc 1, track 14.

2. Edward R. Murrow, *Person to Person* (CBS, 1946), available at Museum of Television and Radio, New York, call number B19148.

3. In another example, he explains a teenage girl's bad mood by saying "her father broke her Chicory Chick," a now perplexing reference to an obscure novelty song he recorded in the 1940s. See Wheaton (1946).

9

State of Grace

Frank Sinatra and American Charisma

T. H. Adamowski

But they hung on his words, smiled and nodded and stared with raised eyebrows at that circle he formed with his forefinger and thumb while the other fingers stood erect like lances and his regal countenance labored to speak; they did not resist, they gladly allowed their emotions to wait upon him and abandoned themselves with a passion that went far beyond anything they would normally have trusted themselves to feel.

—Mynheer Pepperkorn in
Thomas Mann's *The Magic Mountain*

charism [. . . Gk., "gift"] *divine spiritual gift to individuals or groups for the good of the community.*

—*The Harper Collins Encyclopedia of Catholicism*

*I*n 1987 a colleague who had just returned from a sabbatical told me that his plane had been delayed taking off, on a steamy day, in a West African country. While cursing airline, heat, and country, the passengers suddenly noticed the plane that had bumped theirs from the queue: a private jet, sweeping imperiously into position for takeoff. Immediately, excited whispers—based on nothing—swept through the cabin: *Sinatra's* plane! If not forgiven, all was forgotten in a moment of reflected glory on an African tarmac.

About ten years later a young woman dreams she is in the vast corridor of a building she takes to be the Pentagon. Suddenly Sinatra materializes, pursued by dozens of reporters and photographers. Floodlights everywhere. Everywhere, that is, but at the end of the long corridor, where the dreamer dimly makes out the ignored president of the United States. It is, of course, axiomatic for such a dream that a president is always outranked by a Chairman of the Board.

Finally, a 1959 incident in which this essay had its moment of origin. A high school friend learned I had been listening not to our age cohorts' rock and roll music but to Sinatra. He said, mysteriously, that he wanted me to "meet someone," an uncle or cousin, or something. I never did meet him because my friend could not resist describing him: Swaggering along the streets of our Little Italy, in a suit way too sharp for the neighborhood, sporting a fedora, and carrying a trench coat super-casually over his shoulder. Quite unnecessarily, my friend explained, "He's tryin' to be Sinatra."

Each of these examples testifies to a different aspect of Sinatra's charismatic authority over the past five decades as well as to his capacity to evoke what I would like simply to call "desire," some feeling in his audience of want or deficiency—relative to Sinatra—some lack that he could provide. Of course, charisma has generated yards of scholarly definition and moral evaluation, and it is not my intention to rehearse these. I am interested only in what we might call the rich and immediately recognizable texture of the phenomenon.[1] What the desire evoked by Sinatra's charisma may have represented is, of course, a matter on which I can only speculate. But to find traces of the phenomenon itself, the charismatic Sinatra who elicited so many forms of desire, well, this is an easy task. For that, one need only recall the career.

Consider the final segment of his 1966 television "special," "A Man and His Music," Part II, where he performs "Luck Be a Lady Tonight." Sinatra's admirers know the story of this song: that it was sung (as it were) by Marlon Brando in *Guys and Dolls* and that later, with a Billy May arrangement, Sinatra turned it into one of his great "signature" songs. As much as any of Sinatra's taped legacies, the 1966 performance reminds us of what it was like when he was in the "state of grace" that made him the most charismatic American entertainer of the century.

It is a charisma I would restrict to the period after 1953 and Sinatra's return to preeminence in American popular music. Of course, one may quarrel with this restriction, and by another understanding of charisma one might well include the great period of Sinatra's first success, with the wartime bobby soxers. However, while the wartime phenomenon turned on something Sinatra may well have invented for our century, it was, finally, a smaller thing and one he would have to share with a string of successors extending to our own day. The bobby-soxer episode in Sinatra's career partook of that charismatic effect adumbrated long ago by the portrait in Euripides' *Bacchae* of Dionysus, with his mixture of male and female characteristics. I recently saw in a newspaper a close-up photograph, an advertisement as it turned out, of a brooding woman whom, for a moment, I mistook for Elvis Presley. Like the 1940s' Sinatra and the 1950s' Presley, this strange (but increasingly tiresome) fusion of male and female would reappear in Mick Jagger, Michael Jackson, and any number of performers whose talents never matched those of these celebrated pop heirs to Sinatra.

However, what distinguished Sinatra from all later pop charismatics—and from such predecessors as Al Jolson and Rudolph Valentino—is a source and dimension of charisma that, while it may have been intimated in the 1940s, did not arise in its fullness until his return to power, after the period of "troubles" that began for him in the late 1940s.

In this connection it is useful to recall for a moment those grim years when Sinatra was "powerless." Especially revealing about that period are Sinatra's televised performances during the early 1950s. For example, the May 5, 1951, *Frank Sinatra Show,* on CBS, in which Sinatra appeared with Joe Bushkin, June Hutton, Dagmar, and assorted minor figures of the time.

No longer the androgynous "Frankie" of the bobby soxer years, neither is he yet the "Chairman of the Board." His old gestures obsolete and new ones still unfashioned, he relies on bad imitations of the trademark gestures of Jackie Gleason (arms akimbo, as if to say "away we go"). He tries *too hard:* to tell bad jokes, to be likable, to show he is still important. Although his phrasing is often fine and gives intimations of what is to come in the Capitol Records years, his voice sometimes borders on the shrill. This is a man "between jobs," devoid of charismatic authority because of a decompression of self-confidence.

By comparison to those years, then, when Sinatra returned in 1953, it was very much a matter of *power.* Film director and producer Billy Wilder is said to have remarked that when Sinatra arrived at an event, "It's like Mack the Knife is in town and the action is starting" (Hamill 1995: 235). During a televised tribute to the singer, sometime in the 1970s, Orson Welles spoke of the aura of a "bandit chieftain" that Sinatra's friends saw around him. These we may provisionally call reports from reality, from people who knew the real man. However, for those of us not present when this "bandit chieftain" entered a room, Sinatra was not only the grand master of American popular song but also of the art of gesture, supremely able to use gesture to incarnate, via the imagination, all the authority that accrues in America to success, talent, power, sex, and money.[2] For this reason it is prudent to take as provisional even his friends' accounts of the "real" Sinatra; so powerful was Sinatra's imaginative "medicine" that, like his audiences, one suspects that at times even his friends may have seen him through an imaginative filter: bandit chieftain and Mack the Knife.

There have been many great popular singers in America—a few, like Billie Holiday, may even claim to be Sinatra's peers[3]—but Sinatra's charisma was marked by a certain differential: Not all great American singers were Sinatra. When, with a wink and beckoning fingers, he importunes an imaginary Lady Luck not to leave him ("Stick with me baby/I'm the guy that you came in with"), when he slowly turns Juliet Prowse's face toward him while singing "It's All Right With Me," or when, wreathed in cigarette smoke, he turns away from a fading spotlight at the end of "Angel Eyes," each is, of course, an action performed *for its own sake,* in short, a gesture. Thus they are intended to present him not in himself as he really is but, rather, to "de-real-ize" him and make him into the object of the many forms of desire, an emotion that signals to us what we *lack*.

Through such gestures, Sinatra tapped into the national infatuation not only for the Bandit Chieftain but also for the Conquistador, the Aristocrat, the Lover (Triumphant and Despairing), the Man of the People (and first working-class pop singer), the CEO, and, at the bottom of all lines, the Hero—the *American* hero, the incarnation of secular freedom. In the right hands, any one of these roles may have been sufficient to generate charismatic authority and the desire in others to partake of it. With Sinatra all were in play simultaneously to generate the "cool" that uniquely defined his charisma. So rare is the combination that it has generated the cliché that in American show business, "there will never be another Sinatra" (Mallowe 1995: 195). It is indeed difficult to imagine how any other single person will be able, for some future America, to bring audiences into the presence of as many dimensions of the mythology of the Imperial Republic as Sinatra succeeded in doing in the latter half of the twentieth century.

And yet, as I once heard reported of a woman who did not share this experience at a Montreal concert, "*Eh bien,* he is, after all, just a pop singer." True, in a sense, but, *hélas,* beside the point.

No mere "pop singer" generates such intense reactions for so long. Moreover, many mere pop singers have, we know, tried to steal the formula. Trying to be Sinatra, they, too, might swagger, snap fingers, interpolate "Frankisms" in place of a songwriter's lyrics—as did Bobby Darin. One watches such larcenous performances as Jean-Paul Sartre said one watches the performance of a waiter who takes your order just a little too solicitously, who carries his tray with too much élan, who descants the wine with surplus panache. "What's wrong with this picture?" one asks—and then realizes that the man is playing at being a waiter in a café (Sartre 1957: 59). As so many singers—and nonsingers—of a certain period in American popular culture played at being Frank Sinatra.[4]

Even Sinatra occasionally played at being Sinatra, as in his recording of "Old MacDonald," or in "Rat Pack" films. For the most part, however, he simply *was* Frank Sinatra, in the real and imaginary modes. But this "simply" is not without complexity. When, while singing "Luck Be a Lady," Sinatra plays at being a gambler, blowing on imaginary dice in an imaginary casino, rolling them toward the camera, he invites us, by the long look he casts in the direction of the thrown dice, into the imaginary with him, a place from which the everyday world recedes. Nevertheless, such imaginary constructions also always occur *within the world* and depend on our knowledge and perceptions of a certain "real" Sinatra who frequented the casinos of Vegas.

Reality: the place of perception.

What happens when we *perceive*—say, the actual casino floor in the Sands, on a day in 1960? For one thing, we can extract endless bits of data from what we see: Sinatra's suit (its color, texture, etc.), whether, from the expression on his face or his general comportment, he seemed tired, the color of the handkerchief in his pocket, the bored look on the face of his bodyguards, and the infinity of details of the room itself. But in the imaginary, where charisma dwells, we receive a global picture, an image, *all at once.* Travel to your hometown for a perception of your childhood house and the data never stop coming. You might even count the courses of bricks in the perceived house. Call up an image of it, though, *right now,* and you will bring to it only what you need. To try to count the courses of bricks in the imagined house would be a useless passion. By reference to Sinatra's own experiences of the real, Sinatra the maker of imagery produces, through his gestures, a certain kind of gambler: a risk-taking high roller—count on it!— buoyant, sure he will win but, all the same, betraying a flicker of anxiety as he watches the imaginary dice roll on the unreal table before him. And we, responding, bring to that image needs and desires of our own that go begging in the real.

But does charisma work only when we are not in the actual presence of the imagined person? Not at all. To go back to the floor of the casino in 1960, the extraordinary thing that seems to have occurred with Sinatra was, of course, that he was so often not merely "perceived," in the *real,* by his admirers—perhaps, at times, as I have suggested, not even by his friends— when they were in his actual presence. A former pit boss at the Sands Hotel reports, in a private communication, that the crowds in the Copa Room talked, laughed, noisily ate, and so on, even as the other great entertainers walked out onto the stage to begin their shows. The Sands remained a glamour spot the audience *shared with* Dean Martin or Judy Garland. However, just before Sinatra walked out, the crowd always went strangely and expectantly silent. When Sinatra appeared on the floor of the casino, it is no less likely that they were, until that moment, in the perceptual frame of mind. Now, however, the imaginary Sinatra crowded out the real Sinatra so that the gamblers did not "see" fatigue, bored bodyguards, and the like. As for the Sands, it will have formed only the glamorous background for a foreground in which Sinatra—as imagined object—was dominant. (It would not be surprising if this shift toward the imaginary did not also lay behind some of the confusions about what "really" happened on such or such an occasion when the infamous Sinatra temper flared.)

There was a period in American history when middle- and upper-middle-class desire was to be precisely that gambler represented in Sinatra's performance, with by his side a beautiful Lady Luck: freely risking everything, in a place associated with both glamour and crime. Indeed, it was a desire that went beyond the middle classes. The photos of Sinatra that adorned working-class bars in the 1960s and 1970s attested to his continued appeal to that portion of the American population, as well, and his Italian American Hoboken background was as much part of the Sinatra mystique as his jet-setting "lifestyle."

Such desire would begin to fade only when the appeal of Sinatra's particular representations of urban American cool no longer spoke to the children of the various audience cohorts he had generated during the 1940s, 1950s, and early 1960s.[5] For these children, the cool (nomadic by nature) would migrate to a new set of representations that required not tuxedos but T-shirts and jeans. This does not mean, of course, that Sinatra had moved beyond the imaginary for the boomer generation. Rather, for them his charisma had become inverted, and they subjected him to imaginative operations of their own, bringing to the word "Sinatra" only what they needed during the hectic mid-1960s. If, in the jewels and limousines of the rich and famous who jetted to Miami or Las Vegas for Sinatra's openings, the parents might have seen charisma-generating signifiers, many of their children saw only signifiers of capitalist consumerism. For the opinion makers of this generation,

Sinatra's turn to the right could only doom him to the negative charisma attaching to the guy one loves to hate (Adamowski 1998: 26–37).

And yet despite the power of the imaginary to crowd out the real, there was, of course, always a "real" Sinatra, occasionally glimpsed by the rest of us in newsreels or newspaper photos. He might be snarling at a reporter, hurrying to a plane, or leaning over in conference with aides. In a famous photo of 1961, he ascends a stairway holding the hand of Jacqueline Kennedy. He is not at that point, I think, in the "imaginary" mode, for the look on his face suggests he is not attending to the camera. Rather, he is engaged in an action—escorting a beautiful woman up the stairs to a certain destination, in an unguarded moment of revealed pride. Nevertheless, in each of these cases a certain aspect of the real Sinatra is essential to the Sinatra who made himself an imaginary object on certain stages and before certain cameras. After all, it is not for the rest of us to escort the first lady, snarl at the press, or lean forward in a conference room to make a point to attentive men.

Moreover, such episodes turn on another "real" moment, witnessed by millions of Americans in April 1954: Sinatra bounding down the aisle to receive an Academy Award. He is *really* excited. We all knew he had hit bottom, and if we did not know it we learned about it quickly thereafter (again and again and again). Poor boy from Hoboken makes good; girls swoon at his feet. Poor boy from Hoboken blows everything and becomes loser. Loser pursues world's most beautiful woman. In my school, in 1952, we used to laugh at him a little. After 1953 all smiles ceased. The reign of envy had begun.

Thereafter, what mattered for charisma was not merely success but the way in which real success—following hard upon real failure—was linked to a certain way in which Sinatra comported himself when he performed. With all due respect to Ava Gardner's influence with Harry Cohn or to the work of Nelson Riddle and other arrangers, the real Sinatra finally owed his success to himself: to his ability as an actor, especially to his ability as a singer—and what was his fabled "phrasing" if not a consummate sense of *verbal* gesture—and, in everything, to a self-confidence that, even at the lowest point of the troubles, must have always been there.

When Sinatra's affair with Ava Gardner began, there was in it something both pitiful and heroic. He was drifting to the bottom. She was at the top. The prom queen is supposed to go for the quarterback, not the nerd. Photos of Sinatra at this time, including those with the lounge-lizard mustache and the brilliantined hair, betray elements of the kind of image anxiety that causes all forms of charisma to undergo decompression. However, in his diminished reservoir of early 1950s self-confidence, enough remained for Sinatra never to hesitate in his pursuit of Gardner.

Nevertheless, the troubles were essential for those qualities of vulnerability, weakness, and loneliness that would never be far from the new Sinatra character that—under the influence of this residual self-confidence—began to emerge in the early 1950s. Always intimated during the 1940s (his apprenticeship in gesture) by both the softness of his youthful voice and his frail physique, these qualities were profoundly deepened during the troubles and their all-too-public display of a real vulnerability, weaknesses, and loneliness linked to the loss of both his wife and, eventually, that most beautiful woman in the world.

In that first "charismatic" moment, during the war, frailty of physique played an important part. Curiously, it diminished in importance after 1953, although Sinatra remained amazingly thin for years. That early physical vulnerability seems to have been replaced by our collective memory of that later period of human vulnerability, when his own life failures, changing fashions, and other people brought him temporarily to cold earth, experiences we all know in one form or another. Later, when it all turned around, the real troubles would be derealized and made imaginary objects for everyone. It would require no more (and no less) than a hunching of the shoulders or a weary flick of a cigarette lighter—or such magnificent vocal gestures (phrasing) as the interpolated, ever-so-slightly delayed, "of" in "I'm weary all of the time," at the end of "Stormy Weather."

And when it all turned around, the real Sinatra behaved with all the self-confidence that self-reliance—an old American virtue—demands. On the stage of American popular culture, in the imaginary, he became the Conquistador, generating the gestures of sovereign self-assurance; for he had achieved success *twice;* and to be a Conquistador is precisely what so many other entertainers of his era and later were not. From 1953 on the tough-talking performer would turn to imaginary advantage the capital that accrued to him in reality, including the memory—his and ours—of a failure that would live in counterpoint to his defiant confidence.

Let me repeat: When gestures are employed in the service of the imaginary, what occurs is a certain way of suspending the real, placing it, for a time, in brackets. In its place arises not the real object but something that *draws sustenance* from the real to create an image toward which desire may turn. Whose desire? Ours. Through the "language" of gesture—even of tough-guy talk and bravado—the imaginary object plays on an audience as a caress plays on the body of someone we love, to awaken it from reality and to transport it into the imaginary.

Even into imaginary banditry. It is scarcely out of the question that a kid "really" growing up in Hoboken will have made friends who would go on to "careers" in the mob. In the nightclubs of the era they formed part of the ambiance in the way that back-stage drug dealers would for another generation. This is the banality of the real. Of course, in the 1930s there were also *imaginary* mobsters, whose gestures also borrowed selectively from the real. Such tough-talking guys—like Edward G. Robinson, James Cagney, and Humphrey Bogart—would provide Sinatra with "role models" by which to transform his real relationships with mobsters (whatever they were and however they may have been acquired) into the imaginary. My mother used to refer to him as "that hoodlum friend of yours." She meant that in his verbal gestures, before television cameras, in the 1950s and 1960s Sinatra often sounded like a hood (and not like the "nice boy" of the 1940s whom she recalled fondly). She was not speaking of fights or threats or government investigations (to which she paid no attention). Rather, she was responding to the manner in which Sinatra had interiorized a certain kind of 1930s' representation of the hood and made it *part of the act*. This added to his persona a hint of tremendous danger. In turn, such representations fed off all the other things about which we read.

Did these representations speak to a desire? Did Cagney's and Bogart's? Or, later, Marlon Brando's and Al Pacino's? The imaginary gangster bespoke power and ready access to women and money. He even risked death. It all hinted at life beyond the iron cage of reality, an imaginary place where other men quailed before one's toughness. Whatever the reality of the allegations of mob connections turns out, biographically, to have been, in the imaginary the Bandit Chieftain represented the fundamental value Sinatra exuded through all his gestures: freedom.

What mattered to Americans of his era was Sinatra's transmutation of the Bandit Chieftain into Lord of the Rat Pack, during the period that writer Gore Vidal somewhere called "the great national nap." In those days Sinatra's charisma depended on the desire of Americans not to go to bed so damned early, not to be so good, genteel, monogamous, dull, constricted—unfree: "For decades now, Sinatra defined the glamour of the urban night. It was both a time and a place; to inhabit the night, to be one of its restless creatures, was a small act of defiance, a shared declaration of freedom, a refusal to play by all those conventional rules that insisted on men and women rising at seven in the morning, leaving for work at eight, and falling exhausted into bed at ten o'clock that night. In his music, Sinatra gave voice to all those who believed that the most intense living begins at midnight. . . . If you loved someone who did not love you back, you could always walk into a saloon, put your money on the bar, and listen to Sinatra" (Hamill 1998: 14–15).

Long after the rest of the country had dozed off for the night, the Bandit Chieftain and his gang were wide awake and staring: roaring along the highway between L.A. and Vegas, allegedly slugging waiters and passing civilians, and then turning these realities into imaginary advantage at Rat Pack "summits."

It is easy to forget how the Rat Pack dominated the entertainment pages during the late 1950s and early 1960s. Even aspiring Caesars wanted part of the action. Today the Pack is hot again. During the 1950s people were tiresomely good in one way. Now they are otherwise tiresome (counting the fat content in their shopping baskets, railing against smokers, drinking just enough red wine to keep heart disease at bay, etc.). As I think back to that late 1950s' period, I recall nothing so much as the excitement that accompanied every announcement of a Rat Pack summit (or "clan" summit, as they were called in those days). Even my rock coevals took notice. Good citizens of the world often predicted that Sinatra would soon suffer what we now call a lifestyle death. Instead, like the desire he evoked, he grew stronger.

As one of Norman Mailer's characters, in *Harlot's Ghost,* says of a performance by Lenny Bruce, "He seemed to be offering full proof of the proposition that he who gives life to an audience receives life back" (Mailer 1991: 436). Sinatra is an "offstage" character of some importance in this novel. Perhaps it is not entirely an accident that Sinatra's health began to deteriorate noticeably once he stopped performing in public.

Of course, the point of all that excitement turned entirely on Sinatra singing, for despite *From Here to Eternity,* the actor owed his film success to the Sinatra who, in his singing, was even more successful as an actor than the Sinatra who appeared on the screen.

In short, the Pack leader had also to be the auteur of *Songs for Swingin' Lovers* and also of *No One Cares* or *Nice 'n' Easy.* The buoyant lover, the lonely lover, the romantic lover, the seducer. Even the album covers fostered charisma: Sinatra with arms spread to encompass swinging lovers; or leaning against a lamppost; or with finger crooked toward an imaginary dance partner somewhere beyond the album's cover, whom he beckons to come in from the cold of the real world; or lonely at a bar while, around him, others enjoy themselves. That latter cover, for 1959's *No One Cares,* with Sinatra "alone" at the bar—looking into his drink and holding a cigarette, while surrounded by a happy crowd—provides the quintessential representation of the Sinatra whose charisma owed so much to his capacity to evoke loneliness while being at the center of all action.

Such archetypal Sinatra gestures fed off what we had read of the real man and stoked desire in the audience by crowding out from the real man all but certain essentials of the imaginary Sinatra. These absolutely depended on the immensely real Sinatra self-confidence and his catastrophic lapses into gloom. (With the possible exception of Judy Garland, what other entertainer of the time so completely embodied *folie circulaire?*) But beyond reality, they helped create the imaginary domain in which Sinatra ruled as Aristocrat of the emotional life.

Moreover, his myth depended enormously on his aristocratic capacity to spend: money, love, himself. No Calvinist, Sinatra was a throwback to the kind of medieval *Aristoi* who salted the earth with coins to suggest transcendence of money. The stories began appearing in the mid-1950s with regularity: the flamboyant expenditures on airplanes, helicopters, gambling, women—coupled with acts of astonishing charity toward friends and strangers. Indeed, that he did not die a "lifestyle" death thirty years ago could only add to the picture of Sinatra as superhero of the 1950s and 1960s. All of that expenditure—for liquor, in late hours, with women—he survived it all and lived into his eighties, Chairman of the Board.

"Chairman of the (Imaginary) Board": This talismanic epithet also contributed to the myth on which Sinatra's charisma was built. Not merely the Lover, the Kid from Hoboken, the bandit chieftain, the feudal aristocrat, but also the summation, the thing-in-itself: the CEO. How depressed must be half the CEOs in America now that gender-neutral language prevents them from being, like Frank, chairmen of their boards! Among many of Sinatra's admirers it is fashionable to decry this famous moniker, perhaps out of embarrassment for all that it suggests of a Sinatra who was a favorite of corporate America and who issued from a generation more comfortable with money than the generation that followed.

Such embarrassment is a misguided emotion. For all its public relations value, the expression could not have been more consonant with the aura of power that both Sinatra the singer and Sinatra the friend of presidents exuded. The Chairman of a (Real) Board is famously talented, powerful, and wealthy, with gofers available for his every whim, all components of various aspects of the Sinatra myth. If, as a commonplace has it, we cannot separate Sinatra the man from Sinatra the singer, then, surely, we must not forget that if Sinatra the singer owed something to the streetwise kid from working-class Hoboken, he probably also owed something to the entertainer whose every appearance caused the Las Vegas casinos to be filled with CEOs, movie stars, and sheiks.

Moreover, another cliché of the corporate success myth, perfectly consonant with Sinatra's own, is that "it's lonely at the top," and as I have suggested, this solitariness—perhaps already adumbrated by the "boy singer" who steps out from the band to stand alone at the microphone—shadows all of Sinatra's flamboyance. In his music it is never farther away than the next album. On stage, after any burst of up-tempo songs, we learned to await the inevitable announcement of the "saloon songs."

The representation of Sinatra as executive, moving easily in corporate spheres, began taking shape in the mid-1960s, when he was said to be sanitizing his "image." Of course, he was first and foremost Chairman of the *musical* Board, but, as I have said, his success in one area fueled his success in other areas, creating that "differential" that would distinguish him from other great singers. Nothing better in mid-century America than to be Chairman of *some* Board. But to be Chairman *in general!*

The famous story of his post-1953 refusal to shake hands with his old nemesis, Mitch Miller, suggests yet another source of Sinatra charisma, one available only to the Chairman in general. After being dropped by MCA, feeling the indifference of Columbia Records, and being forced to beg for a movie role, suddenly Sinatra seemed to have triumphed over those lesser CEOs, the great corporate producers not merely of records and films but of careers. The "gray-flanneled" "organization man" living in the "lonely crowd" was an archetype of 1950s' middle-class life, but such dutiful and anonymous compliance was famously not part of the real Sinatra, about whom one read. One suspects that the reason his many fights (in the real)—verbal and physical—never cost him much with his public was that such episodes were not so much deplored as *envied.* On stage and record, his gestural representations of self-confidence always took us back to this actual fearlessness of the working-class kid from the neighborhood, indifferent to the gentilities of the class into which he had moved. Moreover, whatever doubts the real Sinatra may have harbored (in the recesses of his privacy) about this almost monstrous self-confidence, the imaginary Sinatra behaved rather like the Robert Duvall character in *Apocalypse Now,* convinced that nothing could harm him.

Not even old age, where fearlessness continued to feed off the real in the space of the imaginary. An old man, his voice always at risk of not being there when he needed it, standing on a stage before thousands of people. We were always nervous: Would it be there, tonight? Surely he sensed our nervousness and, perhaps, even shared it.

We fall asleep—do we not?—by first mimicking sleep. We gesture sleep toward us. In short, we perform a magic trick. If we do it right, we *coincide with* the sleeper we imagine ourselves to be (Merleau-Ponty 1962: 163).

Time and again during these 1980s' performances, Sinatra gestured us into confidence in him by the very manner in which he walked out onto the stage (exactly on time), with that famous cock-of-the-walk prance: the *old* Sinatra as "the old *Sinatra*." First, of course, would come the up-tempo songs, with, often, as an opener, "I've Got the World On a String" or "Come Fly With Me." Yes, they help to loosen the throat and make fewer demands on pitch control. Stuff for ear, nose, and throat specialists. More to the point, the gestures of the swinging Sinatra who opened the show, like those of the would-be sleeper, were a species of white magic, intended both to caress the audience into confidence and—as he aged into a new dimension of vulnerability—to summon, once more, the Voice. Eventually, however, when he announced that it was time for the "saloon songs," a palpable audience tension would return: "Oh, God, Frank," one would quietly say. "Just do 'Strangers in the Night,' not 'Here's that Rainy Day.'"

But they didn't call him *Sinatra* for nothing!

He would turn to the conductor and ask, "Whadda ya got?" Hearing the answer, he would bark, "Shoot." And *of course* it would be something like "Rainy Day" or "Angel Eyes." In the religion in which Frank Sinatra was raised, the *gift* from God to the individual for the good of the community, the *charism* retains great authority, a tribute to the working of grace in the world. It remains one of the most touching achievements of Sinatra's career that, until almost the end, his gestures so often succeeded in opening him to the influence of his mysterious muse, who, once again, would bring him into that secular "state of grace" we call his "charisma" and by which he could overcome the last and fiercest challenge the real offers to the imaginary: the coming of age.

Notes

1. One can never go wrong with the classic accounts of charisma in the work of Max Weber (1978: 1111–70). Both Irvine Schiffer's *Charisma* (1973) and Charles Lindholm's *Charisma* (1990) offer stern warnings against charismatic figures. They lack the tinge of deeply complicating nostalgia for the charismatic figure that can occasionally be made out in Weber's monumental studies of the "iron cage" in which we live.

2. For the purposes of this discussion of gesture, I have borrowed extensively from Jean-Paul Sartre's studies of the "imagination" and his account of sexual relationships in *Being and Nothingness.*

3. Although it may seem odd to call Billie Holiday one of Sinatra's peers as a "popular" singer, I choose this term deliberately. There is a long debate about Sinatra's status as a "jazz singer." There is none about Holiday's. However, when one listens to the recordings of each of these great singers, it is often very difficult to tell why that great and honorific term is applied to the soul-baring woman but not to the soul-baring man. So, I call her a popular singer, the term most often applied to Sinatra. Of course, "jazz singer" is fine, too, as long as it is applied to both of them.

4. And of a later period also, for Sinatra's huge personal authority helped many in the inheritor generation that followed him learn how to be flamboyant rock stars. Although it is nice to have the testimony of so many (Bono, Dylan, Springsteen, Jim Morrison, Elvis Costello, et al.) that they admired Sinatra, it can scarcely be called surprising. Forget for a moment the musical differences between them and consider only the similarity of vocation: they were entering show business at a time when Sinatra dominated it.

5. In a self-congratulatory and immensely knowing article, David Halberstam has recently celebrated Sinatra the balladeer while dismissing any notion that Sinatra was "hip": "There is no such thing as a white hipster. . . . Sinatra's cool always seemed self-conscious" (1995: 155). It would take us too far afield to explore what appears to be a racial "inferiority complex" in this, but Halberstam confuses certain Frankisms of the period ("ring-a-ding-ding," etc.) with a recognition of the actual cool that inhabited Sinatra's rhythms, his unparalleled ability to swing, his nervous energy, and his supercharged alertness. Ironically, these are the qualities that led *Playboy*'s readers, in the same issue in which Halberstam's article appears, to select as the best jazz album of 1997 Sinatra's 1959 concert in Australia with the Red Norvo Quintet.

Part Three

A Riff on Italian American Culture

"I grew up for a few years thinking I was just another American kid. Then I discovered . . . I was a dago. A wop. A guinea . . . like I didn't have a fucking *name*."

10

Sinatra at the Table

Scenes from Patsy's Restaurant

Joe Scognamillo
and Sal Scognamillo

*I*n 1944 war-weary New Yorkers were given a small reason to smile and celebrate when Pasquale "Patsy" Scognamillo founded Patsy's Italian Restaurant in the theater district on West 56th Street. It has moved only once since then (in 1954, to the space next door). In its sixty years of existence, Patsy's has had only three chefs—the late Patsy himself, his son Joe Scognamillo, who has been at the establishment since the tender age of seven, and Joe's son Sal Scognamillo, who has been running the kitchen since 1991.

As a great Neapolitan restaurant, Patsy's has attracted a varied clientele, but is perhaps best known as Frank Sinatra's favorite place to eat, and in fact, his family still enjoys dining at Patsy's whenever they are in town. Sinatra made

Patsy's a mecca of dining alla italiana; *some other regulars included Al Pacino, Robert DeNiro, Mario Puzo, Madonna, and Bon Jovi.*

Here Patsy's is the scena *(scene or stage) to observe Sinatra at work and play in typically Italian American fashion.* [Editor's note.]

JOE SCOGNAMILLO: It was well over 50 years ago [when Sinatra first ate at Patsy's]. I was a little boy, and my father sent me backstage to the Paramount with a big pot of pasta e lenticchie [lentil soup] for a fellow by the name of Frank Sinatra. When I got there, I couldn't understand why all these little girls were screaming outside. Here I have to work so hard, and he's making money on the stage, and the girls are crazy about him and I'm a nice-looking guy. Thank God we got to be very good friends, and the friendship lasted right up to the very end. He was quite a guy.

In 1978 the Yankees won the World Series, and I get a phone call from Billy Martin. "Joe," he says, "we're coming over with the Yankee team. We want to sit upstairs, in the room upstairs." I said, "No problem, Billy." We started to set the table up, but we set them in the front part of the dining room. The back part of the dining room was screened off and closed off. About 47 Yankees and managers and helpers all come pouring in, and I'm greeting them. I take them upstairs, and Billy says to me, "Joey, how are you?" "Fine," I say, "congratulations, it was nice." And he looks at the tables and he sees four tables in the front of the dining room. He says, "Joey, I don't sit here. I sit in the back there." "Billy," I say, "I'm sorry, somebody made a reservation before you, and I can't break my promise." And he said, "Who you got coming? Who's more important than me?" And he walks behind the screen, and there's this beautiful table set up with yellow roses, candles, it's a nice square table to accommodate maybe 18 people. And he says, "Hey, Joe, I want to sit back there. Move us around." I say, "Billy, I'm sorry." He says, "Who you got? The Pope coming in? God coming in? Who is it? Who's more important than me?" I say, "Billy, I can't say."

And throughout the first part of the half hour that they were sitting there, every time I'd walk by—"Yeah, sure, big deal, big deal"—and they were really turning the screws on me. I get the phone call, Frank is leaving the Waldorf and he's on his way over. We have a private entrance going up to the second-floor dining room, and I usually meet Frank on the staircase and take him right up. I did it hundreds of times. Well, anyway, they're all waiting—the Yankees are waiting—to see who's coming. So Frank is there, we open the door, I meet him halfway down the steps, and I want to warn him what's going on. I say, "Frank . . ." He says, "Joey, how are you?" I say, "Fine. Listen, Frank, the Yankees are here." "Yeah, and the British are coming," he says. And he goes right past me, and he comes nose to nose with Billy Martin. The two of them are looking at each other's eyes. And Sinatra looked at Martin and didn't say anything, and he walked right past him.

Now, there's a silence in the dining room. All the Yankees are nice and quiet. And Frank walks behind the screen, they go sit at their table. And Billy calls me over and he says, "Joey, I want to go say hello to Frank." I say, "Let me go talk to him. I don't know. Let me see." I go back, they're enjoying themselves. I say, "Frank, Billy Martin would like to come back and say hello to you. Would it be all right?" "Ah," he says, "all right. He's a Dodger. Let him in." He didn't like the Yankees; he liked the Dodgers.

So anyway, Billy Martin starts and he walks behind the screen, and before you know it, every one of them was lined up to go back there. It looked like communion and confession. At the end of all this, all the Yankees are smiling, and now I'm looking at Billy as if to say, "All right, now you're off my back? That's enough, all right?" At the end of the evening, Frank and his guests finished their dinner and they leave. And he gives me a message: "Tell them dinner's on me." So when Billy calls for the check, I say, "No, no, it's all taken care of." "You mean Frank paid for us?" he says. "What a wonderful man." And he'll always get the front end of the dining room.

If I have one story, I have thousands. I was very, very fortunate to know this man. He's been a great part of our life. His mother and my mother were very close. We've seen his bad times and his good times. We've seen when he would sit alone, and he would ask me and my father to sit with him, not to be alone. He'd say to my father, "See my so-called friends? They're like my shadow. They're only there when the sun is shining." But we didn't forget those days, and neither did he.

One day, before Thanksgiving—we always closed for Thanksgiving. My father would put the signs on the wall, "Closed for Thanksgiving." Who goes to an Italian restaurant on Thanksgiving? You know? Frank comes walking in, and he sat down. He was alone. He sat down, and I came out of the kitchen. At the time, I was the chef. Now the new chef is my son. And he sat down and we talked. He had his dinner, and he says to my father, "Patsy, what are we gonna do tomorrow? What am I gonna eat tomorrow?" My father says, "Frankie, whatever you want." So he calls me out of the kitchen, and he says, "Joey, what are you gonna make for Frank tomorrow?" I say, "We'll make him a nice chicken rollatine, take the bones out and you slice it." He said, "That's great." Okay, he left. My father walked over to the wall and he took all the signs down. He called us all over and he said, "You're all working tomorrow."

And sure enough, Frank comes in the very next day, he sits down. I had his chicken ready. He sat down, my father sat with him. He said, "Patsy, business is quiet tonight." Nobody knew we were open! My father said, "Frank, it's Thanksgiving." What are you gonna do? Later on in life, when he did find out, it was something he cherished for the rest of his life. He said, "You guys gave up your holiday for me. You know, you are my family."

We spent many an evening together. I spent many an evening with him up at the hotel. I sailed on his boat with him. I shared many moments with him. And there was an incident, I'll tell you. Kitty Kelley, she wrote a book. This woman was coming in the restaurant day after day, for maybe about three, four weeks. And the moment she'd sit down, she'd call the waiter over and say, "Tell me something about Sinatra." And she'd call the captain over, "Tell me something . . ." So one of the captains calls me. He says, "Joey, this woman is asking too much about Sinatra. What is it?" I said, "Let me find out." I walked over to the table, and I said, "Excuse me, miss, why is that you're inquiring about Sinatra?" "Well," she says, "I'm writing a book and I would like as much help from you as—" I said, "No, I'm sorry. I know very little about the man. I know he's a good singer. He comes in from time to time, and that's about all you're gonna get." She says to us, "Well, I know he—" I said, "Look, I'll ask you nicely. Please don't come back. Okay?"

A week goes by, and in Liz Smith's column is a write-up saying, "If ever you want to find out something about Sinatra, don't go to Patsy's because everybody dummies up." Fine, okay. I got hit by everybody else; why not by her? A couple of days go by, Frank comes into town. He calls up, he's coming over. We set his table. As he walks in, he hands me the article. He says to me, "Thanks." I say, "We made a pact a long time ago. Friends never say 'thanks.' They just do it." And he never forgot all these things.

There were many, many times where he helped us. He took on the *New York Times* for me. He did a lot of combating for us, and we've shared many friendships. My son, later on in life, got to meet him.

SAL SCOGNAMILLO: Tell the story about the one time that someone tried to pick up his check, James Robinson.

JOE SCOGNAMILLO: Okay, one more little story. Frank Sinatra had been coming into the restaurant, like I said, 50 years, and he has never allowed anyone to take a check. Never. One evening he calls, makes a reservation: "Joey, set my table." "How many you gonna be?" "Four people." I said, "Great." We set up his table, he walks in. He says, "Tonight, I want you to know, I am going to be the guest. The other guy is the host." This shocked me. I said, "Frank, whatever you say." The other couple comes in, we sit them down, he introduces me and so forth. I said, "Fine." We go through a whole course of an evening, fine dining, they enjoyed everything. And the man calls for the check. So I said to the waiter, "Give the gentleman the check. Make sure that you give it to . . ." He gives it to the man, the man slips him a credit card. The waiter goes back and processes it.

I was told by Frank I should never be more than three to four feet away from him at all times. I always had captains and waiters working, but he always wanted me there for anything, for reasons. So the waiter comes running back and he says to me, "Boss, the card's no good. It's been rejected." I said, "Get out of here." I go over to the machine, and I process the card. I swipe the card, and it's denied. I punch it in by numbers—denied. I call it in—denied. Now, I'm embarrassed to high hell. So I walk back to the man and I say, "Sir, your card is here. You are guests of the house." I'm not going to say to him "Your card's no good."

So Frank is laughing. He says, "Why should I be a guest?" Frank says to me, "Joey, what's going on?" I say, "Frank, can I buy you guys . . ." You know, I didn't know what to say. So he says to me, "Tell me the truth." I said, "The card has been rejected." The guy jumps off his seat and he says, "Come on! Frank put you up to this?" Frank is hysterical now, he's laughing. I said, "No, sir, just that . . ." I'm fumbling for words. And he says to me, "You wanna tell me my card is no good? You realize what you're saying?" I said, "I didn't say it." He says, "Prove it to me." Now, Frank is out on the floor, hysterical. So we go back to the unit, and he says, "Swipe the card." I swipe the card, punch it in—denied. American Express card, okay? I say, "Let me show you one more than this. Let me punch it in, in case the machine is screwed up." I punch it in; again it comes up denied. He's getting red in the face, and Frank is laughing in the corner.

So finally he says to me, "Could you call it in?" I said, "Of course." I get on the phone, I say to the young lady, "Young lady, please check this card thoroughly. I'll read the number one at a time, nice and slowly, in English, whatever you want." She goes through the whole routine and she says to me, "The card is denied." She's happy about this. I said, "Wait a minute, don't hang up the phone. The gentleman would like to talk to you." He gets that phone and he's all trembling, and he says to her, "Young lady, did you check this card?" She says, "Yes, I did." She's singing the whole thing, you know? Finally she says, "Look, it's been denied. Is that clear?" He says, "No, no. Listen to me now. The chair you sit on, the building you're in, I own. My name is James Robinson III. I am the president of American Express." He says, "Now, I would like your name."

In the back, Frank is hysterical, he's carrying on. He comes back. Till this day, whenever I see Mr. Robinson, we still laugh about it. We went back to the table, and everybody's now calming down, and I feel better, all right? I don't think that girl works at that office anymore. Sal, do you want to add anything?

SAL SCOGNAMILLO: I didn't have as long a history as my dad did with Mr. Sinatra, but I remember the first time I met him. I've been working at the restaurant about thirteen and a half years, full time, as the chef. As my dad mentioned, he was the chef before me, and before him was my grandfather, Patsy. There's only been three head chefs in all these years. So the first time I met Mr. Sinatra was in 1977. I was fifteen years old. And as my dad had mentioned before, if you've been to the restaurant, there's the main entrance and then there's another door which leads up to the second-floor private dining room, which Mr. Sinatra always went through. And there are doors that you push open and there's a curtain that you have to hold back.

So as it always was when Mr. Sinatra was coming, we'd get the phone call; we'd know he was on his way. My dad said, "Why don't you open the front door for him, lead him up the steps, and bring him into the dining room?" I was real excited to meet him, of course, because I was fifteen and never had met him before. My father told me all about him and, of course, who didn't know Mr. Sinatra? So when he came in, he wanted to say hello to me, and I kept fumbling for the keys to get the door open. I just wanted to get him up into the room, you know? Just get it over with, already. Just get him there, because I didn't want to do anything wrong.

So we came up the steps, he followed behind me, and he kept trying to say hello, which was his way. He always wanted to make you feel at ease. He would go over to you and say hello to you. I mean, Frank Sinatra would say hello to you, you know, it was such a thrill. So we finally get up the steps, and I open the door and I hold the curtain back, and he extended his hand to shake my hand. So I'm holding the curtain with this hand, and I let the curtain go to shake his hand, and the curtain closes right in front of him. You know, fifteen years old, as it is, and meeting Frank Sinatra for the first time, I was just so embarrassed. But he just put me at ease. He made me feel so good. He says, "You're Joey's son. I know your father for a long time."

And subsequently, then, I probably cooked for him at least two dozen times since '85 on, that I was in the kitchen. He would love the stuffed artichokes, which I would prepare with stuffing with bread crumbs, capers, olives, anchovies—everything. I'll write it down! In terms of taking credit for the recipes, they were Grandpa's recipes, so I just followed in their footsteps, and I was very proud to do that. Sinatra would like the arugala salad, the veal cutlet Milanese, which is a scallopini of veal pounded real thin. Grandpa taught me everything. All the pastry that we make, the pasticiotta, the sfogli-atelle, cannolis, cheesecake. That's probably why I'm always overweight, be-cause I work there! I just can't control myself with all the good food. But what a pleasure, to bring this little measure of happiness to this man who, of course, made me happy on so many levels. I mean, who could ask for a better PR man for our restaurant, for our business? And like my dad said, he never forgot. I mean, that Grandpa befriended him, and that Thanksgiving time—he never forgot. Rosemary Clooney is the same way with us. She was a struggling artist who couldn't afford to eat dinner, and . . .

JOE SCOGNAMILLO: Frank brought her in too.

SAL SCOGNAMILLO: And Frank, of course, was the one who brought her in. And Grandpa wouldn't give her a check for so many times, and she never forgot it. Sinatra would tell everyone! Just about five years ago, I remember Sugar Ray Leonard came in, the boxer. And he said, "You know, I just want you to know, Frank Sinatra told me to come here when I'm in New York." And countless people come in because either they've heard that this was one of his favorite restaurants, and things like that. But what a pleasure for me to feed him, and to see him happy with the food. And he would always make it a point to tell me, "Gee, that was great, just like your dad makes." And it just made me feel so good to do that.

11

Mammissimo

Dolly and Frankie Sinatra and the Italian American Mother/Son Thing

John Gennari

*F*rank Sinatra, we all know, is one of the most mythologized tough guys in the annals of American popular culture, a veritable icon of magisterial virility. I've written elsewhere about the intergenerational and cross-racial appeal of this image evidenced in hip-hop culture's appropriation of Sinatra as an honorary "original gangsta" (Gennari 1997: 36–48). Admittedly, there's something strained and maybe a little desperate about the unvarnished male bravado unleashed in such symbolic affiliations, as if hyping oneself into imagined fellowship with the Chairman of the Board will squelch the need for a Viagra prescription somewhere down the road. By foregrounding Sinatra's reputation for mack-daddy puissance, more to the point, we risk camouflaging other facets of his complex personality. Nick Tosches suggests as much in his biography of Dean Martin. There he claims that Frank Sinatra was enthralled by Dino because it was he, not Sinatra, who had cachet with the "racket guys"; that it was Dino who mastered the nuances of *menefreghismo,* the I-don't-give-a-fuck pose of willed nonchalance. Sinatra, according to Tosches, always "seemed to be killing himself over one broad or another," always "seemed to be dispatching others to do his dirty work," and was viewed in New York and Las Vegas mob circles as a "half-a-mozzarella" whose *mammissimo* relationship with his mother raised questions about his manliness (Tosches 1992: 267).

The tag of *mammissimo,* an Italian slang pejorative that translates roughly as "mama's boy," might have been a heavy liability for the man who, as Gay Talese and others observed, seemed to relish his role as the *uomo di rispetto* ("man of respect") and the *padrone,* the honored and feared boss known for going out of his way to redress a wrong or settle a score (Talese 1966/1995: 103). But then again, we're not talking about just any mother: We're talking about Dolly Sinatra, the toughest guy who ever came out of Hoboken, the *real*—and I hope you'll see that I use the term symbolically rather than literally—Original Gangsta.

In the growth industry that is Sinatra biography, it's become a commonplace to locate the source of Frank's combativeness and cunning in the example set by his mother, Dolly, a blizzard of a woman who operated as a political fixer (in Talese's memorable phrase, "a kind of Catherine de Medici of Hoboken's Third Ward" [Talese 1966/1995: 113]), a Prohibition-era saloon keeper, a midwife, and—most notoriously—an abortionist. The Tina Sinatra–produced *Sinatra: The Authorized Movie* features a memorable performance by Olympia Dukakis, whose Dolly is always smacking the young Frankie upside his head, but also hot-wiring her son with passion and ambition. Dukakis's performance makes a strong case for the tough-love school of immigrant bootstrap parenting; she makes us wonder how different mid-twentieth-century American child-rearing practices might have been if Dr. Spock had been raised by an old-school Italian mother. When Dukakis's

Dolly checks her son's self-pitying "I'm-a-nobody" lament with a feral grab of the ear and a rousing "You *are* somebody, you're Frankie Sinatra," you feel a charge of maternal heart and soul that you know is going to carry the young singer to the top.

The unauthorized Sinatra biographies, not surprisingly, have a different take. Donald Clarke, in *All or Nothing at All* (1997), begrudgingly credits Dolly with instilling in her son a feeling for the underdog that ignited his passion for social justice and racial equality (208). But since Clarke otherwise characterizes Dolly as "a small-time gangster who never did anything for anybody unless it was going to bring a payoff" (23), even this small measure of tribute rings hollow. Kitty Kelley's pathography *His Way* (1986) makes the case that his (Frank's) way was actually her (Dolly's) way, and her way was long on selfishness and mendacity. Looming as a hulking ogress over that book's opening scenes, Dolly Sinatra needs less than fifty pages to: (1) scramble her son's psychosexual wiring by dressing him up as a girl; (2) force him to turn to his grandmother's kitchen to stave off anorexia and debilitating latch-key loneliness; (3) terrorize his pregnant girlfriend into a miscarriage; (4) mortify and embarrass him with her ubiquitous abortionist's black bag; (5) disguise her lack of true affection by spoiling him with fancy clothes and lavish sums of walking-around money; and (6) totally emasculate his father, Marty, portrayed as a gentle, asthmatic man of humble Sicilian stock cowed by his wife's imperious Genoese airs. Kelley drools with wonder at the sheer gall of this protean character—Dolly, who knew not only all of the Italian dialects but also the salty language of cigar-chomping Irish pols; who herself cross-dressed as an Irish bloke to defy gender restrictions and attend her husband's boxing matches when he fought under the name Marty O'Brien; who moved the family out of Hoboken's Little Italy into a more respectable neighborhood, only to then deck the place out with "Guinea" furniture (Kelley 1986: 2–48).

John Lahr, in *Sinatra: The Artist and the Man* (1997a), describes Dolly as "a typical *balabusta* [who] controlled the Sinatra household and had a stevedore's heart and mouth," calling Sinatra's sidekick Jilly Rizzo (and many others) "fuckface," reserving for her granddaughter Tina the more endearing nickname "Little Shit" (78). (Lahr is right to link heart and mouth. In Dolly

Sinatra's world, as Italian American writer Barbara Grizzuti Harrison suggests, "cursing often was a measure of affection: 'Okay, you bastards, into the kitchen. I've made some linguine'" [1986: 13]). Of all the biographers, Lahr offers—with a shrewd use of his crucial sources, Pete Hamill and Shirley MacLaine—the most provocative theory about Dolly's influence on Frank's life and art. Arguing that Sinatra "embraced and bullied the world as his mother had embraced and bullied him," Lahr adopts Hamill's argument that Sinatra's relationship with his mother blueprinted his entire tortured romantic history. "I married the same woman every time," Sinatra is said to have told Hamill back in the 1970s, leading Hamill to speculate, "That's Ava. That's all the women. He had this mother who punished and hugged him, and they were all part of the same thing" (Lahr 1997a: 78). Lahr ventures even further in his paradoxical twist on the "mama's boy" theme, claiming—with a decisive fillip from MacLaine's memoir *My Lucky Stars*—that as a singer, Sinatra turned to his audiences for the affection that he craved but never received from his mother. "The stillness, attention, and unequivocal adoration that were never there in Dolly," Lahr writes, "were undeniable in the rapt enthusiasm of his listeners." MacLaine goes even further, intriguingly describing Sinatra's relationship with his audiences as a kind of displaced oedipal fantasy. "His survival was his mother audience," she writes. "He needed her to love him, appreciate him, acknowledge him, and never betray his trust. So he would cajole, manipulate, caress, admonish, scold, and love her unconditionally until there was no difference between him and her. He and she had become one" (Lahr 1997a: 79).

Though psychoanalytic explanations generally leave me with more questions than answers, I must admit to finding something tantalizing in these conjectures about Dolly Sinatra's hold on her son, Frank. But I feel even more strongly that Dolly Sinatra continues to elude understanding, and does so specifically in the way that she confounds and resists sanctioned codes of mothering. Indeed, it may not be going too far to suggest that the strange combination of fascination and disgust with which Dolly Sinatra has been represented fits into larger discourses of mother-bashing that pervade American culture. As persuasively argued by Shari Thurer in *The Myths of Motherhood: How Culture Reinvents the Good Mother* (1994) and by contributors to a recent book of collected essays *"Bad" Mothers: The Politics of Blame in Twentieth-Century America* edited by Molly Ladd-Taylor and Lauri Umansky (1998), there's been a consistent and recurrent public desire to mark as wanting those mothers who fail to live up to sentimentalized ideals of the good mother. The argument does not deny that some mothers simply are *not* good mothers; rather, it suggests that the "bad mother" stigma has been applied to "far more women than those whose actions would warrant the name" (Ladd-Taylor and Umansky 1998: 2). Today we find the stereotype applied almost generically to the welfare mother, the teen mother, and the career woman who spends less time with her children than stay-at-home mothers.

I would argue that a cultural presumption of "good" mothering in the Italian American family has been created by the popular media's hypersentimentalization of an ideal Italian mother who serves symbolically as *everyone's* mother. Who but the most hardhearted among us, after all, didn't laugh and feel a little safer when Danny Aiello's *Moonstruck* (1998) character Johnny Cammereri, who has scotched his marriage plans to go back to Sicily to be with his dying mother, returns to Brooklyn and announces, with just the right touch of operatic schmaltz, that she had miraculously risen from her deathbed and "started cooking for everybody." The Italian slang term for this kind of figure is *mammissima*. In a recent e-mail exchange, I asked a cousin of mine in Italy for her definition of this term. She wrote back: "'Mammissima' is like a big mammy, in the sense of the heart, the mother of all children, the one that always has bread and jam for all—you know, '*mammissima mia*' with a big kiss!"

I found it significant that she used the spelling M-A-M-M-Y. Over here, of course, that word packs plenty of mythological power, albeit in relation to African American rather than Italian American motherhood, that is, the black mammy of Al Jolson's and an untold number of southern white boy's dreams. If we keep our eyes open, we see Italian American analogs to such commodified black mammy figures as the famous Aunt Jemima: recall the ample-bosomed, plump-armed pizza maker Mama [*sic*] Celeste, and the next time you buy your Italian-seasoned bread crumbs, check out that *simpatica* woman smiling out from the top of the Contadina brand container.

Like the black mammy, these are mythical maternal figures whose power resides in the fact that they are available to all of us: We are invited to symbolically feed at their breasts and tug at their housecoats. They are the mothers of all mothers.

Historically, the dutiful, self-sacrificing black mammy of romantic lore was presumed to love her white family and its children every bit as much as her own. Indeed, the black mother lost her sentimental glow as soon as the focus shifted to her relationship with her own children. In the wake of 1965 Moynihan Report, it became respectable even for liberals to blame black "matriarchy"—the pseudoanthropological term for putatively dominant and overnurturing black mothers—for all alleged social dysfunctionality in the black community. Today, while the demonization of black mothers continues in public debates about welfare, we see flickers of sentimental imagery in mainstream media presentations of the black mother. Take basketball as an example. Notice the way NBC, the NBA, and their corporate sponsors together have fetishized Mother's Day, turning that day's game broadcast into a spectacle that intermingles new jack machismo on the court with old-school mother worship in the pre- and postgame player interviews. A few years back, Reebok tried to cut into Nike's share of the basketball shoe market by running a series of advertisements that showed the mothers of NBA stars at home proudly watching their sons on television.

In the mainstream collective imagination, however, it's hard to compete with the Italian mother for sentimental appeal, especially in the world of tough guys. Former New York state senator Alfonse D'Amato and his handlers understood this back in 1980, when they used his mother, Antoinette, in a series of television ads and in a statewide campaign centered on her cookbook *"Mamma" D'Amato's Inflation-Fighting Recipes* (D'Amato 1995: xv, 97). The strategy was brilliant, and by many accounts crucial to D'Amato's upset victory over Jacob Javits: The son may be a vulgar machine politician, the subtext seemed to be, but how untrustworthy can he really be with an old-fashioned Italian mother in his camp? Witness, along related lines, the canonization of Martin Scorsese's mother, Catherine. In a pungent cameo as the mother of Joe Pesci's demonic character in *Goodfellas,* she provides the late-night, spontaneously whipped up dish of pasta for the wise guys who stop by on their way to bury a body. Not the most flattering context, to be sure, but the juxtaposition of wiseguy savagery with maternal humanity comes off as extremely funny—because we know that Scorsese is toying self-consciously with the stereotype of the Italian mother who's always available to tend to the basic needs of her son and of all the sons. Today, thanks to her posthumously published cookbook *Italianamerican* (1997), we all have access to Catherine Scorsese's pasta sauce recipe—and a fine one it is. In a *New York Times* story covering a testimonial dinner in her honor, a number of Martin Scorsese's film-world associates gushed over Catherine's outsized nurturing qualities. "If you could bottle her and spread it around the world," said the screenwriter Nick Pileggi, "there would be no need for social workers" (Hamlin 1997: 3).

Given such powerful assumptions about the humanizing influence of the Italian mother, one of the only ways for her to go wrong is to be *too* nurturing, to be overprotective and smothering and neurosis-producing—to be, in short, a stereotypical *Jewish* mother. Although a Jewish friend of mine says that the only Jewish mothers he knows are Italian, I propose Dolly Sinatra as an example of an Italian American mother who couldn't possibly be confused with the eternally suffering, guilt-mongering, son-eating Jewish mother we know from Woody Allen's films and Philip Roth's novels.

Dan Greenburg, who dramatized his plight as a recovering Jewish son in the satirical training manual *How to Be a Jewish Mother* (1964/1975), offered the following as an illustration of Jewish maternal *weltschmerz:*

> "Ma! Ma!" [says the young Jewish boy running home to his mother].
> "What's the commotion?"
> "The bad boys ran off with my hat."
> "The bad boys ran off with your hat? You should be glad they didn't also cut
>   your throat." (Greenburg 1964/1975: 12).

When I imagine Frankie and Dolly Sinatra in this vignette, I find myself changing the last line to something like:

> "The bad boys ran off with your hat? Let's find the son of a bitch bastards and
> slit their throats."

I jest, of course, but only to celebrate the spirit of an Italian mother who sabotaged hackneyed images of ethnic warmth and projected her spirit far beyond the confines of the flowered housecoat of domesticity. As Grizzuti Harrison put it in a sharp rejoinder to Kitty Kelley's Dolly Sinatra–bashing in *His Way:* "[I]n Italian-American families, tough, noisy women are often the rule," and "it is almost impossible for an outsider to locate the source of power in these families—the whole canny point being to deceive the outside world" (1986: 13).

In her own exaggerated way, Dolly Sinatra typifies the pattern of Italian American mothers who serve not merely as the expressive core and emotional center of the family, but as—in Richard Gambino's apt metaphor—powerful ministers of internal affairs (Gambino 1974: 13). Of course, Dolly Sinatra *also* reigned over half of Hudson County as a powerful minister of *external* affairs, and in this, as in much else, she brazenly scrambled traditional gender codes. Did she also, as the tough guy in the Sinatra household, consign her son Frank to a perpetual, lifelong crisis of masculinity? If so, then maybe we're all in her debt. Duke University professor Thomas Ferraro has argued for a feminine voice at the heart of the Sinatra croon, while Philip Furia has called attention to the "lyrical drag" element of the classic 1950s' Sinatra recordings—the fact that many of the songs Sinatra made his own in the swinging bachelor period were Broadway show tunes from the 1920s and 1930s that had been written for women characters (Scott 1998: B9, B11). In both his musical rhetoric and his screen persona, the mature Sinatra's juxtaposition of brassy ebullience and fragile tenderness—even neediness—captured the anxieties and ambivalences lurking beneath the urbane skinny-black-tie machismo of the Rat Pack years. At all stages of his career, Sinatra's power as a performer owed much to his gift for dramatizing his insecurities and vulnerabilities so compellingly as to call into question whether his tough-guy front was the biggest performance of all. It's this Sinatra whose art nurtures us, this Sinatra who is the mother of us all.

12

Urbane Villager

Thomas J. Ferraro

In memory of Herbert Gans

*I*f, as Pellegrino D'Acierno demonstrates in chapter 14, Italian Americans are marked by betweenness—among America's ethnic minorities the group most suspected of being too Anglo, among America's white majority the group most suspected of being not Anglo enough—then the period of the 1950s and early 1960s was a quintessentially Italian American moment: It was the period after symbolic cultural legitimacy had finally been established—FDR removed Italians from the suspect aliens list, postwar prosperity sponsored blue-collar security, and all-American folk heroes rose from the Italian ranks (Fiorello LaGuardia, Joe DiMaggio, Connie Francis)—but before Italian Americans had "com[e] into their own"—with the eventual rise of an upper middle class, self-consciously ethnic, on the national stage of political, economic, and cultural life. Sinatra's public career spanned the transformation—and, in certain key ways, epitomized what was at stake in it.

In 1958–59, the epicenter of the period I have in mind, when Sinatra was at the height of his iconic majesty, Herbert J. Gans sojourned in the West End of Boston, on the eve of its destruction by urban renewal, producing the 1962 sociological classic *The Urban Villagers.* The West Enders were second-generation Americans of Italian descent and their families: urban villagers who hung together—non-Italians would have said *clung* together—in resistance to what they understood as "the outside world"—meaning mainstream, middle-class America. Yet the status of "ethnicity" was a peculiar matter among them. West Enders were not, Gans insists and illustrates more than once, prone to praise individuals, including public figures, just because they were Italian Americans—in fact, they were more apt to ridicule that form of easy identification (what Gans would later call "symbolic identification").[1] But there was no one in the world they admired and wished to identify with more than the man who called himself the "top wop," Francis Albert Sinatra.

Sinatra's appeal in the West End had much to do with his "persona" (Gans 1962: 192). The West Enders embraced not only his refusal to be embarrassed by his background, but also his willingness to countenance offending the genteel sensibilities of an Anglo-American cultural elite that otherwise, correctly, was taken up with the "classiness" of his singing. Behavior that came across as crass if not exploitative on Beacon Hill and at the *Boston Globe*—Sinatra's romantic exploits, fistfights, Mafia friends, bad ethnic jokes—was taken in the West End as vital attitude. In other words, to *fare brutta figura* on Park Avenue, at least according to the *New Yorker* and the *New York Times,* was to win points on Arthur Avenue, on Canal Street, and in industrial Jersey. Sinatra's public persona was celebrated for demonstrating that you *could* leave the corner without leaving its values behind.

However instinctive Sinatra's public behavior was, by the time of his "Chairmanship" he also understood what was at stake in it for Italian Americans: calling himself the "top wop," he identified his appetites and emotions with the south of Italy—that famous Sicilian temper—and, more important, he identified his disdain of societal niceties with the Italian American urban street corner, what Gans calls "the peer group society." At the Lido in Paris in 1962, Sinatra followed up a quietly majestic rendition of "Ol' Man River" by commenting, "That song was about Sammy Davis's people—and dis song is about mah people." "Dis song" was Rodger and Hart's "The Lady Is a Tramp," and the version he delivered—magnificent. When the Italians step out, he seemed to be saying, they can adopt good taste, put on forms of elegance—"love the theater"—while refusing the policing mechanisms of high society and highbrow culture.[2] Sinatra's version of a post-ghetto ethnicity, then, is not only measured in expressed pride in an Italian American boyhood—strictly middle-class terms—but in fact constituted by the persistence and exemplification of boyhood values—a definitional tautology of what it means to be a "wop."[3]

For Adam Gopnik, as for the better part of the biographers who anticipated and the commentators who responded to Sinatra's death, what made Sinatra great was his transcendence of the street corner as a singer; otherwise, in his life and personhood, he was said to be arrested in "a kind of permanent adolescence." Insisting that "Sinatra was a musician, not a life style" (Franklin, et.al., 1998: 47), the biographers and press have repeated again and again that, *in his music, thank God,* Sinatra was able to exchange his Sicilian temper for royal grace (Lahr 1997b: 83), his vulgar street talk for worldly wit (Clarke 1997: 134), and his "virility, flash, a hint of gangsterism" for "gravity, understatement, and a precise calibration of emotion" (Franklin, et al., 1998: 49). I have heard this dichotomy so often lately, I'm beginning to wonder, was Ol' Blue Eyes just a boy who wouldn't grow up, after all? Of course, nothing would be more genuinely West End than to shrug my shoulders in resignation, as if to say, What can be done and who the f— cares?

In fact, I've been in this explication business too long—I do care. Like Frank, I want to take a swing.

When Gans took up residence among the Italians of the West End, he was astonished—truly astonished—by how they "related" to one another. The West Enders were obsessively communal in a manner that spotlighted individuals in an elegant social chemistry that he barely had language for: He likened it to "display" and "performance" within a "group setting," often the family, but more often the peer group. Although I don't know Gans's background, he was surely convinced that something different was going on in the West End than in, say, Middletown—or, more precisely, given Gans's sociological future, Levittown. As Gans saw it, the Italian American ethos of "performance" has at least three unfamiliar, almost indescribable mechanisms: West End sociability produces "individuality" out of group interaction, not apart from it; the success of an individual provokes quality emulation, variations upon a theme, not sullen resentment; and the aesthetic pleasures of competitive, individuating display strengthens the body politic rather than dividing it against itself.

It is my operating hypothesis that Sinatra, initiated in such rituals at home and as a youth, reproduced them in altered form as a singer for a national marketplace—in his relation to the material, to the audience, to the given occasion. In the final analysis, it is not only the exhilaration in trampiness that identifies Sinatra as Italian American but the exaltedly brilliant way of putting trampiness into the vocalization itself—in which he teases *and* rallies, steps out *and* supports, incorporates *and* distinguishes.

I want to borrow a page from John Gennari—who, by announcing his title a year ago, keyed me in to paying attention to the way Sinatra's relation to his mother is represented. Here is the take of John Lahr, who's often smart and empathetic, building on the take of Shirley MacLaine, who's also smart and empathetic:

> Much would be written in years to come about the Italian side of Frank Sinatra's personality, the need to surround himself with cronies and demanding absolute loyalty, like the *padrone* or clan chieftain, but this has nothing to do with nationality. Italians as a rule are anything but lonely, but Frankie never learned how to make friends the hard way; instead Dolly taught him how to cope with loneliness.
>
> Beyond talent, beyond technique, the palpable but invisible power of every great star stems from the need to be seen and to be held in the imagination of the audience. This is especially true of Sinatra. The stillness, attention, and unequivocal adoration that were never there in Dolly were undeniable in the rapt enthusiasm of his listeners. "Thank you for letting me sing for you" was often Sinatra's exit line at the end of his concerts. In song, he was his best self, and he craved to see that goodness reflected in the ador-

ing eyes of others. "His survival was his mother audience," MacLaine, who often toured with Sinatra, writes. "He desperately needed her to love him, appreciate him, acknowledge him, and never betray his trust. So he would cajole, manipulate, caress, admonish, scold and love her unconditionally until there was no difference between him and her. He and she had become one." Offstage, Sinatra was dubbed the Innkeeper by his friends, because of the largesse of his hospitality; onstage, he operated more or less the same way. He fed others to insure that he got what he needed. (Lahr 1997b: 79)

What irks me is this business of accounting for his success as a function of the mother-driven lonesomeness—it may indeed have had something to do with the force of personality needed to get out of town: "He didn't dream," Tina Sinatra insists of her father's often-repeated account of those days. "He said, 'I'm gonna do it. I'm gonna get across this river. I'm gonna go there and make a name for myself'" (Lahr 1997b: 77). But the psychopathologization of his joy in the spotlight is too easy, especially in light of the old neighborhood: "'In my particular neighborhood in New Jersey, when I was a kid, boys became boxers or they worked in factories; and then the remaining group that I went around with were smitten by singing,' Sinatra said during a 1980 radio broadcast. 'We had a ukulele player, and we stood on the corners and sang songs'" (Lahr 1997b: 78). "Smitten with singing," Sinatra was not so much exceptional as hypertypical, the pathology, if that's what it was, as much cultural as personal, indeed an exaggerated personal drive because it was an internalized cultural appetite.

Consider again the insinuation with which Lahr ends an earlier passage: "Offstage, Sinatra was dubbed the Innkeeper by his friends, because of the largesse of his hospitality; onstage, he operated more or less the same way. He fed others to insure that he got what he needed" (Lahr 1997b: 79). Now compare what Gans saw as the mobility problem entailed in the West End's communal performance aesthetic: "The goods which contribute to the enjoyment of the group and the display of the individual ought to be the best that can be obtained; but the quantity and quality of food, drink, and clothing that are purchased leave little else for other expenditures or savings. West Enders explain that life is too short for any other way of behavior" (Gans 1962: 187).

Sinatra's friends in the City of Angels, most of whom were not Italians, called him the Innkeeper because the only language they had for it was "hospitality"—a word that, as D'Acierno has pointed out, does not have anything like the same valence in Italian (D'Acierno 1999: 706). For an Italian, to do well in food and friendship and clothing is to put on a good face (*bella figura*) for and in front of your friends—it is part fear, part love—and it generates what Italians mean by *rispetto,* respect.

Of course, there can be no question, on some fronts, of Sinatra's extraordinariness. In one sense he was one of those uncommon locals driven to get out—driven, in fact, to leave the corner not by marrying but by taking center stage. And yet the desire to do it as a singer—to sing live and very soon on recordings, and, later, as a radio and television personality, as an actor, and so forth—may have been a function of what Gans identifies as something "artistic" a man was allowed to aspire to without being ridiculed for being effeminate—but there's more to it than that, as women who want to sing and be entertainers, even at the risk of forgoing or postponing marriage and motherhood, indicate. There's something that happens when you sing that turned him on, and that turns most of us on, too.

Bono, lead singer of the rock group U2, recounts meeting Sinatra backstage and finding him embarrassed and tongue-tied until Bono started talking music with him—classical music—and then he turned on, became animated, leapt over the gaps of national difference, generations, and sheer strangerness. Listen, in light of Bono's report, to how Herbert Gans describes the social alchemy of West End "individuality":

> The peer group principle has even more important consequences for personality organization. Indeed, the role of the group in the life of the individual is such that he exists primarily in the group. School officials, for example, pointed out that teenagers were rough and active when they were with their peers, but quiet and remarkably mild and passive when alone. Their mildness is due to the fact that they exist only partially when they are outside the group. In effect, the individual personality functions best and most completely among his or her peers—a fact that has some implications for independence and dependence, conformity and individualism among the West Enders. (Gans 1962: 40)

We can argue with Gans for overemphasizing the distinction between technique and style, but he was on to something, I think, and something not only about what drove Sinatra onto the stage and into the studio and onto the screen but also what he did when he got there—with the music, with the other musicians, and with his audience. The problem is that the language Gans inherited—distinguishing individual from group—is too sociological and too Emersonian. I think the solution lies in the phenomenology of Sinatra's musical performance, although there, too, I risk the circle of hermeneutics beyond language.

What I want to argue is that, in one way, he was more Hoboken when not singing, yet, in another way, he was more Hoboken when he did sing. We've long understood the first part, as John Lahr lusciously summarizes: "Once he was inside the lyric, he had command of the language that he found paralyzing elsewhere. When he opened his mouth in song, he was calm; he was smooth; he was sensitive; he had no hint of the Hoboken streets in his pronunciation; what he called his 'Sicilian temper' was filtered through the charm of lyrics and music into poetic passion" (Lahr 1997b: 83).

I want to argue that, in effect, he was more himself in the action of singing—which was charming but not just charming—because in action in public is where Italian men, at least West End–style Italian American men, *find* themselves. I wish less to credit him either with the achievement of gentility or self-identity—that's for the Anglos and the therapists—as to credit the performances that earned him respect even among the highbrow genteel with the persistence and redeployment of a certain Hoboken logic difficult to talk about analytically because academic intellectualization has not, and still does not, at least not so much, come from Hoboken.

Lahr goes on to emphasize the class distinction: "Sinatra's appropriations of the standards was also the acquisition of the manners of another class. 'It's like stealing a Cadillac—except he's stealing George Gershwin,' Hamill says" (Lahr 1997b: 83). But I'm not sure, in the final analysis, that it is right to say that he stole the songs, exactly—even if Cole Porter and others occasionally felt that way—any more than it is right to imply that when singing he momentarily assimilated. What happened is that he gave renewed life to an established, indeed waning, Tin Pan Alley musical tradition; he took

Cahn and Van Heusen's contemporary stuff to heart, occasionally scored with more exotic contemporary material; wherever it came from, he did not simply do it in his style—as, say, Louis Prima jazzed stuff up, or the post-Trio Nat King Cole eased it down. Rather, in so much of his work, Sinatra fit song and style together, as if they were meant for each other. Lahr is dead-on about that: "With other singers—Vic Damone, for instance, and Tony Bennett—you admired the technique; with Sinatra you admired the rendition. He presented the song like a landscape he'd restored, painting himself into the picture so masterfully that it was impossible to imagine it without him" (Lahr 1997b: 83). A communal individuation, then, rather than a radical separatism, at the level of the music.

And he did not do it alone. Whatever the occasional troubles with Mitch Miller or Nelson Riddle, in general he was enormously generous to the professionals serving him because he liked to work—to play—*with* them. They wanted, desperately, like the boys on the corner, to please each other—not just because he was the man, for it was in his desire for their desire to please that being the "top wop" was constituted. Everything was always, in effect, "live"; he brought friends, family, and prospects into the studio with him. In *Sinatra! The Song Is You,* Will Friedwald takes enormous pleasure in telling the story of a famous big-band singer whose radio show Sinatra once subbed for. When he came on, Sinatra was annoyed because the band, conditioned not to upstage the famous singer, wouldn't play loudly enough. While never doubting he was kingpin, Sinatra nonetheless wanted the band to swing, hard and loud and confidently and happily, *with him*—in concert and for his enjoyment, too (Friedwald 1997: 25). When Gans visited the West End, he knew that showmanship and spectatorship, competition and camaraderie, worked differently there from elsewhere. He didn't quite have the names for it, but he knew he liked it. Gans reports: "It should be noted that what I have called conspicuous consumption and display is not to be equated with the kind of consumption competition which has been noted among the *nouveau riche.* . . . The West Enders do not seek to outdo all others, and thus be the best or numerically the greatest in these displays. Rather, they want to show themselves off, without questioning the right and ability of everyone else to do much the same" (Gans 1962: 83).

In the West End, Gans says that others get to step out next, mildly anxious but anxious to please. I could argue that the relevance to Sinatra is that he adored the best of his peers—Crosby and Holiday, Mercer and Bennett—but that's not the most important point. His listeners feel close to him, determined to emulate, inspired to do their best—not put out by his "topness" but energized: The effect of individuation from the crowd returns to energize those in the crowd to (their own) individuation. It's not exactly what occurs in the closed circle of the West End living room or men's club, but there's a kind of continuity whose affirming effect has so far passed our understanding. Not only did Sinatra find his individualism in song, if that's the same word, but he also created a cultural *corpus christi*—which would not surprise, as James T. Fisher (1997) has so brilliantly explicated, the ethnic Catholic ("lapsed" Catholic) habitués of the Hudson County bars of New Jersey. By *corpus christi* I mean a community of wonder produced out of disparate conditions and temperaments and walks of life, in mystical relation to one another and the body social. In Fisher's model of Jersey culture, there's an embrace of failure and perhaps too much homogeneity—the thrill of Sinatra is the way he produced a new kind of community out of the simultaneous challenge to the ladies to stop being so prissy and to the corner boys to get off their duffs.

This they actually intuited down in the West End. Here's the keenest observation that Gans makes about the appreciation of West Enders for Sinatra: "As a singer, the inflection he gives to the tune and the lyrics is interpreted as arousing his audience to action. As a West Ender said, 'He gives you a little dig in his songs.' At the same time, his singing style has a teasing quality which suggests to West Enders that he is making fun both of the song and of the outside world. To them, he seems to be putting something over on the outside world." (Gans: 1962: 193). West Enders heard in Sinatra's singing a double-edged tease—a dig at respectability, but also at the corner boys, who were made to see that their cult of action can operate in spheres well beyond the corner.

Here's how Mrs. Zirilli's son—from in and around Freehold, New Jersey—recently put it: "My first recollection of Frank's voice was coming out of a jukebox in a dark bar on a Sunday afternoon, when my mother and I went searching for my father. And I remember she said, 'Listen to that, that's Frank Sinatra. He's from New Jersey.' It was a voice filled with bad attitude, life, beauty, excitement, a nasty sense of freedom, sex, and a sad knowledge of the ways of the world. Every song seemed to have as its postscript, 'And if you don't like it, here's a punch in the kisser'" (Lahr 1997b: 94). Now as well as then, among those who got off the corner, among those who never left, and among those who never came close to experiencing it, what is commonly acknowledged and affirmed, from their different vantage points, is the double ironization—the punch in *everyone's* kisser.

At the end of a paragraph explaining how Sinatra used his vocal weaknesses and breakdowns in technique, Donald Clarke slips in a quiet appreciation of how Sinatra could use vernacular and vernacular style—his Jersey accent and his roughneck flash—to powerful effect: "The occasional sound of strain or tiredness, the touch of a New Jersey accent, what Arnold Shaw described as a counterpoint of toughness and tenderness; it is all there in Capitol's superb recorded sound of the mid-1950s, and honest mono at that" (Clarke 1997: 134). Yet what commentators like Gopnik and Lahr and Clarke love to acknowledge—me, too—is the elegance.

Pete Hamill notes, "It is no accident that Sinatra aspired in the music to grace. The ballads, in particular, have a grace to them that is really extraordinary" (Lahr 1997b: 83). I can just hear Gopnik saying "gravity, understatement, and a precise calibration of emotion"—*New Yorker* values one and all, coded Upper East Side, though not exclusively theirs. Also in the *New Yorker,* Alex Ross writes: "But the . . . desolate torch songs . . . seem to come from nowhere. The source of that low, lonely thrum hasn't been identified by Sinatra's multiplying biographers; it may not have to be, because it was a musical effect, an expression of the baritone art" (Ross et al. 1998: 49). Mr. Ross, let me introduce you to the Boss, Bruce Springsteen, corner boy done good, who appreciated the same thing you're hearing, but unlike the maturity-mongers does not hear primarily "sophistication," and unlike the Manhattan aesthetes does not put the achievement of the ballads solely down to "baritone art," and unlike the biographers does not profess to be at a loss regarding where the achievement comes from: "But it was the deep blueness of Frank's voice that affected me the most," recalled Springsteen, "and, while his music became synonymous with black tie, good life, the best booze, women, sophistication, his blues voice was always the sound of hard luck and men late at night with the last ten dollars in their pockets trying to figure a way. On behalf of all New Jersey, Frank, I want to say, 'Hail, brother, you sang out our soul'" (Lahr 1997b: 94).

Amen to that, Bruce.

Notes

1. There is little, if any, identification either with Italy or with the local areas from which the immigrants originally came. Second-generation people know their parents' birthplace, but it is of little interest to them. Excepting a handful of Italian intellectuals and artists, I encountered no identification with Italian culture or Italian symbols. Even those Italians who had made a name for themselves in sports or in entertainment were not praised solely because of their ethnicity. In fact, when a local Italian boxer lost a fight to his Negro opponent, I was told scornfully about a West Ender who had mourned this as a loss of Italian pride. Likewise, there seemed to be no objection to a Jewish singer who had made several hit records of bowdlerized Italian folk songs. "After all," people said, "most of us worked for a Jewish Boss" (Gans 1962: 34).

2. There's doubleness and irony by the score here. For, of course, the kid from Hoboken is at the Lido in Paris making jazz with a sextet, reanimating in immaculate upper-class accent and intonation a Rodgers and Hart "standard," after Elvis and at the moment the Beatles are in Hamburg—he has indeed not only stepped out but, in mobility terms, stepped up. Yet in the midst of this splendiferous rendition he interrupts the song to do a "dirty rat" Bogey imitation, invoking his Las Vegas/L.A. cronies, which—like the complaints about onion soup and the comment about "cherchez la femme" (meaning "why don't you share the broad?") at the other moments during the concert—does indeed come across as a deliberate reminder of the corner. The concert CD is Frank Sinatra, *Sinatra and Sextet: Live in Paris* (Reprise 9 45487–2).

3. In their adoration of Sinatra, the West Enders that Gans hung with understood and reproduced the equation "trampiness is Italian":

> Sinatra is liked first because he is an Italian who is proud of his lowly origin, not so much because of his ethnic background per se—although it is not disparaged—but because he is willing to admit and defend. . . . He has become rich and famous, but he has not deserted the peer group that gave him his start. Nor has he adopted the ways of the outside world. Still a rebellious individual, he does

> not hesitate to use either his tongue or his fists. . . . Also, he shows his scorn for those aspects of the outside world that do not please him, and does not try to maintain appearances required by middle-class notions of respectability. Making headlines regularly for his sexual escapades . . . (Gans 1962: 192).

It's incontrovertible that, with the reference and hint of black vernacular, this reference is to Italian Americans, but it leaves open the possibility of honorific forms of inclusion based on the logic of refusing respectability—of running with the (rat) pack. Certainly, as John Gennari has demonstrated, the inclusion worked in the opposite direction. Not only did *Jet* publish on Sinatra, but black folk I know sent me copies of the *Jet* publication. More tellingly, I am told of a major blues dealer who reports that the only "white folk" always present is Sinatra—and that while they may own the great late-night records of Riddle et al., the records always present are the in-your-face ding-a-ling albums that the Rat Pack persona reaches in this music and that remain, to this day, an embarrassment.

13

Passing for Italian

Crooners and Gangsters in Crossover Culture

John Gennari

The great trombonist Milt Bernhardt once said that "Sinatra sings with the grace of a poet, but when he talks to you, it's all New Jersey." It's a wonderfully evocative statement, but, in fact, it's a false dichotomy: It's the vernacular poetry of New Jersey that *is* the grace. My mother comes from the same area as Sinatra but moved to Massachusetts when she married my father. So I'm kind of the Diaspora of the Diaspora. But my identification with Sinatra has everything to do with coming back to New Jersey as a child. And Sinatra, for me, is indistinguishable, in a Proustian way, from good bread and the wine that's cut with soda until you reach a certain age when you can really drink the wine. It's the memory of my Uncle Abbie, singing over the top of his Sinatra records, karaoke style, before we knew what that was. I grew up thinking that the man's name was "the Great Frank Sinatra." It was drilled into me. That's true. It was "the Great Joe Louis" and "the Great Frank Sinatra." And there's something about that—the boxing, sporting culture, music, tough Italian guys, tough black guys.

I came back to Sinatra through my investment in and study of African American music, jazz, which I think is also a vernacular poetry in which these distinctions between high and low get erased. And the spirit of "passing for Italian" is that, even if you can't trace a blood genealogy to Italy, you can be Italian.

I wanted to get back to Sinatra through jazz, and get him into that book I was writing about jazz, and I couldn't quite figure out how to do it in the context of that project. This essay came out of something that I read in a rap magazine, or hip-hop magazine, and it gave me a kind of a cue to do it through rap, first off, and then get back to jazz.

In a 1995 issue of *Vibe,* the slick photo magazine devoted to rap and hip-hop culture, one of the most hotly debated questions in 1990s' rap aficionado circles—who is the original gangster—was settled once and for all. The last word came down from Bönz Malone, known to *Vibe* readers as a redoubtable arbiter of street authenticity. Malone's original gangster, interestingly, was not one of the usual suspects: not Ice-T or Ice Cube, Tupac Shakur or Schooly-D, not Suge Knight, not even Snoop Doggy Dogg. No, the dopest, phattest, most uncompromising voice of hip-hop masculinity turns out to be Frank Sinatra. "Way before gangster rap, there was already a king on the hill," Malone effused in his article. "A G with the kind of class that makes a person untouchable. No matter where he showed up throughout the country, he would do anything to blow up the spot, always looking for a lamppost so his big band could G off" (Malone 1995: 26).

In Malone's hagiography, Sinatra's music is inseparable from his image, both setting the standard for stylish virility. "His tough Jersey accent redefined the American language," Malone writes, "plus he used his voice, not a gun. It made the girlies stick out them tits like it was a hold-up. Mind you, this was in the '40s, when girls wasn't givin' up the coochie" (Malone 1995: 27).

So keen is Malone's infatuation, so awed is he by the Chairman of the Board's magisterial bearing that he's overcome by racial envy. "I've always wanted to be Italian," he rused, "but I'll have to settle for being black and cool." Malone is being playfully hyperbolic, but his sentiment is actually in accord with a distinct tradition of inter-ethnic identification. One finds the black-Italian crossover fantasy lurking in the imagination of no less an icon of black male cool than Marvin Gaye. "My dream was to become Frank Sinatra," Gaye confesses. "I loved his phrasing. He grew into a fabulous jazz singer, and I used to fantasize about having a lifestyle like his, carrying on in Hollywood and becoming a movie star. Every woman in America wanted to go to bed with Frank Sinatra. He was the king I longed to be. My greatest dream was to satisfy as many women as Sinatra" (Early 1995: 9).

I grew up in an Italian American family in which Sinatra was revered as an icon of success, a tough little *paisan* who became a big shot. "Sure, he can be a bastard," ran my family's party-line response to Kitty Kelley's lurid exposé of Sinatra's pettiness and scummy bedside manners, "but he's done a lot of good for his people." At a family wedding a few years back, when the band played "My Way" and "New York, New York" with a cloying bathos exceeding even that of the late Sinatra himself, my thinly veiled disdain provoked a discussion about whether my seemingly endless years of education had done anything other than deprive me of a sense of my roots. Only recently, with the passing of an uncle—my Uncle Abbie—and my lustful pursuit of his vintage Capitol LPs, has my Italian pride apparently risen back up above family reproach.

In truth, much as I might want to disavow the macho posturing of the swinging bachelor Rat Packer and his scion, the gangster rapper, I must admit to a strong identification with the Sinatra of the snap-brimmed hat, the Oxford gray suit, and the wingtip shoes that, as Gay Talese remarked, seemed to be shined even on the soles. I would also claim allegiance to the Sinatra who, in 1945, sat with W. E. B. DuBois, Mary Bethune, Sterling Brown, Paul Robeson, Duke Ellington, Joe Louis, and others honored by the *New Masses* magazine for their contributions "toward a democratic America." At a certain point, once Sinatra's voice gets under your skin, I guess you stop trying to figure out how the man feted by *New Masses* for his courageous fight on behalf of all minorities is the same one fond of giving his male friends diamond-studded gold cigarette lighters with obscene inscriptions.

I'm going to provide a little historical backdrop here before coming back to Sinatra and his persona. The relationship between Italian Americans and African Americans is no less vexed than other intercultural exchanges in America, and in many respects, it is much more so, owing in no small degree to the fundamental ambiguities of Italian racial identity. A couple years ago, the Miss Italy Pageant exemplified the complex racial inflections of Mediterranean Italian culture and politics. After much fevered debate over the true nature of Italian beauty, the crown was given to a black woman, a naturalized Italian citizen born in the Dominican Republic. In what amounted to an electronic plebiscite, 9 million Italian televoters succeeded in bumping from the judge's panel a fashion photographer who had insisted that a black woman can't win a competition that's meant to reward and represent Italian beauty. Linking the incident to the perennially divisive issue of north-south regional identity, the Italian press did not fail to note that the new Miss Italy's pigmentation was remarkably similar to the dark-hued complexion of the majority of Italians who live south of Florence. It is precisely that suggestion, with its implication of an Italian identity tied more strongly to the Saracen south than to the Teutonic north, that has motivated the Northern League, a politico-cultural secessionist movement that has tapped deeply into the mythology of the Sicilian, the Calabrian, and the Neapolitan as lazy, morally corrupt, intellectually inferior "Other," closer kin to the African savage than to the Florentine prince.

In post-Reconstruction America, in the South, thousands of olive-complected, kinky-haired southern Italian agricultural workers who flocked to Louisiana and Mississippi were of an indeterminate racial status—"a dangerous in-betweenness," as John Higham put it—that consigned them to the strictures of Jim Crow legislation (Higham 1955/1988: 169). In 1899 five Sicilian men, characterized as "black dagos," were lynched for violating protocols of racial interaction in Louisiana. Italians' willingness to work alongside blacks in sugarcane fields and to socialize with blacks created what one historian called "a hindrance to white solidarity" in Louisiana (Cunningham 1965: 24–25).

The cultural fruits of this resistance to white hegemony stretched from early jazz to early rock and roll, from King Oliver, Louie Armstrong, Nick LaRocca's Original Dixieland Jazz Band, and Louie Prima, performing at Matronga's, Segretta's, Ponce's, and Savoca's honky-tonks in New Orleans in the interwar years, to Little Richard cutting his first records at Cosimo Mattasa's J&M Studio in the early 1950s.

Historical ethnographies of the Italian-black relationship typically stress a shared glandular sensibility, earthiness, sensuality, emotional expressiveness, an unembarrassed love of the body, an emphasis on food as cultural mediator. The American sociologist Herbert Gans pointed out that dressing up and the desire for stepping out in style is shared by many Italian Americans and African Americans (Gans 1962: 146). There is also a kind of food connection between blacks and Italians that I took from an interview with the distinguished African American writer Albert Murray. Murray, propagandist of American culture as "incontestably mulatto," is a subscriber to what I'm calling the "polenta is just a fancy name for cornbread" school of culinary hybridity, along with other aspects of black-Italian affinity. This is what Murray says: "Long before there were southerners in the U.S.A., there were southerners in Italy, and it meant a certain climate, a certain hospitality, a certain musicality in the language, and sometimes even a certain kind of violence and tendency to vendetta. In the more learned circles, the European vision of the Italian southerner is much like that of anyone who understands the American South. The feeling is that of an easeful relationship to culture and a spontaneity that says, deep down, the point of learning to cook all this food, and talk this way, and wear these fine clothes, is to have a good goddamn time, man" (Crouch 1990: 248–49).

We need to talk about tension and even violence between blacks and Italians, too. Recall that in Spike Lee's *Do the Right Thing* (1989), probably the most important cultural representation of the balkanized post-1960s urban landscape, the fiery race war that rages at the movie's end is the culmination of a conflict over the symbolic significance of photographs of Frank Sinatra, Dean Martin, Perry Como, Liza Minelli, Al Pacino, Joe DiMaggio, and Luciano Pavarotti hanging on the wall of an Italian-owned pizzeria in a predominantly black Brooklyn neighborhood. The fact that the "Wall of Fame" in Sal's Pizzeria includes no blacks—not even the musicians and basketball players that Sal's racist son admits to worshipping, and from whom he has unwittingly cribbed his styles of speech and gesture—becomes the enabling metaphor for Spike Lee's powerful critique of the colonialist underpinnings of a certain type of Italian-black urban relation.

As W. J. T. Mitchell suggests in a brilliant reading of the politics of public space in *Do the Right Thing*, the conflict over Sal's Wall of Fame shows at once how confidently Italians have come to think of themselves as Americans, as "full-fledged members of the general public sphere" (1994: 388) and how keen is the sense among African Americans of their exclusion from that general public sphere. Although the neighborhood is filled with representations of African American culture—a billboard of Mike Tyson looming over the pizzeria, Magic Johnson T-shirts, Air Jordan sneakers, Afro-centric body ornaments, and the ubiquitous black music soundstream flowing out of Mr. SeZor Love Daddy's storefront radio station two doors down from Sal's—these expressions are figured by Spike Lee as subcultural counterdiscourses angling in from the margin, while the pizzeria symbolizes full ownership of the American dream.

Spike Lee, of course, has himself become a symbol of and a tireless propagandist for black ownership and autonomy in a culture industry that mythologizes that dream. In the documentary film *Hoop Dreams* (1994), we see him at a Nike All-Star camp hyping that message to a group of black high school basketball players. Earlier the players had been subjected to the wildly gesticulating Dick Vitale, who likened the players' ascendancy from the inner-city ghetto to the cusp of NCAA fame, and maybe even NBA fortune, to his own—Vitale's—Horatio Algerish rise to the top of ESPN. We can assume that many of these players were hearing similar rhetoric in recruiting pitches from Rick Pitino, John Calapari, Rollie Massimino, and P. J. Carlissimo, the New Jack Italian American icons whose highly remunerated job it is to manage and supervise black bodies for prime-time TV spectacle.

If Spike Lee sees what keeps Italians and blacks locked in a struggle over public space and mainstream recognition, he also seems obsessed with what draws them together. In *Do the Right Thing* and *Jungle Fever* (1991), blacks and Italians are the kind of tribal enemies who just can't resist testing each other's territorial boundaries and questioning why those boundaries exist in the first place. Even in *Malcolm X* (1992), Spike Lee's effort to create an authentic race hero, he is unable to resist a token nod to black-Italian miscegeny. Playing fast and loose with the Malcolm X autobiography, Spike Lee creates a criminal sidekick for Detroit Red, who sums up his tough-guy rep by announcing, "My mother's black, and my father's Italian. Nobody fucks with me." It is, in fact, this tough-guy pose, this "No, *I'm* the man" status competition that dominates the black-Italian cross-over imaginary.

And lest we think that the allure of this imaginary is limited to male competitors, we have Camille Paglia, that "original gangsta" of academia, to remind us otherwise. Paglia, who greatly values the "emotional truth thing" she sees at the heart of both Italian and African American culture, worships at the altar of pagan goddesses from Aretha Franklin to Madonna, that shrewd and passionate Italian girl who, according to Paglia, was smart enough to perceive in disco a "dark, grand, Dionyesian music with roots in African earth cult" (1992: 7).

Whereas Camille Paglia primitivizes musical blackness, Frank Sinatra classicizes it. Paglia looks south to rhythm and blues for access to the primordial life force. Sinatra looked north, cultivating the Florentine *bel canto* vocal ideal. This is the key. He understood what was happening in jazz and the critical discourse around jazz, and he saw, quite shrewdly, that there was cultural capital to be had in fostering the sense that, in fact, he was a jazz musician. He was a jazz musician; I'm not arguing against that. But the fact that he was perceived as such, and he supplied critics with the rhetoric that they could then use to represent him as such, I think, has something to do with why we're here.

Bootlegging the high-art discourse that attached itself to jazz as it reached the metropolitan intelligentsia in Paris, London, and New York, significantly, Sinatra—unlike Bing Crosby, Elvis Presley, and Dean Martin—has never been seen as a minstrel performer. Partly this is a question of taste and sensibility. When Sinatra ventured outside of the Cole Porter/Harold Arlen/Sammy Kahn/Jimmy Van Heusen stock of swinging ballads and saloon songs, it was not out of envy of Dean Martin's covers of "When It's Sleepy Time Down South," "Carolina Moon," and "Georgia on My Mind."

Sinatra, as several critics have pointed out, sought expressly to distinguish his singing from Crosby's relaxed crooning. In the *bel canto* operatic style that Sinatra emulated, the emphasis—as Arnold Shaw pointed out (Shaw 1995: 29)—is on beauty of tone in additional to emotional expressiveness, on the inventive employment of ornament, and on the smooth use of sustained tone rather than on a declamatory or dramatic delivery. John Rockwell similarly commented on the "broad, artistocratic *As*" in Sinatra's singing, a product, he said, "of the forwardness of his vocal production, the way he lets the tone resonate in his nasal cavities instead of becoming constricted in his throat and chest" (1984: 52).

When Sinatra talks about Billie Holiday as a decisive influence on his singing, he speaks not of "her soulfulness," but of her poetic ability to fit the lyric of a song within the meter (Shaw 1995: 29–30). Like Duke Ellington before him—in fact, that comparison is one I'm surprised hasn't been made more often—Sinatra shrewdly supplied the very rhetoric by which critics and historians subsequently have canonized him. It's no coincidence that Sinatra's post-1980 revival has coincided with the so-called jazz renaissance. "The Lion in Winter," as writer Murray Kempton dubbed Sinatra in a review of a 1993 concert, has gained currency and cachet from the young lion's massively publicized custodial embrace of a so-called jazz tradition.

Listen to Winton Marsalis's antirap diatribes, and hear the echoes of Sinatra's famous rant against rock and roll, as "a brutal, ugly, vicious form of expression, played and written by cretinous goons" (Porter 2002: 320–25). One can only imagine the horror with which Sinatra would greet the suggestion that Rat Pack "chicks" and "broads" are not so far removed from gangster rap's "bitches" and "hos." If Ol' Blue Eyes had taken a measure of gratification from his ascension to pop patriarch, it is not, I would argue, so much the satisfaction of a performer who saw his style win out, as it is the pleasure of the Sicilian *uomo di rispetto,* the man of respect, exacting tribute from his epigones.

14

🎤

Sinatra, the Name Ending in a Vowel

or, "The Voice" as Signifier and Symptom of Italian Americanness

Pellegrino A. D'Acierno

"Of course, it meant something to me to be the son of immigrants," Sinatra said to me once. "How could it not? How the hell could it not? I grew up for a few years thinking I was just another American kid. Then I discovered at—what? five? six?—I discovered I was a dago. A wop. A guinea." An angry pause. "You know, like I didn't have a fucking name." An angrier pause. "That's why years later, when Harry [James] wanted me to change my name, I said no way, baby. The name is Sinatra. Frank fucking Sinatra."

—Pete Hamill, Why Sinatra Matters

The Game of the Name

Frank Sinatra is someone, as he often combatively pointed out, whose name ends in a vowel, someone who as a performer has perhaps been alone in treating both art and life with his name and in his name. As a singer, he put his name on a song in a way only Enrico Caruso and Billie Holiday have done. So definitive and personalized were his renditions that almost every song he sang was a signature piece—the definitive version. So infused with desire and longing were his songs that they desired us as much as we desired them and desired through them. From this perspective, he was perhaps the most autographic vocalist of the twentieth century, that is to say, he never was just a mere performer who reproduced what was prescribed by the lyric and score, always removing performance from the allographic regime, as aestheticians say. Sinatra's singing, regardless of genre, always forced itself to be heard, in effect causing the dimension of listening to be rediscovered. Although he imposed his name through the image-character of his performing self—onstage, offstage, on-screen, off-screen—his real authority over us lay in his solitary, beckoning invitation to be heard. His name, his signature, was in the song. Although musicologists have often emphasized the importance of the verbal element and his diction in his renditions, the recitation of the lyrical text—"what is said"—provided the means for the emergence of the voice; his voice always breaks through the composition and claims us and our longing in his name. If, in the Age of the Mechanical Reproduction and of the technological filter of the microphone, the singer's voice tended to become utopian, appearing to come from nowhere, his voice remained anchored to him indexically. The Voice became his proper name; and the surplus of the Sinatra effect required a proliferation of names: Swoonatra, the Lean Lark, the Voice that Thrills Millions, Ol' Blue Eyes, the Chairman of the Board, and so on. The proper name Sinatra, thus, became the name of names. His signature was in his voice, the Voice, but it was also in his Look—the sequence of Looks he affected as he went from bow tie to black tie, from J. Press madder ties to orange-flecked Sulka cravats—in his Gaze by which he declared his sexual persona, and in his Style and the identity politics at work in that Style.

As a figure who both came from pop culture and transcended it, he has perhaps been alone in putting his name—his *names*—and his biographies on the line, running the risks this entails. Not simply artistic, these risks— political and personal, above all, amorous/erotic—were generated by a provocative and highly contradictory project of self-affirmation that, among other things, made him the target of the right-wing establishment during the 1940s and early 1950s and the object of a pathological FBI sur- veillance that lasted from 1943 through 1980. So under the sign of Sinatra, there operates an aggressive and triumphant "politics of the proper name," to use a term put into play by Jacques Derrida (1985), whom I echo here and throughout. The subtext of those politics is the specter of the improper name, the name marked with class and ethnic Otherness, along with all the stigmatizing names that may be attached to it. To put his name on the line (with everything a name involves and which cannot be summed up in a self), to perform his signatures, to place his name on the extraordinary nar- rative of self-creation through which he achieved America—this is what Sinatra has done and what we have to put on the active record. He did not simply construct the self as a work of art—off-stage as well as onstage—but motivated that self-construction and the elaborate constellation— collision—of personae it entailed into a master identity narrative that spanned six decades and served as a means of mediating between the real and the imaginary for three generations of Americans. In its trans-genera- tional effect, the Sinatran master narrative has reconciled a series of stylis- tic ages and a series of iconographic ages, but, more important, it has rewritten the hegemonic American immigrant myth in a way that exposes the alienation and self-alienation intrinsic to Immigrant American and the myth-function of American exceptionalism. Citizen Sinatra would present himself as an exception to American exceptionalism, and insofar as he was a cultural and even sub-cultural signifier of second-generation Italian America and, by extension, a trans-ethnic signifier of the subaltern "blue- collar" immigrant class, Sinatra would represent Italian American and eth- nic *difference* without apologies to the American dream. Consequently, I regard Sinatra's work and life as constituting a master identity narrative of the Italian American self as it expands into an American "imperial self." It is thus a site where the second-generation self is writ large, with all its strengths and weaknesses magnified a hundredfold, and the site where the Italian American experience and its habitus—its way of operating in the world—first becomes visible and legible.

The Sinatran master narrative was executed as a total work of performance art involving careful scriptings, controlled and autonomous improvisations, as well as constant frame-breaking, including what I shall call, following Erving Goffman (1971), the manufacture of negative experience. It was these violations of scripted behavior that imparted authenticating force to the self-narrative. Indeed, I shall argue that Sinatra's real exemplarity lay precisely in his manufacturing of negative experience and thus in his troubling of the American dream, which he simultaneously embodied and called into question.

In any case, in whatever terms present and future cultural historians and musicologists may calculate the ultimate legacy of Sinatra, the man and the music, their assessments will have to be made with respect to the master identity narrative Sinatra imposed on twentieth-century America and in which the distinction between the music and the man, the public self and the private self, the amorous persona of the singer and the sexual persona of the man, and the imperial self of the Legend and the symptomal self of ethnicity all collapsed or, at least, constantly changed places. This master narrative was written under the sign of passion and in the proper name of Sinatra, the man with one too many names and one too many biographies.

The Game of the Improper Name

Wops don't use maple syrup.

—Ezra Pound

I have begun by playing the game of the proper name not simply because it opens a way to a reading of Sinatra and how he enacts the imperial self through the appropriative act of naming, but also because it foregrounds his reciprocal roles as a signifier and symptom of Italian Americanness. It should be stated that the Italian American identity is essentially nomenclatural—

declared, marked, signed, and delivered through the proper name, even if that name was disfigured during the passage through Ellis Island. Sinatra, of course, refused to change his name, and he defended the "name ending in a vowel" in his appearance (March 1, 1951) before the Kefauver Committee, that "forum for gutter hearsay," as he put it, and where he recognized that an Italian proper name was discreditable, bearing, as it did, the tribal stigma attached to it by the Italian American and, specifically, Sicilian American criminal subculture—namely, the Mafia—which has, in effect, rendered Italian Americans into a discreditable people. Sinatra confided to Pete Hamill: "Half the troubles I've had were because my name ended in vowel. They tried to put me together with all the other stuff that happened. I wasn't the only one. But there I was up on a goddamned stage. I was pretty easy to see, a good target" (Hamill 1998: 44).

What's in a proper name? For Sinatra and second-generation Italian Americans in general, there was the stigmatizing subtext of the Mafia and the equally stigmatizing force of the improper name—wop, dago, guinea. Sinatra constantly stressed the traumatic effect and the omnipresent menace of the improper name as it was imposed as a pejorative by the Other: "Every once in a while . . . I'd be at a party somewhere in Hollywood or New York or wherever, and it would be very civilized, you know, black tie, the best crystal, all of that. And I'd see a guy staring at me from the corner of the room, and I knew what word was in his head. The word was *guinea*" (Hamill 1998: 42).

In addition to Italian American rage, this nomenclatural stigmatization and the process of Othering it imposed produced the reactive ethnicity typical of the second generation: "Sometimes with me, it was a case of if-you-got-the-name-you-might-as-well-have-the-game. . . . You think I'm just some wop wise guy off the street? All right, I'll *be* a wop wise guy off the street and break your fucking head" (Hamill 1998: 49). On the other hand, Sinatra, especially with insiders and most explicitly in the verbal rituals of the Rat Pack, constantly played out the game of the improper name, essentially as a way of depriving these pejoratives of their stigmatizing force and also as a way of expressing tribal connection, more or less as African Americans refer to themselves as "niggers" within the context of other African

Americans. Sinatra was the Top Wop, Dean Martin was "Dag," his airplane "El Dago"; Sammy Kahn transposed the lyrics of Cole Porter's song "You're the Top" into "You're the Wop." In other words, "wop" and the other pejoratives were both the nomenclatural poison and the remedy.

Pete Hamill has developed this material into a canonical "wound of ethnicity" reading of Sinatra. But I believe that one of the keys to understanding Sinatra's identity narrative is establishing a link between the enormous and aggressive naming he affected as a performer and man—friendship and sexual seduction are both essentially ways of imposing one's name on others or the Other—and the stigmatizing process of counter-naming he was subjected to and around which he organized the signs of his social and personal identity. There is a constant combat within Sinatra between his being the subject who actively imposes his proper name and the object who is targeted by the counter-name. Whereas the force of the stigmatizing counter-name is in its power to de-territorialize the self, the force of Sinatra's proper name—the name of names—is in its power to territorialize and re-territorialize. It is precisely the aggressive territorializing self that needs to be placed at the heart of an Italian American reading of Sinatra.

The Lover's Discourse: The Place of the Songs in the Master Narrative

As a way of coming to grips with the implications of the Sinatran identity narrative, it is first necessary to describe the role of his songs in it. Sinatra wrote no official autobiography; instead, he encrypted an unofficial autobiography of his amorous self in the cycle of his songs. That autobiography took the form of an "otobiography" (Derrida 1985)—that is, an autobiography of the Voice addressed to the ear. It has become a commonplace to remark on his impeccable selection of songs—Wilfred Sheed (1986) calls him "the man who saved the standards"—and how he ordered them into LP form to create a narrative. I have already spoken of the appropriative force and the naming of these songs in Sinatra's claiming of them, many of which belong to the highest echelon of American popular song and thus, in terms of class, represented the expropriation by a "blue-collar" singer, the product of immigrant America, of the classical canon of pop songs. Sinatra in effect appropriated the taste culture of the bourgeoisie and even upper-class America, transmitting it through the media to the newly formed mass-mediated American public. There is, for sure, a class allegory embedded in the master narrative, but here I just want to mention Sinatra's appropriation of a class-marked diction. Italian Americans have been systematically stereotyped as barred from language, or, at best, as prisoners of language, as those who break English and are broken by it. Of his generation, Sinatra was one of the few Italian Americans to place himself in the position of struggling with his class image, of which language is the inevitable mirror.

But to return to the problem of putting his name on a song, the way in which he appropriates these songs, makes them his own by personalizing and eroticizing them, especially those involving the amorous catastrophe, infusing them with the Sinatran *tenebroso,* an urban and mass-media version of that dark sound that comes from what the poet García Lorca calls the *duende.* Although he constantly described himself as a saloon singer, an omnibus category for a singer who can turn a booze ballad as well as bounce a song or even belt an anthem like "New York, New York," he is unique as a torch singer, as a voice that articulates the drama of erotic crisis and the solitude of amorous loss. This is, of course, not to overlook the tender celebrations of young love characteristic of his work in the 1940s, in which the whole world would be suspended in the balance of a single kiss; or his post-crooner swinging come-fly-with-me mode, the sophisticated detachment of which might be seen as a defense against the romantic *tenebroso;* or the bittersweet ballads of experience of his mature style; or the aggressive vocals of his middle and old age, from "My Way" (1969) to the "husky murmur" of *Duets* (1993), his ultimate comeback. Indeed, the trajectory of his oeuvre provides a complete anatomy of romantic love as it passes from spring to winter. Within that trajectory are inscribed two histories: the physical history of his voice as it passes from the tenderness of the youthful tenor (technically speaking, he is high baritone), whose velvety crooning approached a whisper, to the raspiness of old age; and his autobiography as an amorous subject as registered in love songs deliberately chosen to correspond to his personal history and inner experience. This autobiography of the vicissitudes of love, the voice, and the Voice is unique in the ephemeral realm of American pop music, and because it is a work of time—the life of a man registered in music—a defiant exception to F. Scott Fitzgerald's "law": "There are no second acts to American lives" (1941: 163). Indeed, it is the passage from the second to the third act that provides Sinatra with his consummate moment as a singer: the cycle of dark songs of exacerbated and unfulfilled desire that enact, in the anatomy of love, the melancholy passage from late summer to autumn. Recorded in the mid- and late 1950s, when Sinatra was in his forties and on the rebound from his marriage to Ava Gardner, this cycle, interspersed with swing tunes, would serve as aphrodisiacs, initiating the American audience into the rites of neo-romantic love. So the trajectory of the amorous discourse as set out in the songs is inextricably linked to the trajectory of the master narrative, mirroring it, anchoring it, glossing it, crossing over to take possession of it, and, at times, even displacing it.

Deconstructing the Chairman of the Board, or, What a Cultural Studies Reading of Sinatra Might Do

> One always perishes by the self one assumes: to bear a name is to claim an exact mode of collapse.
>
> —*E. M. Cioran*, The Temptation to Exist

The current explosion of biographic and interpretive writing and media commentary generated by his death has not only canonized Sinatra but also canonized the way in which he is to be read. In the wake of this monumentalization, it is no easy matter to advance the problem of *what Sinatra means,* to refer to Pete Hamill, who, in his book, has so admirably put this question to himself and also implicitly to us and the communities of memory to which we belong. Sinatra is ultimately the proper name that means too much, the name that designates a surplus. As previously indicated, for me the problem of what Sinatra means involves questioning the dynamics of the borderline between "the work" and "the life," and thus to raise the question of the proper and improper name. But now that the curtain has gone down, we must approach Sinatra retrospectively, a task that requires us to raise the comprehensive question of reading/rereading Sinatra in a more critical and self-conscious way, one that addresses the Sinatra Construct—that is, the set of contradictions he embodied and that have determined, whether consciously or unconsciously, the ways in which he has been read. The substantial body of recent work dedicated to canonizing him, including a miniseries for television and numerous documentaries, has approached him primarily through the conventional biographical trope of the artist and the man. Of the treatments in this mode, those of Pete Hamill and John Lahr are the most illuminating precisely because they maintain a high torsion between the work and the man. On the other hand, the discourse on Sinatra overall is marked by a split between those writers who privilege biography and those who privilege his art, his "otobiography," the biography addressed to the ear. The musicological tradition has produced the more substantive readings. Here I am referring to the line that extends from Henry Pleasants and John Rockwell to Will Friedwald. By the way, both Pleasants and Rockwell advanced the *bel canto* matrix of Sinatra's art of singing, his applied Caruso-ism hybridized by grafts of Billie Holiday and Mabel Murcer, and thus contextualized him within the Italian tradition. The publishing and media mill that has sprung up after Sinatra's death has been diligent in rewriting and filming the master narrative, whether in the positive key of hagiography or the negative key of tabloid exposé camouflaged as behind-the-legend biography. Many of these biographies, especially those issuing from the domain of journalism, oscillate between hagiography and exposé, thereby confirming the reservations Freud expressed toward biography. According to Freud, biographers idealize the hero while trying at the same time to reduce the distance separating them from him. Biographies, Freud argued, never provide any insight into the hero, but rather reveal the infantile attitude that the biographer shares with the reader, one of admiration and narcissistic identification (Freud 1923/1961: 208–12). Indeed, what has been produced, in effect, is a vast fantasy construction in the form of a meta-narrative, a pastiche of recycled materials and newly found anecdotes, punctuated with sermonizings and facile psychobiographizing on the so-called dark side of the Legend. But all this retrospective fictionalization should come as no surprise, since it is a reflection of the Sinatra Construct—that is, the set of contradictions that he always embodied and that have always determined the process by which he was originally consecrated, de-consecrated, re-consecrated, and ultimately canonized as the American Classic.

At this moment it is necessary to move beyond the either/or, pro-or-con responses that made Sinatra into such a site of controversy and contestation and to attempt to graph the many sides of the Sinatra phenomenon. This does not mean bracketing or whitewashing the dangerous side of Sinatra that led him to having been constituted as a "bad object" by his detractors. On the contrary, I shall argue that Sinatra was and remains a site of genuine contradiction that must be articulated and appraised to adequately interpret his works, images, and their effects, especially the effect of what I have called his master narrative, which, among other things, focalizes the tropes of the Italian American identity. Although Sinatra's images and personae would seem to emphasize the social constructedness of identity, masculinity, sexuality, style, and fashion, I want to argue that Sinatra's narrative of self was in great part a deliberate exercise in aesthetic self-fashioning informed by an attitude toward experience that had as its task the "tearing" of the subject from itself in such a way that the self was no longer the subject as such, or that it was made into an Other. In other words, Sinatra was a "technique of trouble," not only to others and the media culture at large but also to himself, and, to a certain extent, his art and life might be seen to be organized around the quest for limit-experiences. All the way, All or Nothing at All. He was an artistic, amorous, sexual, and political adventurer, regardless of the ways in which he would comprise his dangerous experimentation as he became institutionalized and commodified as icon of the establishment and ultimately as its power broker.

What a cultural studies reading might do is take a hard look at Sinatra's genesis and disposition as an artist generated by immigrant culture and the positions he subsequently occupied in the cultural field of production, including his political position-takings. Sinatra's identity politics, even though they are essentially culturalist and thus concerned with the creation of an artistic and personal identity, do have a political content, most concrete early on when he fully embraced the democratic project, becoming one of the first popular singers to politicize his persona. Furthermore, while identity for Sinatra was essentially a matter of Italian American identity, his concerns were never particularist, cutting across ethnic, racial, and class lines and moving beyond identity politics narrowly construed. For Sinatra the personal was the political, and the political was the personal—Hoboken ward politics writ large—and thereby hangs a tale well worth pursuing, for it culminates in a paradox: There can be a Sinatraism of the left and a Sinatraism of the right.

Reading Sinatra as an Ethnic or "New American" Singer

[Sinatra is] a great Italian American, a great American . . .

—*Martin Scorsese*

No one has served more completely as an ethnic signifier than Sinatra, his image coming to mirror the contradictions of second-generation identity. Through him the "ethnic thing"—the ethnic self with all its vulnerability and rage, its strengths and weaknesses—undergoes a tremendous magnification, a universalization of sorts resulting in a mass-media version of the American imperial self constructed in Italian American terms. Whereas DiMaggio, his predecessor as cultural hero, embodied the performing self governed by *sprezzatura* (nonchalance, a Renaissance concept that suggests, among other qualities, what Ernest Hemingway, a great admirer of DiMaggio, termed "grace under pressure") as manifested in the "Streak," that unique record in which the *bella figura* and the work ethic coincided, Sinatra is a more complex figure who constantly introduces the negative into the construction (and maintenance) of his image. Like that other cunning Mediterranean hero of the (im)proper name, Odysseus (literally, to be the bane of many people's existence), Sinatra is a man of many turns but always a technique for troubling others. Sinatra is, in a characteristically Italian way, a man who "makes the scene" by making scenes, but who also makes the private public and thus always put at risk what Goffman calls "the territories of the self" (1972: 28–61). And here, with the notion of a territorial self, we begin to zero in on Sinatra's Italianness, which traditionally has been read, as in Talese's essay for *Esquire* in 1966, as a discrepant but simultaneous occupation of two different worlds: the cosmopolitan one populated by show business people, in which he assumes the role of the swinger; and the traditional one, populated by his inner circle of paisanos, as Talese puts it, in which he assumes the role of *Il Padrone* (the Boss), or, as Talese qualifies, an *uomo rispettato*. Intrinsic to this notion of the man of respect is exaggerated personalism, the display of absolute generosity and fidelity toward the special circle of friends on the condition of reciprocal loyalty: "All the way," "All or Nothing at All." The territorial self draws the line in the sand. Of course, when Sinatra pressed territorial demands on such wider spheres as the media or congressional committees, or even the presidency, he opened the way to territorial violations—what he saw as encroachments on his sphere and what the public saw as violations on his part.

Talese's essay, "Sinatra Has a Cold," is instructive for it is the first piece to read Sinatra from an Italian American perspective. It provides a good antidote to the anodyne and colonizing view set out earlier by Moynihan and Glazer in *Beyond the Melting Pot* (1963). They wrote: "The set of qualities that seem to distinguish Italian Americans includes individuality, temperament and ambition . . . perhaps the ideal is the entertainer—to give him a name, Frank Sinatra—who is an international celebrity, but still the bighearted, generous, unchanged boy from the block" (194). Furthermore, Talese's reading, however implicitly, recognizes that the Sinatran master identity narrative, like all ethnic narratives, is double-voiced, addressed, on one hand, specifically to the Italian American insider—and, by extension, other ethnic insiders—who will read the narrative from an insider's position, and, on the other hand, addressed to the non-ethnic outsider—that is, the American normal who will read and misread it in all sorts of ways.

The enacted master identity narrative—Sinatra was a novelist without knowing it—rises to the realm of serious literature and, even in its present virtual form, can be regarded as the "great Italian American novel," parts of which have already been plagiarized or rewritten, most notably by Mario Puzo in *The Godfather* (1969) and Don DeLillo in *Underworld* (1997). But so far the Italian American reading of Sinatra has remained exploitative and underdeveloped, with Puzo's Godfathering of Sinatra, seconded by Coppola's—typically so, for exploitation is an expression of underdevelopment. Indeed, the complexities and contradictions of Sinatra's lived novel are far more compelling than those of the weak version of it that Puzo, a lesser narrator than Sinatra by far, has appropriated and rewritten in that notorious part of *The Godfather* that passes for a *roman à clef.*

Don DeLillo, the greatest living Italian American novelist, has presented a cameo or snapshot version of Sinatra in his retrospective fictionalization of Sinatra's day at the legendary baseball game in 1951 between the Giants and the Dodgers in which Bob Thompson delivered the "shot heard 'round the world." Sinatra is, as always, situated within a group: This time he is inserted in a box at the Polo Grounds along with Jackie Gleason, Toots Shor, and J. Edgar Hoover, of all people. While DeLillo's Sinatra, sharp- and salty-tongued as the legend goes, gets off a number of witty salvos, his utterances are not top-notch Sinatra—at least not to this writer, for whom Sinatra ranks a notch or two beneath Nietzsche as a supreme midnight philosopher and aphorist. It is interesting that the most revealing view of Sinatra comes through the viewpoint of Hoover: "He [Hoover] admires the rough assurance of these men [Sinatra and Gleason]. It seems flush from their pores. They have a size to them, a natural stamina that mocks his own bible-school indoctrination even as it draws him to the noise. He's a self-perfected American who must respect the saga of the knockabout boy emerging from a tenement culture, from backstreets slant with danger. It makes for gutsy egos, it makes for egos, it makes for appetites. The pussy bandits Jackie and Frank have a showy sort of ease around women" (DeLillo 1997: 29).

This description spins off and riffs on the canonic Sinatra—the outsized self up from tenement culture and, more predictably, the pussy-banditism, Sinatra's sexual persona. Later in the novel, DeLillo will have Sinatra miss the "shot heard 'round the world" as a result of Gleason's gaffe—vomiting on his exquisite slacks and shoes. DeLillo thereby introduces, however implicitly, the business of the *bella figura,* one of the central tropes of Italianness. But all this amounts to a fairly predictable take on Sinatra.

The most profound and thoughtful reading of Sinatra from an Italian American perspective comes not from Italian America but from Irish America, in the person of Pete Hamill, who approaches Sinatra through the grid of the urban ethnicity common to both the Italian and Irish American experience. Hamill writes: "Because [Sinatra] was the son of immigrants, his success thrilled millions who were products of the same rough history. Through the power of his art and his personality, he became one of a very small group that would permanently shift the image of Italian Americans. Many aspects of his character were shaped by that immigrant experience, which often fueled his notorious volatility. More important it infused his art" (1998: 37).

Hamill gets it right: His reading is highly sensitized to the wound of ethnicity as inflicted on Sinatra, and he contextualizes Sinatra and his self-understanding within a larger history of immigrant and ethnic stigmatization. Furthermore, Hamill writes his piece from the position of a genuine insider—not only from his having been let in to the inside of Sinatra's consciousness by Sinatra himself, who regarded him as a confidant and his ultimate biographer, but also from the position of the Italian American cultural identity itself. He brings to bear on his reading of Sinatra a number of tropes that are absolutely critical to our understanding of the man and the artist: *familialismo* and its extension into *padronismo* and *clientalismo; campanilismo,* as reflected in the regional hybridism of Sinatra's parentage—Dolly was Genovese and northern Italian, Martin was Sicilian and southern Italian, the distinction constituting the great divide in the Italian psyche—and the conflict between *la via nuova* and *la via vecchia,* both as reflected in the Sinatra family and Sinatra himself. I am convinced that bringing into play such Italian tropes is essential to a more developed understanding of Sinatra's identity and his identity politics.

"Only My Friends Call Me Wop": Toward an Italian American Reading of Sinatra

I knew Maggio. I went to school with him in Hoboken. . . . I might have been Maggio.

—Frank Sinatra

The way I figure it, there's only three people in the world that matter: Jesus Christ, Frank Sinatra, and me.

—The Sheik in Baby, It's You *(directed by John Sayles, 1983)*

I have already begun to articulate what an Italian American reading of Sinatra might look like by playing out the game of the proper name and by limning some of the contradictions at work in the master identity narrative, thereby locating in him the "divided consciousness" in which the "cursed part"—the secret wound of ethnicity—is embodied and through which it is displayed and ultimately exorcised through the force of his signature. From this perspective, the slogan "My Way" is totally inadequate and misleading as a form of self-presentation and a statement of identity. This is to say that Sinatra's identity and his identity politics must be subjected to a double reading, one that sees him as both a signifier and symptom of Italian Americanness. After all, Sinatra is the Italian American second-generation self writ large, a figure in whom all its ontological securities and insecurities, all its alienation and self-alienation, are magnified, in whom all its resistance to cooption and assimilation and all its compliance to the dominant culture are pushed to a breaking point. He is our double, our secret sharer; through him, the Italian American psychic identity, in its conflicted passage from immigration and exile in the small world of Little Italy to incorporation and "normalization" within the great world of the common culture, becomes legible and visible in a way it does not through the figures of our other triumphant cultural icons such as LaGuardia and DiMaggio. They are relatively straightforward signifiers of Italian Americanness, in whom the discrepancy between the hegemonic version of the American dream and the Italian American version of it collapses. Sinatra instead subverts this facile conflation of American dreams and thus in a more complex way serves as both a signifier and symptom of the Italian American identity, as a figure through whom our unconscious is made to speak. He is our crazy mirror in which our grandiose self is at once authentically reflected and simultaneously distorted and displaced; he is the only Italian American cultural icon of his generation to manufacture negative experience and thus call into question the colonized, conformist self.

Sinatraism, or, the Territorial Self

Of all American performers, Sinatra is the one most intricated in the aggressive performance of the grandiose self. Whereas Arnold Shaw acutely described Sinatra as embodying a "constant counterpoint between toughness and tenderness" (1968: 12), that counterpoint is more fully understood when it is situated within the dynamics of the Italian American territorial self. Having struck the Faustian bargain with the media from the outset, Citizen Sinatra waged a steady agon with the press and other intruders to re-territorialize his preserve—privacy, artistic privilege, and the taste culture (the ideal of "classiness") he upheld, "respect," and the Italian American subculture—that preserve being the very thing that was forfeited as his part of the bargain. Through identification with his confrontational self, the American public came to hold the torch for Ava Gardner; to engage in the career brinksmanship of his repeated comebacks—above all, the first comeback as negotiated by his role as Maggio in *From Here to Eternity* (1955); to appear at the "wrong door" with DiMaggio, our two Italian heroes in search of the American obscure object of desire, whether blonde and breathless or brunette and barefoot; to play the phallocentric game of musical beds with "broads" and starlets in search of the forever lost object of desire; to charm widows in the name of the mutually lost object and to slug the paparazzo who referred to Judy Garland as a "broad"; to engage in the infantile hipsterism of the Rat Pack, the Clan as being one more instance of the territorial self; and, in sum, to play out the board game called "My Way," which connects presidents to Mafiosi, Madonnas to *puttane,* Hollywood to Hoboken via Las Vegas, the *bella figura* to the *brutta figura.* Can all this—not to mention the dilettantish political turn from liberalism to Reaganism—be understood in Italian American terms as an attempt to overcome the marginalized and slighted ethnic self by constructing a grandiose self, defiant and hobnobbing, one that involves the vulnerable young Sinatra hardening, over the years, into the all-attitude tough guy, the Chairman of the Board?

Can the meaning of Sinatra's music be distinguished from the meaning of Sinatra? The question of Sinatra's persona is much more complex than that of, say, Elvis Presley or the Beatles, the two other musical phenomena that have had similar impacts on popular music. Sinatra had the effect of one of those multistable figures studied in gestalt psychology that turns from beautiful maiden to old hag, depending on where one focuses. What Italian Americans, especially of his generation, and other outsiders saw in addition to "the greatest singer in the history of American popular music" (Rockwell

1984: 12) was the following: the man who tries "to do it all in one generation, fighting under his own name, defending underdogs, terrorizing top
dogs" (Talese 1966: 114); the man who throws a punch at a musician who
said something anti-Semitic and who snarls at a Red-baiting columnist, "If
being a Commie means sticking up for the little guy, I'm Red through and
through"; the man who espouses the African American cause two decades
before it was fashionable and does not allow black friends like Sammy Davis
Jr. to be treated with any less respect than he demands for himself; the man
who serves as a "kind of one-man, Anti-Defamation League for Italians in
America." (Some of the above examples are taken from Gay Talese, who
views Sinatra from an Italian American perspective.) What others, especially
the younger generations, saw besides the "greatest singer in the history of
American popular music" was a man whose "My Way" routine had become
a self-parody long before Sid Vicious; a man who was "obviously proud to
be close to notorious hoodlums," to use the words of William Safire of the
New York Times; the man who Bogarts everyone, including Speaker of the
House Sam Rayburn, who, after placing his hand on Sinatra's sleeve and re-
questing him to sing "The Yellow Rose of Texas," received a bit of Hoboken
stichomythia: "Get your hand off the suit, creep!"; the man who, when honored by the President's Medal of Freedom Award and an honorary doctorate
from Stevens Institute of Technology in Hoboken, was ridiculed by *Doones-
bury* cartoonist Gary Trudeau in a series of six strips for flaunting his mobster pals and for the *brutta figura* with the woman dealer in Atlantic City.

What is symptomatic about the negative perception of Sinatra is that it
demonstrates three laws regarding the stereotyping of Italian Americans
within the American imaginary network: They are always already stigmatized
by the generic Mafia taint; they are always regarded as politically incorrect,
regardless of whether they are on the left or the right (the Ferraro/D'Amato
syndrome); they are not allowed to manufacture negative experience, even in
defense of their own defamation, without that aggressiveness being read as a
displaced expression of *mafiosità.* In other words, Sinatraism—understood as
a generic second-generation self-affirming aggressive sensibility, a type of Italian American "Bogartism"—is perceived by the majority culture as "Little
Caesarism." "Doing it my way" is deemed a dangerous way of organizing the

signs of one's personality because it rejects the other-induced self, that authorized by the dominant culture, which, in the Italian American case, is the benign, conformist "Pinocchio-self," that accommodates itself to the other's negative fantasy by constructing itself according to an equally fantastic positive formula. This is not to absolve Sinatra from not distancing himself ethically from stigmatizing associations. Nor it is to propose the famous Freudian loophole: the bow of Philoctetes comes with the festering wound; artistic genius comes with a neurosis or demons not necessarily of one's own choosing. It is simply to indicate that Sinatra's position is symptomatic of the Italian position in the culture at large and that, as the voice of Italian America, he has problematized his identity in such a way as to be one of the few Italian Americans to impose the famous *"Che vuoi?"* on to the majority culture: "What do Italian Americans want?"

Postscript for J. Edgar Hoover, or, Singing the Dagotude Blues

Sinatra is as much to blame as are the moronic bobby-soxers.

—*J. Edgar Hoover*, The Sinatra Files

In *The Italian American Heritage* (1999), I have defined a number of identity tropes and tried to bring them to bear on the reading of Sinatra and other Italian American cultural figures. Such a reading attempts to restore to the ethnic subject those cultural dispositions and codings that tend to be deleted by the common culture or displaced by its regime of stereotypes. This restorative work is, at best, corrective and, when deprived of a critical edge, produces a protective reading that may move us either toward the infantile consolations of hagiography or, what amounts to the same thing, the trap of ethnocentrism. Therefore, an Italian American reading must do much more, and to do so, it must be rigorously critical in examining the process by and the terms in which a figure such as Sinatra is rendered a representative character for the common culture. This is especially true in Sinatra's case. He is the first Italian American figure to lay claims on cultural power without negating his ethnic self or restoring to the strategy of passing.

Although the magic of the Voice gave him immediate entrée into pop culture, his larger claims to a political and cultural voice were fraught with difficulties and were met with resistances that comment on Italian American agency within the dominant culture, especially during the postwar period (1944–1953), when he took a public stance as a socially conscious and committed artist of the left. His social activism, although based on "star power," was not an exercise in celebrity politics but represented an authentic politicization on his part, one that involved his passage from a liberal New Deal Democrat to a more radical position, which was generated by his involvement in "radical Hollywood" and an alignment, however, informal, with the cultural politics of the Popular Front social movement.

The making public, in 1998, of the Hoover-instigated FBI files radically alters our perception of Sinatra. (Excerpts, arranged thematically, from the 1,275-page dossier can be found in *The Sinatra Files,* edited by Tom Kuntz and Phil Kuntz, 2000.) Although their pathological and often wild documentation of Sinatra's activities tells us more about those who compiled them and the cultural unconscious of the Hoover era than about Sinatra himself, they do give real insight into the political Sinatra, who used his star power to support a wide range of "popular" causes and organizations that the FBI and the House Committee on Un-American Activities (HUAC) regarded as fronts for the Communist party. It is this Sinatra—"fellow traveler," not of the Communist party, but of the cultural front—and his negative reception within the America of Hearst, Hoover, and McCarthy that are most exemplary for Italian American self-understanding because they comment on Italian American political agency within the dominant culture. Jon Wiener has provided a perceptive overview of the political Sinatra in his brief essay, "When Old Blue Eyes was 'Red'" (1986), but it remains preliminary, in need of revision and extensive updating in light of the FBI files and our new understanding of radical Hollywood and the cultural front. Such a projected reading needs to situate Sinatra within the generational context of those "plebian" artists and intellectuals from immigrant and working-class families who emerged onto the mass-cultural scene as "New Americans," bearing with them the worldview and social consciousness generated by the ethnic or minority experience. Here I follow Michael

Denning who, in his *The Cultural Front* (1997: 154), correctly identifies Sinatra as one of these "plebian" or "cultural front" stars, placing him in a long list that includes: the singers Billie Holiday and Josh White; the bandleaders Artie Shaw, Benny Goodman, and Count Basie; the filmmakers Elia Kazan, Abraham Polonsky, Edward Dmytryk, James Wong Lee, and Leo Hurwitz; and the Italian American novelist Pietro di Donato and painter Ralph Fasanella.

The mention of Di Donato and Fasanella brings with it the long history of political radicalism at the heart of the Italian American experience—the fullest expression of which is the progressivism of Fiorello LaGuardia and U.S. Congressman Vito Marcantonio, both of whom operated under the sign of Sacco and Vanzetti, who were executed not because of their alienage as foreign bodies or for their anarcho-syndicalism but because they dared to exercise political agency. So just as Hoboken ward politics were passed to Sinatra through his mother's milk, as it were, so was the tradition of Italian American progressivism transmitted to him by the urban and immigrant life-world. And here it is good to recall that Sinatra was quite familiar with this tradition, having been summoned by LaGuardia at the behest of Marcantonio to address the feuding black and white students at Benjamin Franklin High School in 1945. Sinatra is a "fellow traveler" of this tradition, at least until he betrays it, during the 1970s, in the name of another "populism." Furthermore, there is both an Italian and Italian American component to Sinatra's early activism that needs to be examined. All too ironically, the FBI files bear witness to it. A typical example is the press release announcing Sinatra as the guest of honor at the Free Italy Society's annual ball (February 23, 1946), where he would speak on intolerance. He was quoted as follows: "I will be happy to join with my fellow Italian-Americans in the cause of true democracy" (Kuntz and Kuntz 2000: 64). The affair was convened, in fact, to fight domestic fascism as personified by Gerald L. K. Smith, the anticommunist zealot and bigoted leader of the conservative America First Party, the very same Smith who had later sent a telegram (December 16, 1946) to HUAC reporting that Sinatra had participated in a program sponsored by the American Union for Democracy, an alleged front for the Communist party, and who would soon appear at HUAC hearings, where he called on the committee to investigate Sinatra.

All of this material and much more must be brought to a reading of the activist Sinatra. He practices a "politics of the name"—what else?—that initially takes the form of a campaign against racial and ethnic intolerance. Emblematic is the ten-minute short, *The House I Live In* (1945), directed by Mervin Leroy, in which Sinatra, playing himself, takes time out "from radio rehearsals to lecture a group of anti-Semitic boys on the evils of prejudice," as the blurb goes. Here we see the young Sinatra in what would appear to be his most "politically correct" mode, to use an anachronism. He presents an inspirational version of the inclusive American self, informed by the tolerance gained from the ethnic and minority experience. Switching from his audience of bobby soxers to dead-end kids engaged in pack behavior, he offers a corrective street sermon against the evils of the game of the stigmatizing name: Racial and ethnic differences, he points out, "make no difference except to a Nazi or somebody who's stupid." The now-classic title song, "The House I Live In," written by Earl Robinson, appears to be a hymn expressive of music's power to create social harmony. But it is also the nearest Sinatra gets to a protest song in his opus, and its consciousness-raising agenda is not some generic version of the liberal fantasy set to words and music but a specific expression of the ethos of the Popular Front social movement.

The short, which was awarded a special Academy Award in 1946, was a sincere and constructive expression of a politics of conversion. However it may be read as propaganda, a mix of Hollywood liberalism and celebrity dogoodism, it was an authentic expression of Sinatra's tenement democracy and an onscreen version of the kind of youth-oriented social activism he was engaged in offscreen. (The script, written by the outspoken Albert Maltz, who would soon be blacklisted, was based, in fact, on Sinatra's spontaneous visits to high schools where he preached little sermons on tolerance.) The short was also politically correct in its mode of production: All the participants gave their services free of charge, and all the profits were donated to social work with adolescents. But its real political significance was as a declaration of Sinatra's public stance as a leftist.

He would then escalate his project, assuming the vice presidency of the Hollywood Independent Citizens Committee of the Arts, Sciences, and Professions in 1946 and membership in the Committee for the First Amendment (CFA), the short-lived Hollywood organization that sought to organize public support for a group of radical screenwriters and directors before their testimony to HUAC. This activity initiated a long combat against institutional name-calling—that is, Red-tagging and blacklisting. And here our hero finds himself engaged in an elaborate game of the name, played out in the press and in American public opinion, in which he would be both antagonist and victim. Although the game would involve new registers—political, criminal, and moral/sexual—and new counternames—"Mrs. Roosevelt in pants" (shorthand for fellow traveler of the Communist party) and "Frank (Lucky) Sinatra" (an allusion to his fraternization with "Lucky" Luciano and shorthand for fellow traveler of the Mafia "party")—it was, in effect, just a transposed and mass-mediated version of the Hoboken game of the ethnic slur, the same mean-streets game that Sinatra had attempted to combat in his campaign against racial and religious bigotry. At his American Dreaming best, the Sinatra of *The House I Live In* would soon find himself the Red-listed subject of HUAC, "named" twelve times. From this background emerges Sinatra's most exemplary political statement, from a radio broadcast in 1947, in which he criticizes HUAC's witchhunt: "Once they get the movies throttled, how long will it be before the committee gets to work on freedom of the air? How long will it be before we're told what we can say and cannot say into a radio microphone? If you make a pitch on a nationwide for a square deal for the underdog, will they call you a commie? Are they gonna scare us into silence?" Needless to say, the speech is not preserved in the FBI files.

At this point, Angles (his Hoboken nickname)—Red-tagged and Mafia-tarred—is only beginning to learn the rules of the game, and his later politics will be more calculated and opportunistic. The post–New Deal Sinatra does not go all the way to the left, as did Paul Robeson, and, unlike the Hollywood ten, he manages to salvage his career after the notorious "nosedive." He does remain a Democrat through his high-profile adventures with JFK and their immediate aftermath. His last radical gesture is the aborted attempt to hire, in 1960, the blacklisted Maltz as the screenwriter for *The Ex-ecution of Private Slovik.* After that, his politics are personal power politics and thus without content: The turn to the right is a travesty of the original turn to the left; the young man's tragedy, when repeated, becomes the old man's farce. There are many lessons to learn from Sinatra, but the most important are those of the second act (1944–1953). By defying the rules of the game—that is, by refusing to become a "house wop"—Sinatra targeted himself to be the target of Big Brother (the FBI, HUAC, the right-wing press); like the street fighter and cosmic punk Maggio, his cinematic alter ego, he demanded "the Treatment" he would receive. This Sinatra, the one who moved from "New Dealing crooner" to the Red list, summoned into play the American plague of fantasies just as effortlessly as he made the bobby soxers swoon.

15

I Get No Kick from Assimilation

or, "My" Frank Sinatra Problem

Rocco Marinaccio

The extent of Frank Sinatra's current cachet among academics is probably best illustrated by the evolving reaction of my colleagues to the Sinatra music and the Sinatra paraphernalia that have graced my offices over the last sixteen years. I've had various clippings, postcards, and the like; I'm now displaying a particularly beautiful framed poster, with a black-and-white grinning image of the young and bow-tied Frankie set against a yellow and purple background. Everyone these days pretty much thinks it's "cool" and says so when they first see it. Sixteen years ago, however, the reaction was quite different: "That's really funny." "You actually like that guy?" And, most tellingly, "You're such an Italian."

I must admit I was happier with these earlier reactions, particularly the last one. I did indeed believe that my abiding interest in Sinatra was a potent marker of my ethnicity and class background; as Sinatra scholar Leonard Mustazza writes, Italian Americans have long felt "empowered" by Sinatra, "the first Italian-American superstar" and one "who, without shame or apology, has kept his ethnic identity" (1995: 9). The presence of Sinatra in my office was my way of emulating my *paisan* in terms of his historically stubborn refusal to shed his ethnic identity. With *Swing Easy* emanating from my boom box, I knew that no one was going to mistake me for one of the majority of academics with privileged professional backgrounds or for one of those others who shared my ethnic and working-class roots but who quietly (and often quite willingly) obscured them. Despite an increasing interest in ethnicity and class as subjects of inquiry, academia has conventionally resisted acknowledging the variant class and (at least among whites) ethnic identities of its membership, thereby preserving both its self- and public image as an elite institution. When academics look around a meeting table, begin a conversation at a campus function, or generalize about the members of "our profession," they are likely to assume that their colleagues share similar culturally and economically privileged backgrounds. I have heard more disparaging comments about the working classes and have sat silently through more animated conversations about undergraduate idylls in leafy college towns (I commuted three hours a day on New York City buses) or summers in Europe (I was working, sometimes at two jobs) than I care to remember. Thus, as one of the growing numbers of academics with an ethnic, working-class background, I was glad that the Sinatra music playing in my office blocked these conventional assumptions, drew attention to my difference, and thus disrupted the convenient fictions that underlie the academy's elitism.

The problem I face is one of assimilation: In order for academia to maintain its traditional assumptions about ethnicity and class, I need, somehow, to be seen as having abandoned—in fact, transcended—my ethnic and class origins. In this way, I face a problem similar to Sinatra's, whose first professional battle with the forces of assimilation may have been his rejection of Harry James's request that he change his name to Frankie Satin. Sinatra's reply, "[N]o way baby. The name is Sinatra. Frank fucking Sinatra," illustrates his decades-long insistence on being taken both as a serious and influential musician and as the product of working-class Italian America

(Hamill 1998: 38). Those characteristics that came—rightly or wrongly—to be associated with Sinatra's ethnic and class origins were always the most troubling aspect of his incarnation; many Americans—especially in the media—loved the music but wished he would act just a little bit less like a damn dago from Hoboken. It's no surprise, then, that the hostility was the worst during those years of the Rat Pack, the Clan, the Summit. Think of it: Sinatra, one more Italian American, and two Jews—one white and one, of all things, black. All of them from humble beginnings. And they had the world on a string. Shawn Levy's lively history of the Pack's glory days, *Rat Pack Confidential,* vividly documents the hostility of their critics: "Their horsing with race and religion has . . . gotten out of hand," cried Las Vegas columnist Ralph Pearl (you think he'd be *used* to such antics), while show-biz journalist Joe Hyams soberly warned them to start acting like "serious citizens" (Levy 1998: 118, 185). Finally, when, during the 1960 campaign, *Time* magazine intoned, "some of JFK's biggest headaches may well come from the ardently pro-Kennedy clique known as the Rat Pack or Clan," even the normally pugnacious Sinatra felt moved to suggest that "[t]he Clan is a figment of someone's imagination," while Dean Martin sought to quiet mid-America's fears about the group by suggesting that, "[i]f anything it's more like the PTA—a Perfect Togetherness Association" (Levy 1998: 185—86).

I'm willing to bet that Dino really did think that the letters "PTA" stand for "Perfect Togetherness Association." How many other American men, however, could have claimed such obliviousness to suburban life? How many American men would have sorely loved to? It is this obliviousness to the postwar, suburban version of the American dream that underlies the Pack's subversiveness, whether the boys were being reviled by their critics or lionized by their fans. As Frank, Dean, and Sammy rioted through Vegas, Miami, and New York, millions of American men settled into suburban homes, booming families, and humdrum desk jobs. In stark contrast to the suburban ideal, the members of the Rat Pack were resolutely urban and explicitly ethnic. What's more, they showed up drunk for work, and, despite the presence of wives and children, they hardly seemed constrained by the conventional bonds of marriage and fatherhood. In so resisting the dominant narrative of assimilation at mid-century—work hard, get married, have kids, and leave the ethnic urban enclave for a homogenous suburb—Sinatra and the Pack threatened the guardians of middle America. America likes successful immigrants, but it likes immigrants who act like Americans: It's the bargain America offers. Become an American—work hard, go to church, join the Elks Club—and *then* you will be rewarded. This prescription provides the necessary engine for assimilation—how else, in a land of immigrants, to get the teeming masses to compose a society? Poised against this central tenet were Sinatra and his pallies. Could they have been any more self-conscious about their alienation from middle-class life? While America was fleeing its city centers, the Pack haunted Vegas, L.A., New York, and Miami. Rather than lose their ethnic and racial identities, they embodied them. Dino's nickname was, after all, "Dago," one that he often turned on the Leader himself. Sammy's was "Smokey" (and it wasn't referring to the cigarettes). Jewish jokes. Mob jokes. And of course the long-running gag about the diminutive Sammy being presented to Frank or Dean as an NAACP trophy. In so making their ethnic, racial, and religious differences the subject of their onstage patter, the members of the Pack were, in fact, seeing each other and the society at large in the way that the hyphenated American does. The resident of the ghetto or the immigrant neighborhood is acutely conscious of his own hyphenated status and, as a result, far more conscious of that of others. It is usually among the middle to upper classes that such a level of ethnic or racial awareness dissipates, where the assimilated citizen loses his or her ethnic identification and becomes an "American" without the hyphen. And it is in the suburbs, where the ethnic neighborhood fast becomes a dim memory and where Jewish and Italian mothers start cooking recipes out of *Good Housekeeping,* that group identity is shifted to primarily economic status.

As if their self-conscious ethnic and racial difference did not mark them as vigorously anti-suburban, Sinatra and the Pack gleefully flaunted their disengagement from the family lifestyle that is the raison d'être of the suburbs. Indeed, in the late 1950s and early 1960s, Sinatra the middle-aged playboy was the embodiment of everything the American man had been urged to deny himself since the end of World II, when, in the move to establish postwar normalcy, considerable social pressure—in forms as varying as federal housing and education loans, television sitcoms, and helpful tomes such as *The Veteran and His Marriage*—pushed American men to marry, to work hard at the office, and to settle their growing families into a shiny new suburban neighborhood of single-family dwellings. And, as the baby boom and the decline in the divorce rate demonstrate, they did as they were told.[1] Through the 1950s and early 1960s, as American married men faithfully came home to their wives and children (or were, at least, being routinely urged to do so), Sinatra left his family for the world's most beautiful woman and, later, a legendary string of stars, starlets, showgirls, and hookers. As the outpouring of public vilification during the period of his divorce from Nancy and his remarriage to Ava Gardner suggests, Sinatra's rejection of home and hearth flew in the face of the domestic values of the times. In hindsight, however, his departure from the nuclear family makes him seem to have been a man just slightly ahead of his time, for the divorce rate began to skyrocket just as the Pack took the stage in Vegas. Soon it would double that of the 1950s, as American men (and women) sought something beyond the postwar family ideal. We can only wonder how many of the men who got divorces, grew out their hair a bit, and cruised for chicks in the swingin' sixties carried in their minds the inspiration of Sinatra's life-changing cutting of the apron strings.

In this way, Sinatra's very public private life can be seen as an early indication of the growing dissatisfaction with the suburban family ideal, and his carousing lifestyle suggested another way to live and live well. Throughout the Rat Pack era, books with colorful titles such as *The Crack in the Picture Window* and *The Split-Level Trap* typified the growing critique of suburban life and its tendencies to conformity, duty, and homogeneity. Sloan Wilson's Tom Rath, "the man in the gray flannel suit," became an archetype of middle-class male dissatisfaction: All over America family men were playing by the rules, yet going to bed at night with a gnawing sense that they were missing the kind of party Sinatra seemed to be living twenty-four hours a day. These poor slobs, in the Pack's memorable lingo, were the "harveys." So while he may not have been penning any of the controversial media attacks on suburbia, Sinatra's music, movies, and lifestyle nonetheless articulated an alluring alternative to suburban values. Barroom brawler, adulterer and absent father, habitué of America's most sinful urban places, Sinatra drank and smoked his way through the night that all the other nine-to-fivers slept soundly through so they could get up the next morning and go to work just as he was rolling home for some shuteye.

Rejecting the suburban family and its putative rewards, Sinatra's path diverged from those many other ethnic Americans on the way to assimilation. Nowhere, however, was Sinatra's rejection of assimilation—particularly in its 1950s' manifestation—more notable than in his happy abandonment of America's most cherished belief and the prime engine of assimilation: hard work. In *The Man in the Gray Flannel Suit* (Wilson 1955), Tom Rath is repeatedly urged to hustle and is repeatedly chided for failing to do so. His climactic exchange with his boss, himself a great "success story," illuminates the give-it-your-all work ethic that dominated the booming white-collar workplace. Rath begins: "'I don't think I'm the kind of guy who should try to be a big executive. I'll say it frankly: I don't think I have the willingness to make the sacrifices. . . . I'm not the kind of person who can get all wrapped up in a job—I can't let myself be convinced that work is the most important thing in the world.'" His boss, Ralph Hopkins, replies "passionately": "'Somebody has got to do the big jobs. . . . This world was built by men like me. To really do a job, you have to live it body and soul. You people who give half your mind to your work are just riding on our backs'" (277–78).

Such testimony to the necessity of hard work goes back to the dawn of American culture, particularly in the context of the assimilation process. From its earliest formulators—John Winthrop, J. Hector St. John de Crevecoeur, Benjamin Franklin—the American dream has promised success as a result of virtuous industry. St. John de Crevecoeur concludes his famous "What Is An American?" (1782) with the voice of America speaking to the immigrant: "Welcome to my shores, distressed European: bless the hour in which thou didst see my verdant fields, my fair navigable rivers, and my green mountains!—If thou wilt work, I have bread for thee; if thou wilt be honest, sober, and industrious, I have greater rewards to confer on thee—ease and independence" (89–90). It is precisely his earnest labor that will transform the immigrant from a European to that new man, the American.

At the top of the world in Sin City, USA, acting more than anything else like a gang of Lower East Side street urchins who hit the big time, Sinatra and the Pack exposed the greedy heart of the American dream, achieving almost unimaginable success, riches, and power *without* towing the moral line conventional formulations of the dream prescribe. From the days of the Puritans, the moral requirements for material success—honesty, sobriety, industriousness—have been a necessary bit of self-delusion: Without them, the dream and, even, the national mission are reduced to the most sheerly economic terms. Sinatra's crushing blow to this national self-delusion was that he refused to go along with the idealized version of American success, unashamedly illuminating what it really took to make it to the big room. He showed America that success came not from virtue but from innate talent coupled with a hard-knuckled assertion of self, a prescription for success a lot closer to the gruesomely monumental egoism of "My Way" than to the sober industriousness of Crevecoeur or the slavish dedication of Wilson's Ralph Hopkins.

Indeed, sober industry hardly seemed to be the order of the day when the Pack installed a bar onstage at the Sands—what better image to remind us that these guys were hardly sweating for their paychecks? While there will be no argument from this corner that Sinatra was anything but a dedicated and accomplished musician, the Pack's movies and stage shows were certainly pretty loose affairs, and whatever toil might have been involved, Frank (and the whole gang) *seemed,* at least, to just be playing around. Wasn't that, in any case, the point? Over the wild Vegas days and nights during the filming of *Ocean's Eleven*—when the Pack shot the movie by day and caroused on stage at the Sands by night—Sinatra and his pals managed to turn a putative sixteen-hour workday into something more like spring break for grown-ups. Shawn Levy's account of the party shows that what might have been a grueling month and a half was, in fact, dominated by the kinds of insubordination, self-indulgence, and disengagement that a *real* working man dreams about. On the set during the day, Sinatra arrived at his self-appointed hour (whenever that was, and it was usually in the afternoon), rarely worked more than three hours, and even blew town when he felt like it. When the Pack was actually *on* the set, they let the nominal boss, director Lewis Milestone, know who was really in charge. When Sinatra had enough takes of a scene, that was it. When the boys didn't want to memorize the script, Milestone set up off-camera cue cards. When they didn't want even to read the cue cards, Sinatra just ripped pages out of the script. And when they weren't acting they were acting up, tossing cherry bombs and dueling with water pistols on the set.[2] Meanwhile, we should note, American men, particularly those suburbanites who made up much of America's growing managerial class, were being indoctrinated into what sociologist and urban theorist William Whyte calls the "social ethic," in which they were urged to subvert their own interests for the good of the whole, frequently undergoing a barrage of psychological tests on the job to determine their facility to efface themselves (White 1956: 7).

Moreover, at the risk of lobbing a weighty theoretical term into the midst of the Pack's mindless carousing, it might be said that the Pack's stage appearances themselves are, in fact, a deconstruction of the conventional stage show. The Pack's abandonment of sobriety and structure undermines the basic conventions of "professional" performance: Polished dialogue, music, and dancing; the commitment to giving one's all to the audience; politeness to one's fellow performers. Much of what transpired onstage at the Sands—and at the other venues in which the Pack appeared—was a shambles. Sure—Joey wrote some material and was a quasi-MC. But the effect of a Pack performance was the audience's shocked delight in chaos: ceaseless ad-libbing, gleeful fluffing of dialogue, musical numbers that went nowhere, and terrible jokes, many of which, of course, arose during someone's attempts to sing. Every night's performance held the potential for new and more thrilling disorder. Could the boys get through an entire set (and I use *that* word loosely) without even finishing one song? How many lyrics could they butcher? How many romantic tunes could they de-romanticize? How many swinging numbers could they bring to a halt? How many punch lines could they step on? While Frank and Sammy, in particular, regularly had moments of intensely "straight" performing, the presence of these numbers amid the general chaos in fact tends to emphasize the Pack's overall refusal to perform: By giving us glimmers of brilliance, they ultimately show us just how much they are holding back, just how much they are actually *refusing to work*. This is perhaps most vividly demonstrated in the routine ribbing of Sammy, who, more than any of the rest, specialized in the give-'em-your-all style of performing. Suchlike demonstration of the work ethic was too much to remain untrammeled by this crowd, and the group antics (which dominated the second half of the show, after everyone's individual numbers) often focused on undermining Sammy's burning desire to do his job. One moment in particular stands out from the Pack's St. Louis performance in 1965. In his solo segment, Sammy delivers a breathtaking impersonation medley. Later, with all the boys onstage, Sammy ventures to do some more imitations, but with every introduction—"Ladies and gentlemen, Clark Gable"—he is cut off by Frank's pretty mediocre Cagney: "You dirty rat." It's hard, at this point, for the audience member not to *want* to see more of Sammy's efforts, but with the Pack assembled, effort is not the point.

By raking in the big bucks without legitimately working for them, Sinatra was a threat to the national imagination exactly like all those gangsters he said he never knew as well as we all know he did. Particularly during the Great Depression, when honest, hardworking Americans waited in bread lines, took to the rails, and camped out in countless Hoovervilles all across the American landscape, the gangster seemed to show that playing by the rules was for suckers and that there were all kinds of ways to dream your American dream that Horatio Alger wouldn't tell you about but that were, hell, pretty much in the spirit of the thing. Especially if your name was something like Capone, Luciano, Siegel, or Lansky. Writer Robert Warshow's classic delineation of the gangster persona in "The Gangster as Tragic Hero," in fact, rather strikingly captures the brawling Sinatra persona, the Sinatra of "My Way," particularly in its description of "success" gangster style: "brutality at once becomes the means to success and the content of success, a success that is defined in its most general terms, not as accomplishment or specific gains, but simply as the unlimited possibility of aggression" (1948/1972: 132). Sinatra's intimacy with such men, then, was an affront to America not only because he consorted with—and perhaps aided—men who broke the law, but because such powerful criminals only shone more light on the ugly reality of the American dream that Sinatra made brutally plain: Virtue has nothing to do with it.

Perhaps even more threateningly, the Sinatra saga, as it played out for fifty years before an attentive American public, undermines not only the moral facade of the American dream but also the fiction of the immigrant's assimilation to a coherent American identity. The enigma of Sinatra has long been the tension between two seemingly irreconcilable personae: The groundbreaking interpreter of America's greatest, wittiest, most urbane popular music and the dago thug who seemed unwilling (or unable) to leave the streets of Hoboken behind. The conservative writer Joseph Sobran, for example, considers it a "wonder . . . that this uncouth man once sang the best *American* popular songs . . . with such uncanny sensitivity and finesse" (1992: 54; italics mine). This perceived duality, I argue, would not seem contradictory or inconsistent to the immigrant, who generally recognizes the extent to which the "American identity" he or she assumes by means of assimilation has less to do with transforming some "essential character" than with enacting public behavior to a significant degree distinct from private behavior frequently aligned more closely to ethnic and class origins. One might note here any number of examples from immigrant autobiography and fiction. Anzia Yezierska's autobiographical novel *Bread Givers* (1925), a classic of the immigrant experience, traces a young girl's life in America from her arrival at age five from Poland through her "assimilation," which is largely achieved by means of her education and her entry into the ranks of the professional class. At one point in the novel, she attends her mother's funeral clad in her new—and her only—professional suit and is consequently derided for refusing to rend her garments like her more traditional, less assimilated sisters. Her grief, she claims, is no less than that of her sisters, but she needs the suit—the signifier of her "American" identity—when she leaves the private world of the Jewish community for the outside, public world of "America."

Yezierska's recognition of the performative aspect of the "assimilated" American identity ought to shed light on Sinatra's penchant for moving from cocktails with Cole Porter to a pasta dinner with made men. This is what immigrants do: They learn quickly to act "American" when in view of the public and then they go home and speak, eat, love, or fight in accordance with family and ethnic traditions often radically at odds with those of the public sphere. Such a distinction between public and private identities Sinatra would have learned as a boy in Hoboken. His father, after all, assimilated by means of a name change, when the Italian boxer Marty Sinatra became the Irish boxer Marty O'Brien. And indeed young Frankie was known as

"Slacksy O'Brien"—a reference to his love of snappy dressing that suggests the young boy's awareness of image. How many other immigrants knew the performative nature of assimilation, knew that an American identity rests on appearance, not essence? The many names changed at Ellis Island or by immigrants registering at schools or looking for jobs are testament to this. So also is the transformation of Dino Crocetti into Dean Martin and Joseph Gottlieb into Joey Bishop, the kind of transformation, we should remember, Sinatra specifically rejected.

Put simply, Sinatra's problems generally arose because he, at least for most of his life, too often refused to keep his private life private. Rejecting ethnicity as a "private" identity, he sought to live both his assimilated American self and his originary ethnic self in the public eye. So when Kitty Kelley, in her bilious biography (1986), asserts that Sinatra's failure to acquire "Anglo-Saxon sheen" is the core of his problem, she indeed has it right. Although her tone of moral superiority suggests her continued investment in the fiction of assimilation propagated by the mainstream culture, in pointing to American identity as a function of surface, she unwittingly deconstructs the myth of American identity as she is deriding Sinatra for doing so himself. Insisting that a place be made at the heights of American culture for an "unassimilated" Italian, Sinatra flew in the face of our cherished belief that the assimilated immigrant—or anyone who has apparently traversed his class or ethnic origins—is someone *essentially different* from the person he once was. We want to believe that the name change, the gray flannel suit, and, more than anything else, the material success signifies that the person with that funny last name has gotten with the program. How else to rest easily about the millions of foreign born and their children rising up into positions of power and influence? Thus Sinatra's *goombah* persona embodied a perennial American nightmare: The unwashed are climbing out of the tenements and are calling the shots. It's their world, and we just live in it.

Where else is this fear more vividly demonstrated than in the oft-recited narrative of Sinatra's devotion to and rejection by the Kennedys? And who other than Jack and Bobby Kennedy, not far removed from the old sod and even closer to the sleazy world of Joe Sr. and his bootleggers, would be aware of the need to maintain a public perception of distance from the less clearly assimilated Sinatra? The history of immigration in the United States is one of various nationalities arriving in successive waves, often occupying the same neighborhood at different periods in time, as one group moves up and out to be replaced by a more recently arrived one. Along the way of assimilation, each group learns to define itself as American by differentiating itself from the more recently arrived group. In the eastern cities that gave us the Kennedys and the Sinatras, nowhere is this process—and its resultant tensions—more clearly illustrated than by the story of the Irish and the later-arriving Italians. One only need to remind oneself of the compelling title of Noel Ignatiev's recent history of the Irish Americans—*How the Irish Became White* (1995)—to remember the Irish immigrant's hard-fought battle for a place at the American table and thus to understand how the Kennedy alienation of Sinatra was a continuation of a long-standing ethnic relation in which, once again, the anxiety of the Irish American over his own tenuous American identity manifested itself in public efforts to distance himself from the less American Italian.

It is worth considering, then, that twenty years after being tossed away like a bad clam by the Kennedys, Sinatra ended up as the main man at the Reagan White House. There is much at issue here: Differences between the Kennedys and the Reagans, different conceptions of the office of president, and, perhaps, America's progress in accepting cultural diversity. But it must be acknowledged that contemporary versions of Sinatra's life are narrated in a traditional way, as the paradigmatic rags-to-riches immigrant story. In his final two decades, he settled into a more consistent public performance of an assimilated American self. Much of the recent telling of his life, which makes much of his so-called rise from his original ethnic and class status, suggests the widespread public perception of this assimilation. John Lahr writes that "Sinatra's life has been one long slow mastery over his Hoboken origins" (1997b: 77). At a White House dinner for Italian prime minister Andreotti in 1973, Richard Nixon said of Sinatra: "This house is honored to have a man whose parents were born in Italy but yet from humble beginnings went to the very top in entertainment" (Kelley 1986: 417). And the narrative of assimilation to a large degree structures Pete Hamill's consideration of Sinatra's life in *Why Sinatra Matters*: "The life and career of Frank

Sinatra are inseparable from the most powerful of all modern American myths: the saga of immigration. Because he was the son of immigrants, his success thrilled millions who were products of the same rough history. Through the power of his art and his personality, he became one of a very small group that would permanently shift the image of Italian-Americans. Many aspects of his character were shaped by that immigrant experience, which often fueled his notorious vitality. More important, it infused his art" (Hamill 1998: 37).

Elsewhere, Hamill is quoted by John Lahr: "The story of Sinatra . . . [and] of all kinds of people of our time is that they had to cross the bridge either from Jersey or from Brooklyn to Manhattan and have people say 'You fit.'" (1997b: 77). When and how did Frank Sinatra acquire this "fit"? When and how did he become a "good immigrant" after decades of bucking assimilation? I'd say it was in the last twenty-five years, and I'd say it was, in part, because the new culturally sanctioned Sinatra was largely washed of his ethnic identity. Sinatra's various personal and professional debacles in the 1960s and 1970s—the Kennedy campaign, the marriage to Mia Farrow, the mess with Sam Giancana and the Cal-Neva Lodge, and the "retirement" of 1971 and the resumption of his career in 1973 (events punctuated with numerous recordings of all kinds of unsuitable material)—all suggest a man searching for some kind of answer in all the wrong places. What he finally found, I think, was the role of an elder statesman, the "Chairman of the Board," the components of which role all were at peace with America's notions of success: friend of the president, husband of the blond Los Angeles matron, millionaire philanthropist, and cardigan-clad denizen of Palm Springs, painting clowns and flowers in his home studio. At this point, the most visible manifestation of his ethnic identity was his spaghetti sauce; ethnicity, thus, was no longer a threatening fact of the man but quite literally a contained, quaint commodity.

My Frank Sinatra problem, then, is certainly not the Frank Sinatra problem that the Kennedys, Kitty Kelley, and various other Americans have had with him. *My* Frank Sinatra problem might be what I see as Frank's final alienation from his roots. But while I still shudder at the thought of Sinatra at the Reagan inaugural gala, serenading the new first lady—surely a singularly humorless

woman—with, of all things, "Nancy With the Laughing Face," I can understand why he—and many other ethnic and working-class voters—sadly forgot
their roots and joined the Reagan juggernaut against America's disenfranchised.
Finally, *my* Frank Sinatra problem is America's frequent demand that he—and
anyone else who lays claim to America's bounty—be "assimilated." When I
think of the dominant culture's desire to see Frank acquire some of that "Anglo-
Saxon sheen," when I think of the experiences I and many other academics
with ethnic or working-class roots share in an institution that has its way of assimilating us by, somehow, not seeing us, I am wary of what will happen to
Frank Sinatra as he becomes academia's pop text of the moment. I acutely feel
the loss of Sinatra as a marker of my difference from many of my professional
colleagues, and the queasy sensation I get when I see him turned into yet another specimen for academic dissection (even as I run the risk of doing it myself) seems, in fact, to be shared by many in the audience at the Hofstra
conference, where this essay was first presented. The free-for-all atmosphere
that dominated the various question-and-answer sessions powerfully revealed
the profound differences between Sinatra's academic and popular reception, between his academic critics and his (largely working-class) fans. Armed with theories, historical contexts, comparative analyses, and textual close readings, the
scholars made much of Sinatra's many meanings as a conflicted emblem of
American masculinity; as an innovative forger of divergent musical, racial, and
class discourses; and as a proto-postmodernist whose what-the-hell attitude
makes rock and roll's earnestness look positively humanistic. Few of these analyses, however, consistently engaged the hundreds of non-academic fans who attended the three-day conference in earnest. Few of these analyses responded to
their interests and questions, which are typified by one response to my paper:
"They say he was the greatest entertainer of the century. Do you agree?" What
the fans sought from those of us onstage was an affirmation of *their* interpreta-
tions of Sinatra—as the great singer, the high liver, the generous (yet self-
effacing) philanthropist, and ethnic hero.

Not surprisingly, they didn't get it. The days wore on, and panel sessions
grew ever more restive as the fans in the audience grappled to maintain the
legitimacy of their version of Sinatra in the face of what surely must have
seemed a dizzying and only partly accessible series of readings of someone

they believed they *knew*. Even the panel on Sinatra and Italian American culture (with three Italian American panelists), where one might have thought to find a *simpatià* between the paisans in the audience and on the dais, bristled with tension. As the papers proceeded, I didn't need the occasional interruptions from the audience to realize their growing dissatisfaction. Even as the academic in me enjoyed the work I was hearing, the working-class Bronx Italian in me knew that this audience was not going where it wanted to go—again—and was not happy about it. So, after ninety minutes of postmodern theories of subjectivity, sociological analyses, and a number of references to Sinatra and the Mafia, I was not surprised when a member of the audience stood up and declared that she was tired of hearing about Frank and the mob and insisted that we remember that "We are all Italians and we are beautiful." That woman, I thought, knows what Sinatra means to her, and it wasn't—at least apparently—the same for the Italians on the dais, despite their best intentions. One speaker had, in fact, expressed prior to his talk his genuine pleasure in sharing, for the first time after years as an academic, his work with a preponderantly Italian American audience. "There's a lot of love in this room," he said as he began to speak. After his talk, I could only ask him if he had been attending the same conference as I had been.

I don't mean to suggest, however, that the frequent divisions between the audience and the scholars at this panel or at the conference as a whole point to some kind of critical illegitimacy. What I do want to draw attention to, however, is the way in which the academy—even that presumably hip, politically informed side of the academy that studies popular culture—shares with the mainstream society the inescapably conservative end of *assimilating* those subjects marked by class and ethnic identities divergent from its own. What the largely ethnic, non-academic audience sensed—rightly, I think—was their hero being reconstructed by the academics in their own images and for their own purposes. This phenomenon points to a troubling reality in the academic study of popular culture. While the study of popular culture has been seen as a hallmark of the democraticization of academic practice, the ruffled fan feathers at the Hofstra conference demonstrate the way in which such study often rests on co-option of the popular artifact. Frank Sinatra—like Elvis and Madonna before him—must, in some way, be *assimilated* into academic discourse—rather than be understood as he is understood in his original ethnic and class context—in order to become a legitimate object of interest or, even, pleasure. Good intentions no doubt abound and much worthwhile work no doubt is done in the various minority and popular cultural studies fields, yet it can also be argued that this work, in commodifying racial or ethnic identity and in constructing its authoritative readings of minority or popular figures, parallels the practice of "the melting pot" by undermining the very identity it wishes to explore and delegitimizing the interpretive authority of the popular audience.

Thus, like those popular biographers and music critics who wrestle with Sinatra's loutish behavior in the face of his ethereal singing, like the "American" who trembles at the seemingly unassimilated Sinatra calling the shots in L.A., Vegas, or—shudder—Washington, D.C., the literati desire an assimilated Sinatra: They are as anxious as the mainstream about the outsider Sinatra's masterful appropriation of the insider's cultural property. Perhaps the most apt (and certainly the most entertaining) example of Sinatra anxiety is John Picard's 1994 *Iowa Review* story, "Sinatra: A Memoir." In it a Johns Hopkins professor of classics meets and befriends Sinatra, having been summoned to Vegas by one of Sinatra's cronies. The Leader, it seems, has read some of his work and wants to talk. As the story begins, the narrator articulates all of the signs of the "elite" Sinatra fan. He expresses his greatest fondness for the Capitol recordings (the story is, in fact, set in 1959, thereby erasing any reference to the "My Way" era schlock). He's not interested in the swaggering pose and the legendary personal saga, but in the "pure"—in fact, somehow *literary*—aspects of the artist: "interpretation of lyrics, subtlety of phrasing, emotional nuance" (4). Most important, he echoes the recurrent disgust at Sinatra's "low" company and behavior and the typical inability to reconcile the vulgar (i.e., ethnic and working class) character with the sophisticated song stylings. But, on becoming an "unofficial member of the Rat Pack" (6), the narrator resolves the enigma of Sinatra:

> From the first stop of the tour I found myself summoned at all hours of the day and night. He would be pacing back and forth in his suite between shows or after an evening of heavy drinking or in the middle of an assignation. In-

variably, some of his lackeys would be present, the sharkskin-suited toughs who laughed at all his jokes, lit his cigarettes, procured female companionship; or some robed young woman sitting with her legs tucked under her, snapping her cigarette over an ashtray, glaring at the intruder. He would dismiss them with a wave. Often his first words to me would reflect a residual crudeness: "What is it with broads?" or "Who the hell needs this screwy business?" But as we got onto some more elevated subject, most often a continuation of some previous discussion (the French Revolution, Tu Fu, *Sputnik,* Watteau—his interests were stunningly wide-ranging), a change would come over him. He would begin to lose his restiveness, stop his pacing and eventually light on some chair or sofa. After half an hour most traces of his profane, hipsterish speech would have vanished, replaced by an articulate and refined mode of expression—although never entirely. I remember poignantly, for example, his referring to Robspierre as "one rebarbative cat." (3)

Here the story brilliantly resolves the perennial quandary of Sinatra's elite critics and fans by reassuringly representing the assimilated, "cultured" Sinatra as the "real" Sinatra, who is "a thinker, a polymath, a savant, an intellectual in the best sense of the word" (Picard 1994: 2). It is amazing, in fact, how many of Sinatra's friends and critics want to establish his intellectual mettle. Comedian Alan King, for example, a guest of honor at the Hofstra conference, was frequently quoted in the press commenting on Sinatra's affinities for the kind of critical discussion the conference featured. And Pete Hamill opens *Why Sinatra Matters* with a real-life scene reminiscent of Picard's fictional one: After dismissing some bimbo for her slim grasp of Hollywood history (she's never heard of Joan Blondell), Sinatra's interest turns to debating the relative merits of Fitzgerald and Hemingway (turns out he's a *Gatsby* fan). The thug is just a pose; he has, in fact, largely transcended his original ethnic, working-class identity, keeping only "traces" of that identity as a bit of piquant color to his "refined" personality (not unlike that spaghetti sauce he peddled during the Reagan years). And his intellectual nature finally explains the music: The "pathos and pain" of the Capitol recordings, the narrator muses, are the result of his intellectual alienation, "perhaps as much as his difficulties with Ava" (Picard 1994: 5). Sinatra's need for an intellectual life is so great, in fact, that the narrator worries that Sinatra is "becoming overly dependent" on him. Dependency problems aside, however, now that Sinatra has finally, for the first time in his life, "begun taking himself seriously as an intellect," the narrator finds "his singing ha[s] never been better" (3, 12). And, of course, with the full awakening of his intellectual life, Sinatra steadily withdraws from the vulgar ethnic community of his Rat Pack cronies into such a model of ivory-tower isolation that even the narrator begins to feel a little "stifled": "I enjoyed our talks as much as ever, but I needed a break once in a while, something I'm not sure he ever understood" (7). Here, finally, is the Sinatra to suit the fondest wishes of the elite: His "romanticized view of the intellectual life," which takes him even beyond the capacities of your everyday classics professor, is the root of his extraordinary song (7). As sad, lonely, and frustrated as the rest of us alienated intellectuals, he finally establishes his disgust for his low-rent cronies: "Dean doesn't even know when the Civil War was," he says, and "Sam thinks Rabelais is a type of cheese" (7).

I must admit to having had a desire to hear just such a dismissal usher forth from Sinatra's lips myself. Sure, I do wish he hadn't hung around with murderous creeps. I could certainly have lived without his slugging relatively powerless people like journalists and waiters around. And I hate the fact that he was so mean to Lauren Bacall. I'm not, finally, immune to the appeal of Picard's fantasy, just as I'm not finally immune to the desire to add my voice to the ever-louder conversation about Sinatra going on today in the academy. What I hope, however, is that our collective honesty about and interrogation of these desires to see a different Sinatra—a more "refined," a more "American" Sinatra—than the one he generally forced us to deal with for so many years will pave the way for a more genuinely inclusive conversation about class and ethnicity. Will we find ways to understand and to value Sinatra's class and ethnic origins in conjunction with his musicianship? Will we find ways to understand and to value Sinatra's meanings to ethnic and working-class Americans, distinct from those meanings made by academics? As we came to the end of the twentieth century—Sinatra's century—he, perhaps more than any other figure of his time, may have provided us with the occasion for a more enlightened look at ethnicity, class, and identity in American culture.

Notes

1. The boom in the birth rate is, by now, common knowledge, but it is perhaps worth illuminating the declining divorce rate after the war. Statistical formulations of course vary, but, in general, the divorce rate through the 1950s declined to pre-1940s levels, which Barbara Dafoe Whitehead attributes to "[t]he post-war campaign for domesticity, combined with a generous package of government benefits for married GIs" (1997: 43).
2. Levy's account also illuminates the fabulously lucrative financial arrangement Sinatra wangled for *Ocean's Eleven*. He received $30,000 for bringing the story to Warner Brothers (even though it was Lawford who had originally purchased the idea from Gilbert Kay), $200,000 for appearing, and one-third of the gross receipts (which netted him about $1 million). Add to this take his 9 percent ownership of the Sands, which boomed during the weeks of filming and Pack appearances.

Coda

"One can be a *paisan* or a *padrone*—but not both."
—Anonymous

16

Prophet, Padrone, Postmodern Prometheus

Moral Images of Sinatra in Contemporary Culture

Edmund N. Santurri

"**F**rank Sinatra was a bad man." That judgment shadows and haunts every popular celebration of this extraordinary figure's achievements. The subtitle of a June 1995 *Village Voice* feature issue captured with some economy the culture's profound ambivalence toward the man: "American Music's Greatest Singer and Most Notorious Bully," the title proclaimed. *Bully*, yes, a familiar characterization, but other images rush to mind. Sinatra as crude, self-indulgent, narcissistic, obscene, abusive, tempestuous, volcanic, violent, alcoholic, adulterous, promiscuous, decadent, sybaritic, lascivious, misogynistic, exploitative, tyrannical, mean-spirited, cruel, sadistic, vindictive, paranoid. Sinatra as gangster groupie, as presidential pimp, as powermonger and idolator. Sinatra as punk, as two-bit hoodlum, as "spoiled brat" (Clarke 1997: 90). These are just some of the moral images that fund and complicate the popular consciousness of Frank Sinatra.

Of course, there are the loyal Sinatra fans, the Sinatraphiles whose aesthetic appreciation, ingenuous affection, heartfelt admiration, and sense of fairness inspire moral counterpoints to the "bad man" indictments. In these moral *apologiae pro vita Sinatrae*, "Ol' Blue Eyes" is the misunderstood man, the secret benefactor and philanthropist who silently assisted countless individuals in need and who raised billions for charitable causes, the indefatigably loyal father, friend, and associate, the tireless advocate of civil rights and egalitarian social arrangements, the vigorous proponent of world justice and peace whose principled commitments prompted him to serve as a money runner for Zionist patriots in the 1940s and yet later to establish a meeting center in Nazareth for both Jewish and Arab youths. For the most adamant apologists, Sinatra's episodes of bad behavior are finally peripheral to the central character, sideshows to the main event, or at the very least comprehensible given a capacious rendering of his personality and circumstances. If the man consorted with mobsters, this was unavoidable for nightclub and casino performers of the 1940s and on. If he was often domineering or excessively demanding in his personal relationships, this was the result of rigorous standards of loyalty applied both to himself and to others. If he was given to serial sexual liaisons, crude displays, temperamental outbursts, brooding withdrawals, these were at worst the underside of creative personality and genius, periodic eruptions of charismatic energy, spillings over of the same erotic power that fueled his art, expressions of the very manic-depressive sensibility that made for his greatest musical achievements, the exuberant songs for swinging lovers, the searing ballads lamenting love lost. If Sinatra's anger seemed boundless at times, this was the anger of a righteous indignation gone awry, the consequence of a moral sensibility under siege in a world where virtue is not rewarded after all. Under such adverse conditions, moral outrage easily turns into something indiscriminate, outrage without an object, outrage sans phrase.

This last image of Sinatra as a tragic hero whose moral fall was occasioned by hostile forces of a larger fallen world figures significantly in historian Jon Wiener's depiction of the man as a kind of political prophet victimized by right-wing agents virulently opposed to his progressive politics (1991: 263–79). According to this account, Sinatra starts out in the 1940s as a subversive political radical launching jeremiads against various forms of racial discrimination and social intolerance in America. He makes the film short, *The House I Live In* (1945), gives courageous anti-discrimination speeches in tension-filled, newly desegregated high schools, aligns himself with radical factions within the already leftish Hollywood Independent Citizens Committee, and supports Henry Wallace's presidential candidacy in 1948. As a consequence, Sinatra becomes the quarry of the right-wing establishment. He is labeled a communist in deliberations of the infamous House Un-American Activities Committee and attacked by the right-wing press as a "Red" sympathizer with violent tendencies and Mafia ties. Shortly thereafter, and as a result of the baiting by the right wing, his career goes into a tailspin only to recover with his performance in the 1953 film *From Here to Eternity.* His political activism continues with his support of JFK's presidential campaign and his hiring of blacklisted left-wing writer Albert Maltz for a projected film on Private Slovik, an American soldier executed for desertion, but right-wing operatives make an issue of the hiring, and Sinatra finally drops Maltz, apparently in response to pressure from the Kennedys themselves, whose patriarch Joseph P., was also a rabid anticommunist. After J. Edgar Hoover reveals to Bobby Kennedy the JFK-Sinatra-Judith Campbell–Sam Giancana quadrangle, the Kennedys drop Sinatra from their list of intimates. He responds by supporting Hubert Humphrey against Bobby in the 1968 presidential campaign, but the Humphrey people also regard Sinatra's reputation as a political liability and urge him away from the campaign. In 1972 he is investigated for alleged mob ties by a congressional committee headed by Democrats no less—one, indeed, a liberal, a friend of the Kennedys, and indebted to Sinatra for previous campaign support (John Tunney). The evidence proves inconclusive, and Sinatra walks away without further damage—except to his reputation.

Out of a sense that the Democrats had betrayed both him and their principles, Sinatra eventually turns to the Republican party, which he comes to see as the real agent of populism and whose standard bearers, Presidents Nixon and Reagan, accord him the public celebration and respect he never received from his Democratic friends. In Wiener's words: "Beaten down as an activist leftist, his career destroyed by the right-wing press, [Sinatra] made a stunning comeback, then found himself snubbed and abused by the liberals whose views he shared. Only then did he sign up with his old right-wing enemies" (1991: 263). Coming from a left-wing historian, these remarks are intended to present Sinatra's political shift as a moral fall—but Wiener also intimates a degeneration in terms less controversial: "[Sinatra's] turn to the right," he observes, "coincided with a deepened contempt for women and his most offensive public behavior ever" (269). The suggestion here is that Sinatra's political experience embittered and demoralized him—*literally* demoralized him, severely damaging his moral character, which became, ironically enough, the casualty of events set in motion by his earlier moral endeavors. There are many ways to kill a prophet, it would seem.

This picture has its attractions and carries a degree of plausibility, but there are obvious complications. First, while it is reasonable to think that the unfair treatment Sinatra received from his conservative enemies and less than faithful liberal friends might have brought out his worst tendencies, those tendencies were his, after all, and they were evident from the very beginning—for example, the nasty temper, the insensitivity in his treatment of women (particularly his first wife) (Taraborrelli 1997a: ch.1–13). Second, though the right-wing press did do considerable damage to his reputation and career, Sinatra brought much of the problem on himself with his brazen, reckless, and ostentatiously bad behavior. For example, while his enemies in the press certainly traded on rumor and undoubtedly exaggerated the extent and depth of his mob associations in the 1940s, Sinatra invited the distortions with his imprudent decision to visit Lucky Luciano in Havana. While Sinatra's violent attack on conservative columnist Lee Mortimer may have been provoked by Mortimer's unjust treatment of him, Sinatra did punch the columnist in the head in full view of a horrified public. While he was hounded by the press for his marital infidelity, Sinatra was ostentatiously unfaithful to his wife, and his affair with Ava Gardner was as damaging to his early career as anything.

A third difficulty with the political prophet-as-victim reading is that Sinatra's ethical and political history seems more equivocal at points than the reading makes it out to be. For example, given what we can now gather, Jack Kennedy, though a Democrat, was hardly a political liberal in any straightforward sense of the term, and Sinatra's attraction to "Chicky Boy" (Sinatra's pet name for JFK) seems to have had less to do with a shared interest in civil rights and more to do with Kennedy's power, charisma, and fondness for raucous boys-will-be-boys parties and serial sexual escapades with beautiful women. This is not to deny that Sinatra had genuine political and moral convictions but only to suggest that he was also deeply interested in power, personality, and influence, that this interest shaped his political commitments, and that noting these facts complicates our assessments of his political and moral history.

Most important, there was something ambiguous, troublesome, about Sinatra's egalitarianism from the very beginning. While there can be little doubt that he was genuinely outraged by racial and ethnic discrimination and that this outrage drew fuel from his own experience of discrimination as an Italian American as well as from his class consciousness of being, initially at any rate, an outsider to power and privilege (Lahr 1997a: 40), Sinatra's egalitarian gestures always carried a hint of elitism, condescension—and the personal beneficiaries of his democratic patronage sometimes paid a considerable price. Donald Clarke overstates the point but instructs nonetheless when he says: "On the plus side was [Sinatra's] instinctive feeling for the underdog; he hated racism, anti-Semitism or injustice of any kind. . . . But his hatred of injustice was in the abstract. When it came to individual underdogs, they were either his friends or his enemies, and woe to them if they stepped out of line; neither strangers nor close friends were immune" (1997: 208).

These remarks overstate the criticism because certainly Sinatra's defense and assistance of some "individual underdogs" demonstrated a substantial degree of concern beyond an "abstract" commitment to social justice. His support of Sammy Davis Jr. is a principal case in point. Yet Sinatra's relationship with Davis also illustrates the ambiguous character of Sinatra's egalitarianism. On one hand, no one did more than Sinatra to destroy the racist barriers to Davis's social and professional advancement. On the other hand, the hierarchical character of the Sinatra-Davis relation was painfully obvious—as Davis's wife May Britt persistently protested to no avail (Levy 1998: 274). Sinatra was the lord of the realm, who demanded unqualified devotion from all his vassals, including Davis. When Davis went too far and criticized Sinatra publicly, the lord ostracized the vassal until Davis begged for forgiveness. There were other patterns of deference and subordination in the Sinatra-Davis relation. For instance, it is hard not to wince at the accounts of Sinatra's public racial jokes at Davis's expense—even though the jokes seemed bereft of genuinely racist motivation and were clearly part of an act incorporating the kind of good-natured barbs one innocuously hurls at the best of friends (Zehme 1997: 79). Yet the reason the jokes are unsettling despite their apparent lack of authentically racist intention is that they reinforce the patterns of subordination constitutive of Sinatra's relation with Davis. Sinatra, the lord, had the right to make jokes, racial or otherwise, at his vassals' expense, and this was a prerogative he exercised indiscriminately—without regard, one might say, to race, ethnicity, or religion. Moreover, only the most privileged among the vassals were permitted by the lord to respond in kind. From all indications, Davis was not so permitted. Dean Martin, Joey Bishop, and Don Rickles apparently had more freedom, though there were other patterns of subordination in place with Bishop and Rickles. Martin seems to have been the one individual who had achieved a certain independence and virtually equal standing with Sinatra in the circle of close associates (Levy 1998: passim). In sum, and to shift the metaphor so that it matches his particular ethnic history, Sinatra's American democratic egalitarianism was always qualified by a kind of Mediterranean noblesse oblige with its various patterns of deference and subordination.

Almost a quarter century ago, author Gay Talese traced the roots of this Mediterranean disposition and comportment to Sinatra's Sicilian heritage (Talese 1966/1995: 99–129). In Talese's account, Sinatra's personality combined features of the Italian *padroni* (the bosses, the masters), who lorded unambiguously over their charges, with elements of the traditional Sicilian *uomini rispettati* (men of respect), "men who are both majestic and humble, men who are loved by all and are very generous by nature, men whose hands are kissed as they walk from village to village, men who would *personally* go out of their way to redress a wrong" (103). As man of respect and *il Padrone,* Sinatra was both beneficent patriarch and ruthless overlord. His profound acts of generosity to those in need cut a "*bella figura,*" and were, like the gestures of his Sicilian prototypes, exercises at once in both paternalism and power, fellow feeling and pity, care and condescension (Lahr 1997a: 59–60). For his splendid generosity, he expected in Sicilian style an unqualified and unilateral devotion, expressed in public forms of recognition that honored his place of privilege and authority. Sinatra was, as grand *patriarca,* the pinnacle of his moral community, the undisputed focal point of moral endeavor, the source of the most extraordinary benefaction, the rightful object of the most profound consideration, affection, and veneration. Subjects who failed to show the requisite deference could expect swift and decisive retribution. As Italo-hierarch, Sinatra was both communal judge and executioner, who punished wayward servants imperiously, expeditiously, precipitously, ruthlessly. He was quick to anger in response to insult or slight, and his precipitous rage was of a piece with his brilliant decisiveness, awful and arresting and submissively received by those around him. To understand Sinatra rightly, one might argue, is to understand him precisely in these Sicilian terms. In Sinatra and his associates, one easily insists, we encounter the inhabitants of an alien Mediterranean moral world that resists commensuration with American mainstream moral standards and sensibilities.

At this point, one is likely to hear the argument that the typical moral indictments of Sinatra's character require substantial qualification precisely because they abstract unduly from his Italian cultural surroundings. The indictments, in this view, would reflect a kind of ethnocentrism that judges Sinatra's character and action in terms foreign to his way of life, that is, in the terms of American bourgeois morality. Certainly there is a degree of wisdom in this argument. Indeed, one might press the point further and propose not only that we should be reticent about invoking American bourgeois moral standards in assessing Sinatra's life but also that American bourgeois society has something to learn morally from the Mediterranean ethos reflected in much of Sinatra's behavior. For instance, Sinatra's rigorous conception of interpersonal loyalty had a decidedly Italian character, and while one might be tempted to dismiss his version of *omertà* (the code of silence) as little more than an underworld doctrine permitting honor among thieves, one perhaps should be open to the possibility that sometimes there is honor among thieves and that occasionally the honorable thing to do is to protect the dishonorable friend or at least to recognize a tragic moral cost in betraying one's *paisano* for the sake of one's principles—difficult as this recognition may be for the American bourgeois moral consciousness with its relentless neo-Kantian emphasis on principled impartiality and its resistance to privileging special relations and particular associations in the formulation of moral judgments (Zehme 1997: 72).

Still, while we might concede that certain indictments of Sinatra reflect ethnocentric biases and ethical myopias of various kinds, it would be something of a stretch to suggest that Sinatra's Sicilian ethos rendered him largely immune to standard moral critiques rooted in American bourgeois sensibilities. For one thing Sinatra was, of course, Italo *American;* he lived in both the Italian and American bourgeois moral worlds, and that fact burdens any extenuation or justification of his behavior founded on observations of cultural difference. Yet even if one grants the controversial point that Sinatra was often decidedly Italian in moments when he is judged most negatively, that concession still leaves open the question whether the judgments are morally sound. Indeed, if the common moral consciousness can recognize some truth in Sinatra's Italian ways (e.g., regarding interpersonal loyalty), it can also recognize some error in those ways and some truth in American bourgeois moral ways. For instance, if we see something right in Sinatra's "Sicilian" outrage over Sammy Davis's breach of loyalty with the latter's public dissing of the "Chairman," we also appropriately cringe at the "Sicilian" severity of Sinatra's retributive response. If we commend Sinatra's Italian generosity, we also rightfully regret its patronizing, condescending, and oppressive expressions (Lahr 1997a: 40). If we marvel at the *bella figura* of his supreme beneficence, we are also reasonably appalled by his patriarchal presumptuousness, by the price he extracted for his gifts, by the high prerogatives he assumed, by the demeaning treatment of his friends, by the abuse, by the violent eruptions, by the typically acquiescent, indeed obsequious, responses of his associates.

All of this may seem obvious enough. Indeed, even within the most unassimilated of Italo-American communities, there was considerable moral ambivalence over the excesses of Italian patriarchy (Orsi 1985: 120–29). Yet in some accounts of Sinatra one detects at times an uncritical celebration of certain arguably Mediterranean flourishes in his character or perhaps an implicit special pleading rooted in the judgment, "That's just the Italian Frank." A perfect example is the famous incident of the porcelain birds (Talese 1966/1995: 104; Zehme 1997: 189). The setting is a party at the home of Sinatra's ex-wife, Nancy. A young female guest accidentally breaks one of Nancy's cherished pair of alabaster birds. Sinatra's daughter (also named Nancy), exclaims in momentary panic, "That was my mother's favorite." Father Frank, disturbed by his daughter's insensitive, if understandable, reaction, gives her his infamous steely-eyed look of angry disapproval, walks over to the scene of the crime, knocks the remaining bird off the table and breaks that one, too, puts his arm around the young guest, and says, in full view of an arrested audience, "That's O.K., Kid." A *bella figura,* indeed—brilliant, decisive, dramatic, and genuinely, if precipitously, calculated to ease the distress of his mortified guest. The performance of a moral virtuoso? Perhaps, but what about the elder Nancy's feelings? The birds were her "favorite," after all, not Frank's (at least so far as we know). Did he really have to break the second alabaster to make the point? In fact, while this incident is typically presented as an especially creative moment in a history of moral performances, Sinatra's grand gesture, for all its Italian theatricality, strikes the detached observer as morally ambiguous at best, a display of insensitivity as well as kindness, a flamboyant act that draws maximal attention to the agent's status as hero of the story and reaches for dramatic impact even at the moral expense of disregarding the interests and feelings of his former wife.

But such moral reservations, some might protest, are rendered insignificant, petty, by the sheer artistry, drama, power, and personality expressed in the moment. "How many people would have the imagination to do that?" Gay Talese asks in a recent memorial interview recounting the alabaster event (Talese 1998: 60). Imagination, creativity, charisma, genius, art, power, personality—these are the normative categories, it might be insisted, that apply centrally in any evaluation of Sinatra, the character, the artist, the man. Conventional moral criteria—finally—are beside the point. Sinatra was, in this account, less *il Padrone*, less a prisoner of ethnic and cultural form, and more a culturally transcendent creative force, an Hegelian "world-historical individual" who shaped the movement of the spirit in history and stepped on anything in his—and its—path, a magnificent, life-affirming, will-to-power who swept away the conventional, the mediocre, in supreme acts of creativity or who took up the ordinary and radically refashioned it to make it great. He was the Nietzschean *übermensch,* beyond good and evil in the standard sense of those terms, a generator of value utterly his own rather than a slave of value imposed by the world.[1] If he shocked and offended conventional morality, this was a price appropriately and justifiably paid for supreme human achievement, for exquisite art, for personality and creativity of the highest magnitude. As jazz pianist Marian McPartland has noted: "All the other stuff in his life, maybe if he hadn't been like that, he wouldn't have been such a great singer. It all melts in together, his experiences. I can't imagine a guy singing like that who's going to be a quiet, well-behaved, normal guy. In many ways he was normal. Of course, a lot of other people chase women today, even presidents, but Sinatra did make an art form of it, then he took all that stuff and put it into song" (Primack 1998: 32). Here is an image of Sinatra invited by the man himself in recordings like "My Way" and "That's Life," both of which depict the singer as a kind of Promethean hero proclaiming and preserving his individuality through sheer self-exertion, persistence, and defiance, and emerging victorious despite the impediments of the everyday world. Indeed, those recordings themselves, it might be proposed, serve as demonstration pieces of the man's enormous talent for lifting the ordinary and transforming it through sheer force of personality into something beyond the ordinary. In these recordings we have a singer whose vocal instrument has seen better days, who, despite singing flat in crucial musical moments, takes up songs with undistinguished melodies and the most banal, self-serving, painfully embarrassing lyrics and "puts them over," transforms them by sheer exertion of will and power of personality into rousing anthems of egocentric celebration and indelible cultural markers of the myth of heroic individualism (Friedwald 1995: 424, 445–47). No wonder Sinatra would refer to "My Way" in concert as the "*national* anthem," and he who creates national anthems that are essentially songs to himself can only inspire awe and wonder. Again, moral criticism seems utterly beside the point. Indeed, if such considerations persuade, they persuade a fortiori when the truly great musical performances are in full view. Sinatra's life has given us, after all, the art songs, the *lieder*, of American popular music. There may be certain moral regrets about that life, but they are simply overwhelmed by the aesthetic brilliance of the career.

Naturally, Sinatra's achievements as musical artist would be at the center of any appreciation of him as Promethean figure beyond ordinary moral assessment. But in certain quarters there is also the urge to see him as an artist in a larger sense and thus to enhance his Promethean status in effect. If Bill Zehme's treatment in *The Way You Wear Your Hat* (1997) trades on something more than a tongue-in-cheek, coffee table-book, conceit, it celebrates the singer precisely as one whose entire way of life was a work of art with its own uniquely fashioned, internal rules of comportment and engagement. To be sure, Zehme does connect Sinatra explicitly with a "lost art of livin'," and this might suggest a celebration of the man as the bearer of an important tradition threatened by extinction in a devitalized age. Yet what comes through mainly in Zehme's depiction is an image of Sinatra as a kind of postmodern innovator, a craftsman of existential meaning and value in a world objectively dispirited, "disenchanted" in philosopher Richard Rorty's sense of that term (Rorty 1989: passim). In this account, to appreciate Sinatra's life as *art* is precisely to appreciate it as *his* highly nuanced, idiosyncratic, contingent expression. As practitioner and sage of this art, Sinatra was, of course, a splendid exemplar and purveyor of taste and excellence, but the standards were largely of his own making, and they are illuminated in thick description of his particular living his particular life.

The way he wore his hat, mixed his drink, held his glass and cigarette, planned his wardrobe, flashed his steely blue-eyed smile, dated, courted, seduced, loved his women, the way he coined and spoke with self-confidence and panache the insouciant Rat Pack speak with its "bird," "pallie," "Harvey,"

"Clyde," "coocoo," "ring-a-ding-ding" lexicon, the way he defended his friends and punished his enemies, the way he wined and dined with presidents and gangsters, the way he held a crowd in thrall at every concert, and, yes, of course, the way he sang "One for My Baby," "Angel Eyes," "Night and Day," "Tramp," "Skin"—all of these stylistic flourishes and others were uniquely his own and made his life in toto the supreme art it was. To cloud celebration of that life with moral reservation, in the present account, is to retreat from life itself unimaginatively and complacently to the conventional. As New York cabaret singer Mary Cleere Haran recently observed, Sinatra may appall us with his "seduction-through-insult" singing of "Tramp" to Rita Hayworth in the 1957 film *Pal Joey,* but he mainly enthralls us (and Hayworth)—even though we sense deep down that in hurling the lyrical insult Sinatra is doing no more than being himself. Haran's words: "Rita calls him 'Beauty,' and his songful seduction is indeed a thing of beauty—cold and glittering and perfect. . . . [I]n that indelible moment, Rita Hayworth's reaction is ours. She illuminates why a strong, independent woman has put up with so much bad behavior. This crumb could sing—beatifically" (1995: 10). And could live poetically, one might add. Life as beauty, as erotic exuberance, as unadulterated vitality and personality, as art, simply overwhelms moral considerations. Or so the argument would go.

For all its allure and suggestiveness, this construction of Sinatra as postmodern Prometheus invites two critical responses at least. First, whatever concessions are made rightly to the view of the man as prodigious fashioner of cultural meaning and value, it is also true that he was at times as much a creature as a creator of the culture in which he lived. After all, in insisting on having things his way and celebrating the same with "My Way," Sinatra arguably was doing little more than playing out the narcissistic fantasies of mid- and late-twentieth-century American society. As Clarke notes:

> I would maintain that Frank Sinatra, in his clumsy, violent, often ugly way, has been the master of the *zeitgeist* of the twentieth century. He not only gained fame, wealth and power, but influenced the lives of countless millions with his art; thus he touched all the bases, accomplishing things that most people, in one way or another, would like to do, and he did it his way. But his way was according to the rules of the society in which he lived: it was just that

some of the rules were written and some unwritten. . . . [H]e has been a par-
adigm of our century because he has been neither more nor less confused . . .
than the rest of us. As individuals we may disapprove of his friendships, his
womanizing, or his occasional violence; but as a society, when we look at Sinatra we see what we would like to see in the mirror: the guy who has it all, and
can still effectively say, "Who, me?" (1997: 261–63).

Of course, to see Sinatra as the product and expression of an entire culture's
egocentric individualism may go some way toward extenuating his moral of-
fenses or at least tempering moral criticism of his own egocentrism, but such
mitigation naturally comes at the expense of diminishing his status as world-
historical individual. In this treatment he is counted as just one, admittedly
prominent, social member whose aspirations and excesses mirror the move-
ments of the herd.

Nonetheless, the fact of Sinatra the artist remains, and for some that may
be enough to ensure his status as postmodern Prometheus. Yet here I am inclined to say with Dostoevsky that buried deep within the psyche of every
übermensch is an underground man, which is to say really (and here is the second critical response) that the very idea of an *übermensch* is a social fiction,
an ideology. Yes, there are the Caesars, the Napoleons, the Picassos, the Caru-
sos, the Sinatras if you will, and culture often tells a certain story about them,
magnifying their lives in a kind of storybook way, constructing images of the
Man-God (to use Dostoevsky's expression) in narrative gestures glorifying the
possibilities of the human *qua* human. But these stories are fairy tales, of
course, cultural self-deceptions, wish fulfillments that obscure the underside
of human accomplishment. Buried deep within the psyche of every *übermensch* is an underground man, which is to say that behind all grand achievements are limited human beings, vulnerable, anxious, vainglorious, corrupt,
petty, spiteful, resentful, violent, guilt-ridden—the list goes on.

Certain biographical accounts of Sinatra's private life, seamy and sala-
cious as they may be, fuel this Dostoevskian deconstruction of the entertainer's life and career. Sinatra may have appeared on stage and screen as the
supremely self-confident, creative artist, the Man-God who achieved aesthetic transcendence, but behind the scenes this Man-God (we are told by

Gay Talese himself) was run aground by a "cold." On a day he needed to tape an important network show, he suffered from nasal congestion. He couldn't perform—at least as he would have liked to. He responded by becoming a mean-spirited, brooding, petulant tyrant, who lashed out at those around him (Talese 1966/1995: 108–12). More generally, Sinatra was, by his own account, an "eighteen-karat manic depressive," and his emotive oscillations seemed to have been triggered by the most trivial of contingencies (Hamill 1995: 231). In his ugliest moments we have a picture of a man vulnerable, conflicted, tossed by mood swings, torn by hostility, seething with resentment—and other signs of psychic fragmentation manifest themselves in certain stories he tells about his life. When he says to Pete Hamill that he genuinely loved all the many women he made love to, the admission sounds less like the confident assertion of an extraordinary bon vivant and more like the self-deluded rationalization of a Kierkegaardian aesthete, a Don Juan whose serial sexual encounters reflected a life swept away by impulses and events not fully within his control, a life lived by a character lacking the genuineness of identity constituted by sustained interpersonal commitment (Hamill 1995: 234). "A lover of all is a lover of none," one is tempted to say in response, and a self that tries to love all in that way, Kierkegaard taught us, is no self at all—much less a super-self. Yet, ironically enough, in Sinatra's remark to Hamill one also detects a glimmer of self-recognition, a faint expression of remorse over the failure to sustain relations, and with his intermittent admissions of guilt and gestures of repentance, however indirect or muted, Sinatra undermines his image as vibrant *übermensch* beyond good and evil. "Conventional" morality, it would appear, leaves its traces. Compunction and self-conviction remain—however buried in layers of self-deception. Just before Sinatra's death, biographer Taraborrelli reported:

> Like many people when they near the end of their lives, Frank Sinatra has had an opportunity to reflect upon his long life, and in doing so he has realized that he does have some regrets. Apparently, Frank is sorry about some of the things that have occurred during his lifetime. For instance, associates say that he has never completely reconciled in his heart the matter of Peter Lawford. One business associate says that he heard Sinatra say, "I shouldn't have done that to Peter. Why was I such an ass?" He also seems to regret having left

Nancy so many years ago, for Ava—but he has regretted that for years. "I was an idiot," he once said to Jilly [Rizzo]. "How could I have hurt Nancy that way?" (1997a: 511).

Finally, the image of Sinatra as *übermensch* is clouded by the character of his march toward death—and particularly by his dogged insistence on performing whatever the conditions, almost until the bitter end. Of course, there was something remarkable about his Dylan Thomas-like raging against the coming night, his stubborn delight in entertainment and public adulation, his Sisyphean resolve to work despite the substantial erosion of vocal skills and general physical deterioration. Yet in Sinatra's perseverance toward the end there was also pathos, and there was denial. Disturbing images linger: the indisputably bad vocal performances that parodied his greatest moments (notwithstanding the counterclaims of aficionados); the botching of lyrics even with a teleprompter, which he could not read because of cataracts; the failure of the reunion tour with Dean Martin, who seemed to recognize the end of things and had the good sense to quit over Sinatra's objections; the floundering 1991 performances with Steve Lawrence and Eydie Gorme; the collapse in Richmond; the rambling speech at the Grammy awards ceremony cut off in midcourse without warning by his own manager before a large TV viewing audience. All of these events and others seemed born of a desperate resolve to keep the inevitable end permanently at a distance (Taraborrelli 1997a: 480).

Death denial, anxiety, self-deception, finitude, guilt, the underground. "Human, all too human," one is prompted to say in ironic reversal of the Nietzschean line. When all was said and done, this *übermensch* was one of us.[2]

Notes

1. My reflections in this section were stimulated by an exchange with philosopher Brian Schuth in April 1995.
2. I am indebted especially to William Werpehowski of Villanova University for ongoing exchanges about the significance of Frank Sinatra in contemporary culture.

Works Cited

Adamowski, T. H. 1998. "Love in the Western World: Frank Sinatra and the Conflict of Generations." In Leonard Mustazza, ed. *Frank Sinatra and Popular Culture: Essays on an American Icon.* Westport, CT: Praeger, pp. 26–37.

Adams, Frank S. 1944. "Wallace, Truman at Madison Square Garden." *New York Times* (November 1), pp. 1, 16.

Agnew, Spiro T. 1980. *Go Quietly . . . Or Else.* New York: William Morrow.

Alter, Jonathan. 1998. "The Power and the Glitz." *Newsweek* (May 25), p. 64b.

"American Music's Greatest Singer and Most Notorious Bully." 1995. *Village Voice* 40, no. 25 (June 20).

Anderson, Clifford. 1995. *The Stages of Life.* New York: Atlantic Monthly Press.

Armbruster, Ann. 1995. *The Life and Times of Miami Beach.* New York: Alfred A. Knopf.

Bellelli, Guglielmo. 1991. "Une emotione ambigue: la nostalgie." In *Cahiers Internationaux de Psychologie Sociale* 11 (September): 59–76.

Belmonte, Thomas. 1999. "The Contradictions of Italian-American Identity: An Anthropologist's Personal View." In Pellegrino D'Acierno, ed. *The Italian American Heritage: A Companion to Literature and the Arts.* New York: Garland, pp. 3–20.

Berman, Edgar. 1979. *Hubert: The Triumph and the Tragedy of the Humphrey I Knew.* New York: G. P. Putnam's Sons.

Bliven, Bruce. 1995. "The Voice and the Kids." In Steven Petkov and Leonard Mustazza, eds. 1995. *The Sinatra Reader.* New York: Oxford University Press, pp. 30–33.

Bogart, Stephen Humphrey. 1995. *Bogart: In Search of My Father.* New York: Dutton.

Boyer, Paul S. 1995. *Promises to Keep: The United States Since World War II.* Lexington, MA: D. C. Heath.

Brownstein, Ronald. 1990. *The Power and the Glitter: The Hollywood-Washington Connection.* New York: Pantheon Books.

Clarke, Donald. 1997. *All or Nothing at All: A Life of Frank Sinatra.* New York: Fromm International.

Coleman, Ray. 1995. *Sinatra: Portrait of the Artist.* Atlanta, GA: Turner Publishing.

Cook, John W., and Heinrich Klotz. 1973. *Conversations with Architects.* New York: Praeger.

Crouch, Stanley. 1998. "Sinatra Gave Music the Closeup." *New York Daily News* (May 17), p. 49.

———. 1990. *Notes of a Hanging Judge: Essays and Reviews, 1979–1989.* New York: Oxford University Press.

Cunningham, George. 1965. "The Italian: A Hindrance to White Solidarity in Louisiana, 1890–1893." *Journal of Negro History* (June): 24–25.

D'Acierno, Pellegrino, ed. 1999. *The Italian American Heritage: A Companion to Literature and the Arts.* New York: Garland.

D'Amato, Alfonse. 1995. *Power, Pasta, and Politics: The World According to Al D'Amato.* New York: Hyperion.

DeLillo, Don. 1997. *Underworld.* New York: Scribner.

Denning, Michael. 1997. *The Cultural Front: The Laboring of American Culture in the Twentieth Century.* New York: Verso.

DeRamus, Betty. 1998. "Sinatra Helped Sick Joe Louis Keep on Fighting in Las Vegas." *Detroit News* (May 19), sec. E, p. 1.

Derrida, Jacques. 1985. *The Ear of the Other: Otobiography, Transference, Translation.* New York: Schocken.

Early, Gerald. 1995. *One Nation Under a Groove: Motown and American Culture.* Hopewell, NJ: Ecco Press.

———. 1989. "Listening to Frank Sinatra." *Prairie Schooner* 63 (Fall): 108–10. Reprinted in Leonard Mustazza, ed. 1998. *Frank Sinatra and Popular Culture: Essays on an American Icon.* Westport, CT: Praeger, pp. 109–10.

Fisher, James T. 1997. "Clearing the Streets of the Catholic Lost Generation." In Thomas J. Ferraro, ed. *Catholic Lives, Contemporary America.* Durham, NC: Duke University Press, pp. 76–103.

Fitzgerald, F. Scott. 1941. *The Last Tycoon.* New York: Charles Scribner's Sons.

———. 1925. *The Great Gatsby.* New York: Charles Scribner's Sons.

"Frank Sinatra in Gary." 1945. *Life* (November 12), pp. 45–46.

Franklin, Nancy, Adam Gopnik, Alex Ross, et al. 1998. "Talk of the Town." *New Yorker* (May 25), pp. 47–49.

Freud, S. 1940/1964. *An Outline of Psycho-Analysis.* London: Hogarth Press, vol. 23, pp. 141–207.

———. 1930/1961. "Address Delivered in the Goethe House at Frankfurt." In *The Standard Edition of the Complete Psychological Works of Sigmund Freud,* vol. 21. London: Hogarth Press, pp. 208–12.

———. 1930/1961. *Civilization and Its Discontents.* London: Hogarth Press, vol. 21, pp. 59–145.

———. 1923/1961. *The Ego and the Id.* London: Hogarth Press, In *The Standard Edition of the Complete Psychological Works of Sigmund Freud,* vol. 19, pp. 3–66.

Friedwald, W. 1997. *Sinatra! The Song Is You.* New York: Da Capo Press.

———. 1995. *Sinatra! The Song Is You: A Singer's Art.* New York: Scribner's.

Gambino, Richard. 1974. *Blood of My Blood: The Dilemma of the Italian-American.* New York: Doubleday.

Gans, Herbert J. 1962. *The Urban Villagers: Group and Class in the Life of Italian-Americans.* New York: Free Press.

Gennari, John. 1997. "Passing for Italian: Crooners and Gangsters in Crossover Culture." *Transition* 72 (Fall): 36–48.

Giddins, Gary. 1998. *Visions of Jazz.* New York: Oxford, pp. 220–231.

Giddins, Gary., ed. 1995. "Sinatra at 80." In *Voice Jazz Supplement* 10, *Village Voice* 40, no. 25 (June 20), pp. 1–19.

Goffman, Erving. 1971. *Relations in Public: Microstudies of the Public Order.* New York: Harper & Row.

Goldstein, Norm. 1982. *Frank Sinatra: Ol' Blue Eyes.* New York: Holt, Rhinehart and Winston.

Gordon, Richard E., et al. 1961. *The Split-Level Trap.* New York: Random House.

Greenburg, Dan. 1964/1975. *How to Be a Jewish Mother: A Very Lovely Training Manual.* Los Angeles: Price Stern Sloan.

Greenwood, Leonard, and Jeannine Stein. 1987. "Sinatra Given L.A. NAACP Award Despite Rights Protest." *Los Angeles Times* (May 15), part I, p. 22.

Grizzuti Harrison, Barbara. 1986. "Terrified and Fascinated by His Own Life." *New York Times Book Review* (November 2), p. 13.

Halberstam, David. 1995. "Sinatra at Sunset." *Playboy* (April), pp. 75–76, 154–156.

Hall, Stephen S. 1983. "Italian-Americans: Coming into their Own." *New York Times Magazine* (May 15), pp. 28–29, 32–34, 44, 49–54.

Hamill, Pete. 1998. *Why Sinatra Matters.* Boston: Little, Brown.

———. 1995. "Sinatra: The Legend Lives." In Steven Petkov and Leonard Mustazza, eds. *The Frank Sinatra Reader.* New York: Oxford University Press, pp. 227–39.

Hamlin, Suzanne. 1997. "Remembering an Italian Mother Just as She Would Like." *New York Times* (February 19), sec. C, pp. 3, 5.

Haran, Mary Cleere. 1995. "Pal Frank." In *Voice Jazz Supplement* 10, *Village Voice* 40, no. 25 (June 20).

Heard, Alexander. 1960. *The Costs of Democracy.* Chapel Hill: University of North Carolina Press.

Hersh, Seymour M. 1997. *The Dark Side of Camelot.* Boston: Little, Brown.

Higham, John. 1955/1988. *Strangers in the Land: Patterns of American Nativism.* New Brunswick, NJ: Rutgers University Press.

Holden, Stephen. 1998. "Frank Sinatra Dies at 82; Matchless Stylist of Pop." *New York Times* (May 16), pp. A1, B16–17.

Howlett, John Frank. 1980. *Frank Sinatra.* London: Plexus.

Ignatiev, Noel. 1995. *How the Irish Became White.* New York: Routledge.

Jameson, Frederic. 1969–70. "Walter Benjamin, or Nostalgia." *Salamagundi* 10–11 (Fall-Winter), pp. 52–68.

Kahn, E. J. 1995. "The Fave, the Fans, and the Fiends." In Steven Petkov and Leonard Mustazza, eds. 1995. *The Sinatra Reader.* New York: Oxford University Press.

Kane, Gregory. 1998. "Sinatra's Talent Crossed All Racial Lines." *Baltimore Sun* (May 20), sec. C, p. 1.

Keats, John. 1957. *The Crack in the Picture Window.* Boston: Houghton Mifflin.

Kelley, Kitty. 1991. *Nancy Reagan: The Unauthorized Biography.* New York: Simon and Schuster.

———. 1986. *His Way: The Unauthorized Biography of Frank Sinatra.* New York: Bantam Books.

Kempton, Murray. 1995. "Sinatra, The Lion in Winter." In Steven Petkoff and Leonard Mustazza, eds. 1995. *The Frank Sinatra Reader.* New York: Oxford University Press, pp. 179–180.

King, Alan, with Chris Chase. 1996. *Name Dropping: The Life and Lies of Alan King.* New York: Scribner's.

Klein, Edward. 1996. *All Too Human: The Love Story of Jack and Jackie.* New York: Pocket Books.

Kuntz, Tom and Phil Kuntz, eds. 2000. *The Sinatra Files: The Secret FBI Dossier.* New York: Three Rivers Press.

Kutler, Stanley I. 1997. *Abuse of Power: The New Nixon Tapes.* New York: Free Press.

"L.A. Branch of NAACP Gives Sinatra Achievement Award." 1987. *Jet* (June 1), p. 56.

Ladd-Taylor, Molly, and Lauri Umansky, eds. 1998. *"Bad" Mothers: The Politics of Blame in Twentieth-Century America.* New York: New York University Press.

Lahr, John. 1997a. *Sinatra: The Artist and the Man.* New York: Random House.

———. 1997b. "Sinatra's Song." *New Yorker* (November 3), pp. 76–95.

Lapidus, Morris. 1979. *An Architecture of Joy.* Miami: E. A. Seeman.

Levy, Shawn. 1998. *Rat Pack Confidential: Frank, Dean, Sammy, Peter, Joey, and the Last Great Showbiz Party.* New York: Doubleday.

Lindholm, Charles. 1990. *Charisma.* Oxford: Blackwell.

Mailer, Norman. 1991. *Harlot's Ghost.* New York: Random House.

Mallowe, Mike. 1995. "The Selling of Sinatra." In Steven Petkov and Leonard Mustazza, eds. 1995. *The Frank Sinatra Reader.* New York: Oxford University Press, pp. 194–212.

Malone, Bönz. 1995. "O.G.: Frank Sinatra Didn't Take Orders; He Took Over." *Vibe* (September), pp. 14–18.

Masciangelo, Pier M. 1990. "La nostalgia: una dimension de la vide psiquica." *Revista de Psicoanalisis* 47, no. 3 (May-June): 546–57.

McFadden, Robert D. 1998. "Hoboken to Hollywood and Beyond: Mourning the Man and the Magic." *New York Times* (May 16), p. B18.

McGilligan, Patrick, and Paul Buhle. 1997. *Tender Comrades: A Backstory of the Hollywood Blacklist.* New York: St. Martin's Press.

Merleau-Ponty, Maurice. 1962. *Phenomenology of Perception* (Colin Smith, trans.). London: Routledge and Kegan Paul.

Mitchell, W. J. T. 1994. *Picture Theory: Essays on Verbal and Visual Representation.* Chicago: University of Chicago Press.

Moynihan, Patrick, and Nathan Glazer. 1963. *Beyond the Melting Pot.* Cambridge, MA: MIT Press.

Mueller, Mark. 1998. "Nat King Cole's Widow: Sinatra Championed Rights." *Boston Herald* (May 20), p. 50.

Mustazza, Leonard. 1998a. "Comment: Seeing Red: A Sinatra Scholar Examines the FBI's Political Probe into Ol' Blue Eyes." Available at http://www.aponline.com (December 11), pp. 1–7.

———. 1998b. "Frank Sinatra and Civil Rights." Paper presented at Hofstra University conference, "Frank Sinatra: The Man, The Music, The Legend," November 12–14, Hempstead, NY.

———. 1995. "Sinatra's Enduring Appeal: Art and Heart." In Steven Petkov and Leonard Mustazza, eds. 1995. *The Frank Sinatra Reader.* New York: Oxford University Press, pp. 3–14.

Mustazza, Leonard, ed. 1998. *Frank Sinatra and Popular Culture: Essays on an American Icon.* Westport, CT: Praeger.

O'Donnell, Kenneth P., and David Powers with Joe McCarthy. 1970. *"Johnny, We Hardly Knew Ye": Memories of John Fitzgerald Kennedy.* Boston: Little, Brown.

Olinick, Stanley L. 1992. "Nostalgia and Transference." *Contemporary Psychoanalysis* 28, no. 2 (April): 195–98.

Orsi, Robert. 1985. *The Madonna of 15th Street: Faith and Community in Italian Harlem, 1880–1950.* New Haven, CT: Yale University Press.

Oudes, Bruce, ed. 1989. *From the President: Richard Nixon's Secret Files.* New York: Harper & Row.

Paglia, Camille. 1992. *Sex, Art, and American Culture.* New York: Vintage.

Parmet, Herbert S. 1983. *JFK: The Presidency of John F. Kennedy.* New York: Penguin Books.

Patterson, James T. 1996. *Grand Expectations: The United States, 1945–1974.* New York: Oxford University Press.

Petkov, Steven. 1995. "Ol' Blue Eyes and the Golden Age of the American Song: The Capitol Years." In Steven Petkov and Leonard Mustazza, eds. 1995. *The Frank Sinatra Reader.* New York: Oxford University Press, pp. 74–88.

Petkov, Steven, and Leonard Mustazza, eds. 1995. *The Frank Sinatra Reader.* New York: Oxford University Press.

Picard, John. 1994. "Sinatra: A Memoir." *Iowa Review* 24, no. 3 (Fall): 1–12.

"*Playboy* Interview with Frank Sinatra," February 1963. Available at http://members.aol.com/artanis103//play-interview.html.

Pleasants, Henry. 1974. *The Great American Popular Singers.* New York: Simon and Schuster.

Porter, Eric. 2002. *What Is This Thing Called Jazz?* Berkeley: University of California Press.

Primack, Bret. 1998. "Frank Sinatra Through the Lens of Jazz." *Jazz Times* 28, no. 4 (May): 32.

Pugliese, Stanislao G. 1996–97. "The Culture of Nostalgia: Fascism in the Memory of Italian-Americans." *Italian American Review* 5, no. 2 (Autumn/Winter): 15–26.

Puzo, Mario. 1969. *The Godfather.* New York: Putnam.

Quirk, Lawrence J., and William Schoell. 1998. *The Rat Pack: The Hey-Hey Days of Frank and the Boys.* Dallas: Taylor Publishing.

Regan, Donald T. 1988. *For the Record: From Wall Street to Washington.* New York: Harcourt Brace Jovanovich.

Reeves, Richard. 1993. *President Kennedy: Profile of Power.* New York: Simon and Schuster.

Reeves, Thomas C. 1992. *A Question of Character: A Life of John F. Kennedy.* Rocklin, CA: Prima Publishing.

"Relationships of Sinatra with Blacks that Book about Him Does Not Highlight." 1986. *Jet* (October 13), pp. 56–63.

Rider, Jacques le. 1992. "Viennese Modernity and Crises of Identity." *Psychohistory Review* 21, no. 1 (Fall): 73–108.

Rockwell, John. 1984. *Sinatra: An American Classic.* New York: Random House.

Rorem, Ned. 1989. *Settling the Score: Essays on Music.* New York: Doubleday.

Rorty, Richard. 1989. *Contingency, Irony and Solidarity.* Cambridge: Cambridge University Press.

Rudin, Max. 1998. "Reflection on the Rat Pack." *American Heritage* (December).

Sadie, Stanley, ed. 1981. *The New Grove Dictionary of Music and Musicians,* 20 vols. London: Macmillan.

St. John de Crevecoeur, J. Hector. 1782/1988. "What Is an American?" In *Letters From an American Farmer.* New York: Penguin.

Salinger, Pierre. 1960. *With Kennedy.* Garden City, NY: Doubleday.

Sarris, Andrew. 1986. "Sinatra: Screen." Liner notes to CD package *The Voice: The Columbia Years 1943–1952.* Columbia Records (C4K–40343).

Sartre, Jean-Paul. 1965. *The Psychology of Imagination.* New York: Citadel Press.

———. 1957. *Being and Nothingness: An Essay on Phenomenological Ontology* (Hazel E. Barnes, trans.). London: Methuen.

Schiffer, Irvine. 1973. *Charisma: A Psychoanalytic Look at Mass Society.* Toronto: University of Toronto.

Scott, Janny 1998. "Even Scholars Say Its Witchcraft." *New York Times* (May 16), pp. B9, B11.

Shaw, Arnold. 1995. "Sinatrauma: The Proclamation of a New Era." In Steven Petkov and Leonard Mustazza, eds. 1995. *The Sinatra Reader.* New York: Oxford University Press, pp. 19–29.

———. 1982. *Sinatra, the Entertainer.* New York: Delilah.

———. 1968. *Sinatra: Twentieth-Century Romantic.* New York: Holt, Rinehart and Winston.

Sheed, Wilfred. 1986. "Album Notes" for *Frank Sinatra: The Voice, The Columbia Years, 1943–1952* (Columbia).

"Show Biz Legends Reunite on U.S. Concert Tour." 1988. *Jet* (March 7), pp. 56–58.

Sinatra Live in Paris. 1994. Reprise Records.

Sinatra, Frank. 1991. "The Haters and Bigots Will Be Judged." *Los Angeles Times* (July 4), sec. B, p. 5.

———. 1958. "The Way I Look at Race." *Ebony* (July), pp. 35–44.

———. 1947. "As Sinatra Sees It" (Letter of the Week). *New Republic* 6 (January), pp. 3, 46.

———. 1945a. "Let's Not Forget We're *All* Foreigners." *Magazine Digest* (July): 8–10.

———. 1945b. "What's This About Races?" *Scholastic* (September 17), p. 23. Reprinted in Leonard Mustazza, ed. 1998. *Frank Sinatra and Popular Culture: Essays on an American Icon.* Westport, CT: Praeger, pp. 23–25.

Sinatra, Nancy. 1995. *Frank Sinatra: An American Legend.* Santa Monica, CA: General Publishing.

———1985. *Frank Sinatra, My Father.* New York: Pocket Books.

Sobran, Joseph. 1992. "The Man Who Was Sinatra." *National Review* 7 (February): 54–55.

Talese, Gay. 1998. "A Swinger with Swagger." *People* 49, no. 21 (June 1): 60.

———. 1966. "Frank Sinatra Has a Cold." Originally published in *Esquire.* Reprinted in Steven Petkoff and Leonard Mustazza, eds. 1995. *The Frank Sinatra Reader.* New York: Oxford University Press, pp. 99–129.

Taraborrelli, J. Randy. 1997a. *Sinatra: Behind the Legend.* Secaucus, NJ: Birch Lane Press.

———. 1997b. *Sinatra—A Complete Life.* Secaucus, NJ: Rose Books/Carol Publishing.

Thurer, Shari L. 1994. *The Myths of Motherhood: How Culture Reinvents the Good Mother.* New York: Houghton Mifflin.

Tosches, Nick. 1992. *Dino: Living High in the Dirty Business of Dreams.* New York: Dell.

Vare, Ethlie Ann, ed. 1995. *Legend: Frank Sinatra and the American Dream.* New York: Boulevard Books.

Vecoli, Rudolph J. 1978. "The Coming of Age of the Italian Americans: 1945–1974." *Ethnicity* 5: 119–47.

Viscusi, Robert. 1996. *Astoria.* Toronto: Guernica.

Warshow, Robert. 1948/1972. "The Gangster as Tragic Hero." In Warshow, *The Immediate Experience.* New York: Atheneum.

Weber, Max. 1978. *Economy and Society: An Outline of Interpretive Sociology,* vol. 2 (Guenther Roth and Claus Wittich, eds.). Berkeley: University of California Press.

Wheaton, Glenn. 1946. "Songs by Sinatra." Music by Axel Stordhal, with the Benny Goodman Sextet and Janet Waldo and the Pipers. Produced by Mann Holiner for Old Gold Cigarettes (CBS, January 30). Available at Museum of Television and Radio, New York City, call number RB16555.

Whitehead, Barbara Dafoe. 1997. *The Divorce Culture*. New York: Knopf.

Whyte, William H. Jr. 1956. *The Organization Man*. New York: Simon and Schuster.

Wiener, Jon. 1998. "His Way." *The Nation* (June 8), p. 38.

———. 1991. *Professors, Politics and Pop*. New York: Verso.

———. 1986. "When Old Blue Eyes Was 'Red.'" *New Republic* (March 31), pp. 21–23. Reprinted in Ethlie Ann Vare, ed. 1995. *Legend: Frank Sinatra and the American Dream*. New York: Boulevard Books, pp. 64–69.

Williams, Paul. 1994. *Tommy Dorsey, Frank Sinatra: The Song Is You*. New York: BMG Music.

Wilson, Earl. 1976. *Sinatra: An Unauthorized Biography*. New York: Macmillan.

Wilson, Sloan. 1955. *The Man in the Gray Flannel Suit*. New York: Pocket Books.

Yezierska, Anzia. 1925. *Bread Givers*. Garden City, NY: Doubleday.

Zehme, Bill. 1997. *The Way You Wear Your Hat: Frank Sinatra and the Lost Art of Livin'*. New York: HarperCollins.

Contributors

T. H. ADAMOWSKI is Professor Emeritus, Department of English, University of Toronto, and the author of scholarly articles on William Faulkner, D. H. Lawrence, Jean-Paul Sartre, and others.

JANICE L. BOOKER is a writing instructor at the University of Pennsylvania College of General Studies. She has also taught creative writing and journalism at Temple University and Arcadia University, as well as at community adult education venues. Ms. Booker lectures extensively on literary personalities and the literary salon at universities, libraries, and cultural institutions. She is a former radio producer and broadcaster, television talk show host, and the author of several books and many freelance articles for national periodicals. Her most recent book is *Philly Firsts* (Camino Books, 1999). Janice Booker is a native Philadelphia, a graduate of Temple University's Department of Journalism, and a long-time ardent Sinatra fan.

DOUGLAS BRINKLEY currently serves as director of the Eisenhower Center for American Studies and is professor of history at the University of New Orleans. Three of his biographies—*Dean Acheson: The Cold War Years* (Yale University Press, 1992), *Driven Patriot: The Life and Times of James Forrestal*, with Townsend Hoopes (Alfred Knopf, 1992), and *The Unfinished Presidency: Jimmy Carter's Journey Beyond the White House* (Viking Press, 1998)—were chosen as Notable Books of the Year by the *New York Times*. His recent publications include *The Bernard DeVoto Reader* (editor, with Patricia Limerick, Yale University Press, 2000), and the introductions to *War Letters* (New York: Scribner, 2001), as well as *36 Days* (New York: New York Times, 2001). He is also the author of *Rosa Parks* (Viking, 2000), the *American Heritage History of the United States* (Viking Press, 1998) and *FDR and the Creation of the United Nations*, with Townsend Hoopes (Yale University Press, 1997). Other scholarly contributions include *Rise to Globalism: American Foreign Policy Since 1938* with Stephen E. Ambrose (Viking-Penguin, 1997), *The Majic Bus: An American Odyssey* (Harcourt Brace, 1993; Anchor Doubleday, 1994), and edited works on Dean Acheson, Theodore Roosevelt, Jean Monnet, and the Atlantic Charter. Dr. Brinkley has also written extensively for *Newsweek, Time, American Heritage,* the *New Yorker,* the *New York Times,* the *Wall Street Journal,* the *Atlantic Monthly, Foreign Affairs, Foreign Policy,* and other journals. His most recent works include *Wheels for the World: Henry Ford, His Company, and A Century of Progress* (Viking Press, 2002); *Mississippi: Making of a Nation* with Stephen Ambrose (National Geographic Society, 2002).

PELLEGRINO D'ACIERNO is professor of Italian and comparative literature at Hofstra University where he directs the Italian studies program. He has taught a wide range of courses in comparative literature, critical theory, cultural studies, cinema, and Italian intellectual history at Columbia University, New York University, and Cornell University, as well as Hofstra. He has been named a Visiting Distinguished Professor of Italian and Cultural Studies at Columbia University and has held visiting appointments at Yale University, Rice University, and the Southern California Institute of Architecture. He was awarded the Prix de Rome by the American Academy in Rome in 1989 and was named a Guggenheim Fellow in 1996. Among his publications are *Filippo Tomasso Marinetti and the Freedom of Poetry* (Scribner's 1993) and *The Itinerary of the Sign: Scenes of Seeing in Giotto's Fresco Cycle in the Scrovegni Chapel* (SCI-Arc Press, 1998). He is the editor and primary author of *Italian American Heritage: A Companion to Literature and the Arts* (Garland, 1999) and editor of *Carl Gustav Jung and the Humanities* (Princeton University Press, 1990). He is completing *Invisible Cities: From the Postmodern Metropolis to the Cities of the Future* and *Strange Loops: Cinema and Architecture as Spatial-Temporal Practices.*

JOSEPH DORINSON is professor of history at Long Island University's Brooklyn campus. A noted authority in the field of popular culture, his research specialties span sports history (in particular, the Brooklyn Dodgers and African American sports heroes), humor studies, Russian immigration, Brooklyn and Jewish history, and World War II movies and music. He is the co-editor of *Jackie Robinson: Race, Sports and the American Dream* (M. E. Sharpe, 1998). Among his other publications are "Paul Robeson (1898–1976): A Centennial Symposium" (co-edited) in *Pennsylvania His-*

tory (Winter 1999); "Ethnic Humor: Subversion and Survival" in *What's So Funny? Humor in American Culture* (Scholarly Resources, 1998); the book *Anyone Here A Sailor? Popular Entertainment and the Navy* (Bright Lights Publications, 1994); "Brooklyn: The Elusive Image" in *Is Anyone Here from Brooklyn* (Fradon, 1990); and "Racial and Ethnic Humor" in *Humor in America* (Greenwood, 1988).

THOMAS J. FERRARO is associate professor of English at Duke University. He is the author of *Ethnic Passages: Literary Immigrants in Twentieth-Century America* (University of Chicago Press, 1993); the editor of *Catholic Lives, Contemporary America* (Duke University Press, 1997); and a contributor to *The Columbia History of the American Novel* (1991), *The Italian American Heritage* (Garland, 1999), and *Scribner's Encyclopedia of U.S. Cultural and Intellectual History* (2001). At Paula Cohen's invitation, he joined the first-ever Sinatra panel at the Modern Language Association. He is now writing a book on the media arts and what cultural studies has to fear about Italian America.

JOHN GENNARI is assistant professor of English and ethnic studies at the University of Vermont. His essay on the Afro-Italian actor Giancarlo Esposito appeared in *Common Quest* (Winter 2000). He has written extensively on music and American culture with an emphasis on jazz, including *Canonizing Jazz: An American Art Form and Its Critics* (forthcoming University of Chicago Press).

GASPAR GONZÁLEZ received his Ph.D. in American Studies from Yale University. Currently associate editor of *Street*, an arts and culture weekly in Miami, he has written for such publications as *Miami New Times, The Miami Herald, New York Newsday*, and *The Texas Observer* and is the author of two forthcoming volumes: *The Manchurian Candidate: Cold War Politics and Cultural Production*, with Matthew Frye Jacobson (University of Minnesota Press) and *Barnstorming American Culture* (University of Tennessee Press).

ROB JACKLOSKY is an associate professor of English at the College of Mount Saint Vincent in the Bronx. He has published scholarly essays on Matthew Arnold and short fiction in the *Sonora Review* and other literary journals.

ROCCO MARINACCIO is associate professor of English at Manhattan College in the Bronx, where he teaches twentieth-century American literature and culture. He has published recent work in contemporary literature and American literature and is completing a book manuscript on Objectivist poetry and proletarian literature.

LEONARD MUSTAZZA is Distinguished Professor of English and American Studies at Penn State University's Abington College in suburban Philadelphia. He is the author of four books on Frank Sinatra, including *The Frank Sinatra Reader* (Oxford University Press, 1995) and *Ol' Blue Eyes: A Frank Sinatra Encyclopedia* (Greenwood, 1998).

MICHAEL NELSON is professor of political science at Rhodes College. His articles have appeared in, among others, the *Journal of Politics, Political Science Quarterly, Public Interest,* and *Washington Monthly,* where he formerly served as editor. More than 40 of his articles have been anthologized in works of political science, history, and English composition, and he has won national writing awards for his articles on music and baseball. His most recent books are *Governing Gambling: Politics and Policy in State, Tribe, and Nation,* with John Lyman Mason (Century Foundation Press, 2001), and *The Elections of 2000* (CQ Press, 2001). Other recent books include *Alive at the Core: Exemplary Approaches to General Education in the Humanities* (Josey-Bass, 2000) and *The American Presidency: Origins and Development, 1776 - 1998* with Sidney M. Milkis (CQ Press, 2003).

STANISLAO G. PUGLIESE is associate professor of modern European history at Hofstra University and a former visiting research fellow at the Italian Academy for Advanced Studies at Columbia University. He is the author of *Carlo Rosselli: Socialist Heretic and Antifascist Exile* (Harvard University Press, 1999) and *Desperate Inscriptions: Graffiti from the Nazi Prison in Rome* (Bordighera Press, 2002). He is the translator of Andrea Bocelli's autobiography, *The Music of Silence* (HarperCollins, 2000) and the editor of *Fascism, Anti-Fascism, and the Resistance in Italy* (Rowman & Littlefield, 2004), *The Most Ancient of Minorities: The Jews of Italy* (Greenwood, 2002), as well as *The Legacy of Primo Levi* (forthcoming, Palgrave Macmillan). He is currently writing a biography of the Italian antifascist writer Ignazio Silone, to be published by Farrar, Straus & Giroux.

EDMUND N. SANTURRI is professor of religion and philosophy and director of "The Great Conversation" at St. Olaf College in Northfield, Minnesota. He is the author of *Perplexity in the Moral Life: Philosophical and Theological Considerations* (University of Virginia Press, 1987) and co-editor of *The Love Commandments: Essays in Christian Ethics and Moral Philosophy*

(Georgetown University Press, 1992). He has also published a number of essays on theological ethics, moral philosophy, and intellectual history. A longtime Sinatra fan, he published "Christian Theology and Frank Sinatra" in the December 1992 issue of *The Cresset* and "Theology and Music in a Different Key: Meditations on Frank Sinatra and Eros in a Fallen World," in *Frank Sinatra and Popular Culture* (Praeger, 1998).

JOE SCOGNAMILLO is the son of the late Pasquale "Patsy" Scognamillo, founder of the famous restaurant at 236 West 56th Street that bears his name. Joe Scognamillo served as chef at the family restaurant from 1952 until 1984.

SALVATORE SCOGNAMILLO is the son of Joe Scognamillo and the grandson of Patsy Scognamillo. Sal, who has been chef since 1984, is only the third chef in the history of the restaurant, following his grandfather and father. He is the author of *Patsy's Cookbook: Classic Italian Recipes from a New York City Landmark Restaurant* with a foreword by Nancy Sinatra (Clarkson Potter, 2002).

Index